Sports, Society, and Technology

Jennifer J. Sterling • Mary G. McDonald
Editors

Sports, Society, and Technology

Bodies, Practices, and Knowledge
Production

Editors
Jennifer J. Sterling
University of Iowa
Iowa City, IA, USA

Mary G. McDonald
Georgia Institute of Technology
Atlanta, GA, USA

ISBN 978-981-32-9126-3   ISBN 978-981-32-9127-0   (eBook)
https://doi.org/10.1007/978-981-32-9127-0

This Palgrave Macmillan imprint is published by the registered company Springer Nature Singapore Pte Ltd. The registered company address is: 152 Beach Road, #21-01/04 Gateway East, Singapore 189721, Singapore

Acknowledgments

This project was made possible with funds provided by the Homer C. Rice Chair in Sports and Society and the School of History and Sociology at the Georgia Institute of Technology. The editors are also grateful to the collection's contributing authors for their patience and perseverance as well as their willingness to share provacative and important ideas.

Contents

Notes on Contributors

Mark Cooper is Assistant Professor at the University of California, Davis, in the Department of Human Ecology and the Department of Animal Science. His work frequently engages questions of materiality, legibility, and political ontology. His research examines the role of measurement and metrics in the ordering of social, economic, and environmental systems and the limits and implications of quantification.

Katelyn Esmonde is a Hecht-Levi Postdoctoral Fellow at Johns Hopkins University's Berman Institute of Bioethics. Her research focuses on wearable fitness technologies, the ethics of obesity prevention, and feminist approaches to health research.

Kathryn Henne holds the Canada Research Chair (Tier 2) in Biogovernance, Law and Society at University of Waterloo. She is also Fellow of the Balsillie School of International Affairs and Australian Research Council Discovery Early Career Research Fellow in the School of Regulation and Global Governance at Australian National University. She is the author of *Testing for Athlete Citizenship: Regulating Doping and Sex in Sport* (2015), and her research is featured in *the American Journal of Bioethics*, *Law & Policy*, *Signs: A Journal of Women in Culture and Society*, and *Theoretical Criminology*.

Shannon Jette is Associate Professor at the University of Maryland. Her research focuses on social, cultural, and historical aspects of knowledge production in the disciplines of kinesiology, medicine, and public health. She is particularly interested in studying exercise and fitness practices as technologies of health that have the potential to shape how we understand and experience our bodies.

Andi Johnson is Senior Lecturer in the Department of History and Sociology of Science at University of Pennsylvania, where she also serves as senior fellow for the Leonard Davis Institute of Health Economics. Andi teaches undergraduate students in the Health and Societies Program and the Science, Technology, and Society Program. Her main area of research concerns the history and anthropology of physiology, exploring epistemological and political intersections of science and sport in the twentieth and twenty-first centuries. Andi's work has appeared in *Biosocieties, Health Affairs, Journal of the History of Biology*, and *Social Studies of Science*.

Roslyn Kerr is Senior Lecturer in Sociology of Sport and Dean of the Faculty of Environment, Society and Design at Lincoln University in Christchurch, New Zealand. She is the author of *Sport and Technology: An Actor-Network Theory Perspective* (2016) and has a long-standing interest in the role of non-humans, such as technologies, in the production and performance of sport. While much of her writing has drawn on the work of Bruno Latour and other actor-network theorists, she is broadly interested in a range of French sociologists, having also published sport-focused articles on Michel Foucault and Pierre Bourdieu.

Samantha King is Professor of Kinesiology and Health Studies and Gender Studies at Queen's University. Her work on the embodied dimensions of consumer culture has appeared in *Social Text, Ethnic and Racial Studies*, the *Sociology of Sport Journal*, and the *International Journal of Drug Policy*, among other venues. Her book, *Pink Ribbons, Inc: Breast Cancer and the Politics of Philanthropy* (2006), is the subject of a National Film Board documentary by the same name. She is co-editor of *Messy*

Eating: Conversations on Animals as Food (2019). Her work explores the place of protein in contemporary food and fitness cultures.

Mary G. McDonald is the Homer C. Rice Chair in Sports and Society and Professor in the School of History and Sociology at the Georgia Institute of Technology. Her research focuses on American culture and sport including inequalities as related to gender, race, class, and sexuality. Her publications have appeared in such venues as the *Sociology of Sport Journal, Ethnic and Racial Studies, Sociological Perspectives*, and the *International Review for the Sociology of Sport*. A past president of the North American Society for the Sociology of Sport, she directs the Sports, Society, and Technology program at Georgia Tech.

Madeleine Pape is Postdoctoral Fellow in the Science and Human Culture program at Northwestern University. She completed a Ph.D. in Sociology from University of Wisconsin-Madison. Her research examines debates over epistemologies of sex and gender and how these are influenced by the actions of governing bodies, with a focus on international sport and biomedicine in the United States and Canada. Prior to her graduate studies, Pape was a track athlete who competed for Australia in the 800 m at the 2008 Olympic Games in Beijing and the 2009 World Championships in Berlin.

Christopher Rosin is Senior Lecturer in Rural Social Science at Lincoln University in Christchurch, New Zealand. His interests in non-human actors are based on the research of the influences of audit metrics in agrifood production systems, which have relevance for the sociology of sport as well. This research and analysis draws on theoretical insights from convention theory, actor-network theorists, and Deleuzian perspectives on assemblage.

Jennifer J. Sterling is Lecturer in the Department of American Studies at the University of Iowa. She joined the Sport Studies faculty after completing her Ph.D. in Kinesiology (Physical Cultural Studies) at University of Maryland and a postdoctoral fellowship with the Sports, Society, and Technology program at the Georgia Institute of Technology. Her research interests revolve around the disciplinary intersections of Sports Studies, Science and Technology Studies, and Visual Culture. In particular, her research explores how techno-scientific visualization practices, including medical imaging and data visualization, shape understandings of physically active bodies and affect inequalities.

Nicholas Taylor is Associate Professor in the Department of Communication at North Carolina State University. His work applies posthumanist and feminist perspectives to qualitative research on the intersections of media and subjectivity; specific interests include competitive, spectatorial gaming (esports), domesticity and digital play, and the ways adult artists and enthusiasts engage with LEGO. He is lead editor, with Gerald Voorhees, of the first collection on masculinities and digital gaming (*Masculinities in Play* 2018) and lead editor of a forthcoming volume on LEGO makers and craftspeople (*LEGOfied: Building Blocks as Media*).

Matt Ventresca is Postdoctoral Associate in the Faculty of Kinesiology and Integrated Concussion Research Program at University of Calgary. His research is focused around the sociocultural study of media, science and technology, and pain and injury in sport cultures. His project investigates how neuroscientific research, media coverage, and athletes' experiences come together to create complex and sometimes contradictory processes of knowledge production around sport-related brain injuries. He is the co-editor of the forthcoming book, *Sociocultural Examinations of Sports Concussions*, and his work has appeared in journals such as *Sociology of Sport Journal* and *Communication & Sport*.

Gavin Weedon is Senior Lecturer in the Department of Sport Science in the School of Science and Technology at Nottingham Trent University. His current research explores the ecological and biomediated dimensions of embodied practices, spanning studies of telomere biology, genetic testing, and whey protein powder. His sociological research on sport and exercise has appeared in journals such as *Cultural Studies↔ Critical Methodologies, Journalism: Theories, Practice, Criticism*, and the *International Review for the Sociology of Sport*.

Carlin Wing is Assistant Professor and Chair of Media Studies at Scripps College. Her work as an artist and scholar connects everyday gestures to global histories in contexts of play, game, and sports. Her current book project, *Bounce: A History of Balls, Walls, and Gaming Bodies*, follows an array of bouncing balls through the histories of electronic and non-electronic games, across the spectrum of play, game, and sport, and into the domains of physics, material science, animation, and computing in order to describe the worldviews and cultural contests that have been embedded in the architectures, instruments, and gestures of games of ball.

List of Figures

Introduction: Sports, Society, and Technology

Jennifer J. Sterling and Mary G. McDonald

There are a growing number of scholars working at the intersections of Science and Technology Studies (STS) and Sport Studies. This work does not represent a new phenomenon as STS scholarship has previously engaged physical culture while critical Sport Studies scholars have long pointed out how technology and science impact physical activity and human movement including sports. However, the recent growth in inter-disciplinary interactions between these two fields, examples of which are represented in *Sports, Society, and Technology: Bodies, Practices, and Knowledge Production*, is noteworthy. The chapters, therefore, help to illustrate that the study of sports, society, and technology is empirically, theoretically, substantively, methodologically, and disciplinarily diverse and important.

J. J. Sterling (✉)
University of Iowa, Iowa City, IA, USA
e-mail: jennifer-sterling@uiowa.edu

M. G. McDonald
Georgia Institute of Technology, Atlanta, GA, USA
e-mail: mary.mcdonald@hsoc.gatech.edu

© The Author(s) 2020
J. J. Sterling, M. G. McDonald (eds.), *Sports, Society, and Technology*,
https://doi.org/10.1007/978-981-32-9127-0_1

Taken as a whole, *Sports, Society, and Technology* uniquely addresses the complex entanglements of sports, society, and technology. Sport is a particularly well-suited object of this analysis given its connection to popular pleasures and its capacity to act as a site of ideological meaning making. In addition, the rapid development of technologies and their expanding applications in sports further compels the use of critical, and interdisciplinary, analyses to explicate the social, cultural, political, and historical contexts of an expanding technoscientific landscape. A growing convergence between STS and Sport Studies helps to propel established topics in new directions by offering each discipline new ways to address emerging sporting technologies, phenomena, and related issues.

In this introductory chapter, we briefly discuss important themes and approaches within critical Sport Studies and STS that predate and help to inform this collection. We begin by clarifying terms, pointing toward a brief, and shared, epistemological history between the fields. Foregrounding the book's thematic organization, we conclude the chapter with a discussion of these productive collisions before introducing each of the authors' contributions. Far from definitive, this chapter is strategically selective as a way to introduce some past themes and frames to help contextualize the emerging topics, issues, theories, and methodological concerns that inform the interactions between Sport Studies and STS, and are highlighted individually and collectively by the *Sports, Society, and Technology* chapters.

Tracing Technoscientific Sporting Pasts and Futures

As is the case with most scholarly tracings, we acknowledge that characterizing academic areas of study in terms of their objects of study is a daunting, if not impossible task, particularly in an era of increased interdisciplinarity. Any attempt to name and discuss dynamic elements of a field—themes, paradigms, and ways of knowing—inevitably involves exclusions. That is, in a "world of multiplicities, in which naming, defining, and mapping are acts of ontological politics" we recognize our actions "give or take explanatory power and authority" (Felt et al. 2017a, p. 4). Therefore, any attempt to construct any field of study is best seen as creating what Max Weber (1949) called "ideal types," or abstractions that can help illuminate a phenomenon but are simultaneously dangerous for simplifying and reifying a complex social process. With this caveat in mind, this tracing—partially and suggestively rather than exhaustively—highlights what we see as key themes and movements within the social studies of sports, science, and technology.

Both critical Sport Studies and STS are historically closely aligned with sociology and have been influenced by broader shifts in the academy toward embracing interdisciplinary ways of knowing which draw from, among others, anthropology, communication, critical race, literary, gender, and cultural studies. Scholars of both sport and science and technology have similarly looked at phenomena as socially constructed and contested. Feminist scholars were among the first critics to expand the study of sport—given the historical exclusion of large numbers of women from sports—to include notions of physical activity, recreation, and the (moving) body. In doing so, feminists, joined by other critical scholars, also interrogated the very notion of sport itself. While fans may recognize sports as rule-bound, organized, and highly competitive, feminists have suggested that sport is eminently tied to power relations of gender, race, class, and nation. For example, late nineteenth- and early twentieth-century myths of female physical malady structurally relegated many women to less physical leisure pursuits. Understanding this process opened up new questions such as "what counts as sports" and "who counts within sports" and "why" (Coakley 2017).

Much as with "sport," scholars of technoscience have likewise moved away from common-sense notions of science as a means to discover natural laws grounded in the scientific method, and of technology as the "relative straightforward application of science" (Sismondo 2010, p. 8). As with strands of Sport Studies, many STS scholars draw upon diverse disciplinary perspectives to conceptualize an active process whereby scientists and engineers engage in researching the material world, which exists—much like sport—as the product of cultural, political and economic contexts and discourses. While never unified, scholars in both fields have produced critiques (influenced by sociological perspectives in the 1960s, 1970s, and 1980s) that challenge logical positivism's emphasis on quantification and tendency to abstract social phenomena. These parallel developments are reflected by sport scholars who have convincingly, and increasingly, exposed the ways in which sports science has reproduced common-sense notions about the body often grounded in dominant ideologies of race, gender, class, and sexuality. And this scholarship, in turn, has spurred critical sport scholarship to embrace more expansive notions of technology—beyond discursively reductive interpretations of Foucauldian technologies of the body (1986) and toward a (re)consideration of how the discursive and material both interact and are enmeshed.

Thus, a robust range of critical studies of sport has explored the place of science and technology in sporting cultures.[1] For example, research has interrogated scientific racism through an examination of the white historical obsession with the black athletic body, a body partially produced by scientific racism. In a similar way, feminist scholars have shown how medical opinion historically helped to construct the female body as anatomically incapable of physical exertion. Aligned with Anne Fausto-Sterling's (2000) work within STS, other feminist scholars have demonstrated the ways binaries of male and female as well as culture and nature are remade in sports science practices including those around gender verification in sport. As contemporary scholarship illustrates, powerful medical discourses continue with flawed attempts to verify the gender of athletes participating in elite women's events. Ideologies of sex, gender, and sexuality continue to influence the International Association of Athletics Federations's quest to verify the gender of female sexed bodies, the most recent iteration of which is in the quest to confirm the alleged hormonal advantage (hyperandrogenism) of muscular and successful women (see the chapter by Pape in this collection). These writings compellingly argue that science and technology, like sport, are far from neutral arbitrators, but are rather embedded in social and political relations.

Sport Studies scholars have additionally undertaken critical examinations of risk and injury in sport, as well as the cultural, ethical, and economic pressures which contribute to doping and the use of performance enhancing substances, topics more commonly approached through scientific methods in exercise science and sports medicine. These "laboratory" spaces of exercise science and sports medicine have also been interrogated as important, but understudied, sites of knowledge production (see the chapter by Johnson in this collection). A smaller corpus of research has also explored ethically and ontologically confounding statuses—cyborgs, posthumans, transhumans, and bio-others—as products of human-technology interactions. These include internal and external human-made modifications produced by equipment, prosthetics, and pharmaceuticals. Human–more-than-human collisions are further engaged in scholarship investigating broader empirical sites such as athlete and fan interactions with built and natural environments as well as with animals in sports. Research on sporting mega-events such as the Olympic Games and the FIFA World Cup is also increasingly engaging political and ethical questions around the use of security technologies to ensure safety. Finally, though quantification has long been defined as one of the characteristics of modern sport (Guttmann 1978), more recently scholars have responded to a "digital turn" via research on digital media, esports, (exer)gaming, (bio)metrics, and the quantified sporting self.

This scholarship reflects shifting conceptualizations and materialities of science and technology—from time-keeping, equipment, and training, to doping, cyborgs, and sex testing, to the digital era's focus on biometrics. Yet few critical Sport Studies scholars have engaged these issues through the lens or frameworks of STS, such as those marked by close and in-depth attention to the practices of science and technology. Likewise, sport's entanglement with science and technology has infrequently garnered the attention of STS scholars. For example, there is no substantial engagement with sport in any of the chapters that constitute four editions of the *Handbook of Science and Technology Studies* (see, for example, Felt et al. 2017b), which map the breadth of scholarship and epistemological shifts within the field of STS. As such, the absence of sport is noticeable. This state of affairs further points to the continuing need to elevate and interrogate scholarship which productively engages both fields.

In comparing the emerging scholarship of the two disciplines, it could be argued that STS is more likely to approach science and technology from a production or object-oriented perspective or that STS scholars have been quicker to respond to the need for critical studies of big data and technological quantification, and that Sport Studies scholars are more interested in embodiment. However, growing evidence of cross-over between scholars in the two fields suggests that this distinction may instead be most useful in illuminating the increasing and productive influence of each discipline on the other and the potential for their ongoing and future convergence.

Collisions and Contributions

A potential site for continued convergence relates to issues around methodological, epistemological, and ontological sensibilities exemplified through STS approaches such as actor-network theory (ANT) and new materialisms. Far from the only approaches used within STS, we highlight these two as examples of modes of analyses that are also grounded in epistemological and ontological concerns, which allow for a more expansive approach to both new and existing sporting phenomena. Often identified with STS more broadly and with the work of STS scholars Bruno Latour and Michel Callon, and sociologist John Law in particular, actor-network theory or ANT is a "disparate family of material-semiotic tools, sensibilities and methods of analysis that treat everything in the social and natural worlds as a continuously generated effect of the webs of relations within which they are located" (Law 2008, p. 141). Thus, "actants" in networks are conceived of as both human and nonhuman as ANT incorporates the materiality and interests of objects and things into analyses. After all, as Sismondo (2010) explains, science and technology often "works" by "translating material actions and forces from one form to another" (p. 83). Additionally, objects and things are clearly given meaning as they interact with human actors and, as such, both the material and semiotic constitute networks—that is, networks offer a type of material-semiotic analysis.

Rosalyn Kerr's (2016) *Sport and Technology: An Actor-Network Theory Perspective* is illustrative of the productive application of ANT in tracing the influence of things—in this case, technologies within sport—while noting the highly individualized and unstable character of networks and assemblages; human and nonhuman combinations "that have vastly different qualities and capacities from singular parts" (p. 25). Kerr's scholarship on gymnastics has shown, for example, that nonhumans are central in gymnastics networks. This includes the use of cameras and apparatus that help shape bodily activity in the sport while showing that the (often authoritative) coach is not the most, or only, important human or nonhuman actant in this network. Popularized in the 1980s, Kerr (2016) explains how early renditions of ANT were rich in ethnographic thick descriptions, which helped to detail the myriad of actants involved in the production of science and knowledge. ANT has since gone through many iterations and is not without its critics who, for example, point out the problematic symmetry often granted to human and nonhuman actions and interests without an associated concern with relations of power.

STS approaches also overlap with new materialisms, a development that has activated an ontological turn in Sport Studies (see the chapter by Henne in this collection), a turn that works to decenter anthropocentric Enlightenment fantasies of humans as always and everywhere the most important actants. Broadly conceived, (new) materialisms suggest that bodies are not simply material but also ensconced within the material world and processes, thus counteracting scholarship that mainly centers on representation and interpretation. This relational ontology suggests that different bodies—animate and inanimate—are not separate but instead "intra-act" in a dynamic process of becoming (Barad 2007). This framework helps to disrupt notable Western binaries often reproduced in dominant ontologies, including those often guiding Sport Studies scholarship, such as active-passive, material-discursive, masculine-feminine, nature-culture, and subject-object (McDonald and Sterling 2020). As Jane Bennett has written, this focal point additionally "draws human attention sideways, away from the ontologically ranked Great Chain of Being and toward a greater appreciation of the complex entanglements of humans and non humans" (Bennett 2010, p. 112). Actor-network theory and new materialisms are among the many STS-inspired methodological, epistemological, and ontological influences evident throughout the productive collisions represented by each of the *Sports, Society, and Technology* chapters, and applied to a wide-ranging set of emerging themes, issues, debates, and concerns located at the intersection of sports, science, and technology.

Chapter Introductions

Sports, Society, and Technology: Bodies, Practices, and Knowledge Production illustrates contemporary investigations of sports, science, and technology through a myriad of different topics and methods within the ten chapters that follow. Contributing authors include scholars from Sociology, Gender Studies, Legal Studies, Environmental Science, Media Studies, Communications, and Kinesiology, in addition to Sport Studies and STS programs, representing the aforementioned emergent, diverse, and necessary (inter)disciplinary entanglements.

The anthology is organized into two thematic parts—Practices, Productions, and Knowledges and Bodies/Matter. While there is considerable overlap between the focus of each part, the chapters in the Practices, Productions, and Knowledges segment highlight the complex role of human and nonhuman actants as well as the attendant knowledge formations that constitute sport, science, and technology processes. The chapters in this first part often decenter the human body as a primary point of analysis, thereby disrupting anthropocentric accounts that are too often reproduced in contemporary sport scholarship. Chapters in the second part, Bodies/Matter, are grounded in feminist sensibilities which collectively demonstrate ontological understandings of bodies as multiple, material, and ensconced within the material world.

Part 1: Practices, Productions, and Knowledges

In the opening chapter of Practices, Productions, Knowledges, "True Bounce: Stories of Dunlap and the Rise of Vulcanized Play," Carlin Wing offers a historical tracing, locating evolving rubber technologies as essential to modern sport's constitution and the ideological promotion of fair play. By focusing on changes within the Dunlap brand over time, Wing examines material science and manufacturing, arguing that the quest to produce a consistent or "true" bounce in such objects as tennis balls is far from mere play but rather ensconced within technologies of industrial development and imperial power relations.

While the first chapter of this part is "object-oriented"—a common approach within STS that is less frequently applied to sport and fitness settings—the next four chapters additionally explore practices of knowledge production. Andi Johnson's "Manufacturing Invisibility in 'the Field': Distributed Ethics, Wearable Technologies, and the Case of Exercise Physiology" offers a rare ethnography of exercise scientists' networked activities in the laboratory and "field." Discussing the implications of exercise scientists' physiological knowledge production, Johnson in particular notes how the use of miniaturized instruments helps to produce their own invisibility in field settings and subsequent scholarship.

Next, Matt Ventresca critically examines sport's "concussion crises" in "The Tangled Multiplicities of CTE: Scientific Uncertainty and the Infrastructures of Traumatic Brain Injury." In doing so he shows how neuroscience's inability to determine the exact cause and effect mechanisms that produce brain trauma (e.g. chronic traumatic encephalopathy) exposes not only scientific uncertainty but ultimately an inability to capture the brain's material complexity. Rather than continuing to privilege neurological ways of knowing, Ventresca instead argues for the need to embrace critical socio-cultural perspectives that examine, challenge, and seek to change collision sports infrastructures of harm—the values and violent contexts which place athletes' bodies and brains in danger.

While Ventresca analyzes the politics of uncertainty produced in quantitative scientific studies of sports concussions, the next chapter hones in on cultural work performed through seemingly definitive systems of measurement within sports. In "The Agency of Numbers: The Role of Metrics in Influencing the Valuation of Athletes," Roslyn Kerr, Christopher Rosin, and Mark Cooper explore how sporting metrics exist as unique forms of sporting information—so much so that particular evaluative metrics acquire a "life of their own" by reducing player performances to numeric values. Drawing upon Latour's notion of the immutable mobile as well as Deleuze and Guattari's concept of territorialization, the chapter charts how metrics serve as useful sites to explore performative power and to theorize nonhuman agency in sport and beyond.

Finally, Nicholas Taylor's ethnography examines collegiate e-gaming as embodied and digital sites of identity making, technique development, and intense competition. In "The Numbers Game: Collegiate Esports and the Instrumentation of Movement Performance," Taylor suggests that unlike collegiate and professional sports, these *League of Legend* players merge the roles of athlete and analyst into a single hybridized identity. Taylor concludes the chapter by briefly discussing the problematic but increasing linked network of knowledge production between video games, sports, and the military where embodied performances are digitally transformed into "moving dots." Taylor's investigation is important in documenting the increasingly prominent place of esport within the broader sports landscape, as well as its diversity and hierarchies. As with other chapters in this part, his analysis further uncovers the powerful capacities of linked corporeal and material networks within technoscientific sporting landscapes.

Part 2: Bodies/Matter

The second part, Bodies/Matter, begins with Kathryn Henne's chapter, "Possibilities of Feminist Technoscience Studies of Sport: Beyond the Cyborg Body" which opens a much needed dialogue between feminist Sport Studies and feminist STS frameworks. Engaging with rich histories of feminist thought, she also draws from both sport and technoscientific studies more broadly. In particular the chapter examines how feminist scholars have applied STS concepts such as the cyborg, agential realism, and assemblage to sport, while also considering how feminist Sport Studies's emphasis on embodiment, sport, and physical activity offers important conceptualizations for understandings of science, technology, and society.

Samantha King and Gavin Weedon's chapter flows well from Henne's discussion as the authors deploy an important tenet of feminism via Mol's ontological conceptualizations regarding the ways in which multiple bodies come into being through diverse practices. "Enacting Bodies: The Multiplicity of Whey Protein and the Making of Corporealities" traces a popular protein supplement favored by fitness enthusiasts, from a toxic by-product of dairy (cow) production to its materialization as a seemingly healthy commodity. This exploration is important in troubling individualistic and human-centered notions of embodiment while also making visible the often-toxic impact of whey on the natural environment, thus further highlighting the importance of human-nonhuman ecological relationships.

In "The (In)Active Body Multiple: An Examination of How Prenatal Exercise 'Matters,'" Shannon Jette and Katelyn Esmonde also use Mol's conceptualization to map the multiple ways that prenatal exercise comes to matter socially, politically, and materially. In particular, they investigate which ontologies are performed in healthcare contexts, and the privileging of "the over-nutrition hypothesis" and a linear model of causality to emphasize the need for mothers to engage in prenatal physical activity to maintain an "appropriate" weight for the health of their future children. Far from innocent practices the authors illustrate how a narrow notion of an idealized maternal body emerges from the multiple possibilities available. In doing so, this chapter rearticulates a history of STS scholarship that exposes the politicized framings of women's reproduction capacities as well as STS and Sport Studies scholarship that takes the materialization of (multiple) bodies seriously.

Madeleine Pape continues a focus on feminist scholarship in her chapter, "Ignorance and the Gender Binary: Resisting Complex Epistemologies of Sex and Testosterone," where she interrogates and reveals how sexed bodies impose binary categories onto a far more complex and indeterminate reality. Drawing on interviews with international track-and-field stakeholders, including athletes, coaches, managers, media personnel, and officials Pape examines how this elite sport community understands organizations' attempts to regulate those women athletes with naturally occurring high testosterone. Informed by a growing body of scholarship around the social construction of ignorance, this chapter explores the institutional process whereby stakeholders resist alternative ways of knowing and protect their epistemic commitments to binary sex.

In the section's and collection's final chapter, "Screening Saviors?: The Politics of Care, College Sports, and Screening Athletes for Sickle Cell Trait," Mary G. McDonald explores how a required health screening of US college athletes for sickle cell trait is embedded in a longer history of racialization and racist science. Designed to identify and monitor individual athletes during intense exercise which might result in ill health, this individualized focus obscures larger structural problems regarding the National Collegiate Athletic Association's (NCAA's) racialized labor practices and inattention to other matters of athlete health. McDonald's examination further reveals the politics of care as well as the precarious use of health screening within sport spaces and beyond while helping to trouble notions of (dis)ability, health, and risk.

Individually, each of the above chapters makes their own unique contribution related to their objects of analysis, concepts and theories engaged, and methods utilized, illuminating and interrogating complicated relationships between science, technology, and sporting cultures. Collectively, this anthology highlights the benefits of Sport Studies and STS convergences, particularly in this era of increasingly technologized societies and sporting cultures. In assembling this collection of emerging scholarship it is our hope that *Sports, Society, and Technology: Bodies, Practices, and Knowledge Production* additionally propels established topics in new directions and generates further questions, conversations, and analyses.

Note

1. We realize we are providing very general themes (and an incomplete account at that) as our purpose is to provide examples that reveal the diversity of topics covered to date. It would be impossible to fully document the related and substantial body of scholarship that predates and informs this anthology in the limited space of this introduction. However, there are books and anthologies which provide useful introductions, overviews, and analyses. These include but are not limited to Vertinsky's (1994) examination of nineteenth-century medical ideologies and women's physical activity; Young's (2004) edited collection on risk and injury; Tolleneer et al. (2013) on doping and sports and Henne (2015) on doping and sex regulations in sport; Miah's (2004, 2017) interrogation of both gene doping and sports-digital relationships; Magdalinski (2009) and Fouché (2017) on sporting bodies and technology; Lupton's (2016) exploration of the quantified self and self-tracking and Millington's (2017) examination of the datafication of contemporary fitness; and Taylor's (2012) unpacking of esports. For an excellent introduction to the critical Sociology of Sport see Coakley (2017).

References

Barad, K. (2007). *Meeting the universe halfway: Quantum physics and the entanglement of matter and meaning*. Durham, NC: Duke.

Bennett, J. (2010). *Vibrant matters: A political ecology of things*. Durham, NC: Duke.

Coakley, J. (2017). *Sport in society: Issues and controversies*. New York: McGraw-Hill.

Fausto-Sterling, A. (2000). *Sexing the body: Gender politics and the construction of sexuality*. New York: Basic Books.

Felt, U., Fouché, R., Miller, C., & Smith-Doerr, L. S. (2017a). Introduction. In U. Felt, R. Fouché, C. Miller, & L. S. Smith-Doerr (Eds.), *The handbook of science and technology studies* (4th ed., pp. 1–26). Cambridge, MA: MIT Press.

Felt, U., Fouché, R., Miller, C., & Smith-Doerr, L. S. (2017b). *The handbook of science and technology studies* (4th ed.). Cambridge, MA: MIT Press.

Foucault, M. (1986). *The history of sexuality: Vol. 3. The care of self*. New York: Pantheon Books.

Fouché, R. (2017). *Game changer: The technoscientific revolution in sports*. Baltimore, MD: Johns Hopkins University.

Guttmann, A. (1978). *From ritual to record: The nature of modern sport*. New York: Columbia University Press.

Henne, K. (2015). *Testing for athlete citizenship: Regulating doping and sex in sport*. New Brunswick, NJ: Rutgers University.

Kerr, R. (2016). *Sport and technology: An actor-network theory perspective*. Manchester: Manchester University Press.

Law, J. (2008). Actor-network theory and material semiotics. In B. S. Turner (Ed.), *The new Blackwell companion to social theory* (3rd ed.). Oxford: Blackwell.

Lupton, D. (2016). *The quantified self: A sociology of self-tracking*. Cambridge: Polity Press.

Magdalinski, T. (2009). *Sport, technology and the body: The nature of performance*. London: Routledge.

McDonald, M. G., & Sterling, J. (2020). Feminist new materialism and the troubling waters of the 2016 Rio de Janeiro Olympic and Paralympic Games. In J. Newman, H. Thorpe, & D. Andrews (Eds.), *Sport, physical culture and the moving body: Materialisms, technologies, ecologies*. New Brunswick, NJ: Rutgers University.

Miah, A. (2004). *Genetically modified athletes: Biomedical ethics, gene doping and sport*. London: Routledge.

Miah, A. (2017). *Sport 2.0: Transforming sports for a digital world*. Cambridge, MA: MIT Press.

Millington, B. (2017). *Fitness, technology and society: Amusing ourselves to life*. London: Routledge.

Sismondo, S. (2010). *An introduction to Science and Technology Studies*. Malden, MA: Blackwell.

Taylor, T. L. (2012). *Raising the stakes: E-Sports and the professionalization of computing games*. Cambridge, MA: MIT.

Tolleneer, J., Sterckx, S., & Bonte, P. (Eds.). (2013). *Athletic enhancement, human nature and ethics: Threats and opportunities of doping technologies*. New York: Springer.

Vertinsky, P. (1994). *The eternally wounded woman: Women, doctors, and exercise in the late nineteenth century*. Urbana, IL: University of Illinois Press.

Weber, M. (1949). "Objectivity" in social science and social policy. In M. Weber (Ed.), *Essays in the methodology of the social sciences* (pp. 50–112) (E. A. Shils & H. A. Finch, Trans.). New York: The Free Press.

Young, K. (Ed.). (2004). *Sporting bodies, damaged selves: Sociological studies of sports-related injury*. Bingley, UK: Emerald.

Part I

Practices, Productions, and Knowledges

True Bounce: Stories of Dunlop and the Rise of Vulcanized Play

Carlin Wing

Dear Dunlop

In the summer of 2013, Raneem El Welily wrote a "Dear Dunlop" letter. Of sorts. The 24-year-old Egyptian squash champion atted Dunlop Sport, tweeting that they were ruining her life. Their terrible squash balls were "not even round." She attached photographic evidence of the offending objects. The image shows a collection of Dunlop Pro squash balls, some obviously shy of a regular spherical shape. Many had been discarded with the white stamp of the Dunlop brand still fresh. Other players had also noticed the problem. It was not simply that the balls were bouncing too fast or too slow. Their elasticity, shape, and lifespan were all unpredictable. In an interview in the fall of 2013, longtime top American player Latasha Khan said, "It's dramatic. Some just take off. And other ones are so heavy that they just die. You can't warm them up" (L. Kahn, personal communication, Oct 3, 2013). Kahn said this was affecting both the duration of matches and who was winning and losing. Malaysian

C. Wing (✉)
Scripps College, Claremont, CA, USA
e-mail: cwing@scrippscollege.edu

J. J. Sterling, M. G. McDonald (eds.), *Sports, Society, and Technology*,
https://doi.org/10.1007/978-981-32-9127-0_2

17

Raneem El Welily ✔ @RaneemElWelily · 18 Aug 2013   ∨
Dear @DunlopSport ur terrible squash **balls** r ruining my life These'll all go to
waste!! Not even round #BadQuality

💬 3   ⟲ 27   ♡ 20

Fig. 1 Screenshot of an August 13, 2013 tweet by Raneem El Welily addressed to Dunlop Sport

champion and women's world number one, Nicol David, said the ways the balls were changing shape made her think that if the balls did not already have expiration dates, that they should have them (N. David, personal communication, Oct 2, 2013). David's Malaysian compatriot, Wee Wern Low, who had just joined David in the top ten rankings the year before, laughed as she described her coach telling her not to blame the ball during practice. Her reply to him: "No, I'm serious. Some of them are really just not round and some are fliers as well. For some reason one ball can be like a normal bounce and from the same box you can get another ball that just keeps flying around like nobody's business. It is crazy" (W. Low, personal communication, Oct 2, 2013). At the time of her post, El Welily was chasing the number one ranking, a spot that had been held continuously by David since 2006. To achieve her quest, El Welily needed Dunlop's balls to be the constant she had come to depend on, not suddenly strange objects. She needed a *true bounce*: a bounce that is regular, reliable, and predictable. The Dunlop Pro balls had become untrue.

A squash ball is a small thing, literally and figuratively. Squash is a minor sport that aspires to but has never been included in the Olympics. Developed in England in the early nineteenth century and spread around the world by the British Empire, the game's history is reflected in the current women's and men's world squash rankings with top players hailing from England, Egypt, Australia, Malaysia, India, Canada, Hong Kong, New Zealand along with a scattering of European countries. Squash was the first British game to be played from its outset with a rubber ball. The ball used today is about the size of a table-tennis ball but with a thicker shell. It has almost no bounce until the rubber is warmed up through repeated contact with racket strings and court surfaces. The regularity of the shape, size, behavior, and durability of these small pneumatic objects may matter only to professional squash players. But it matters a lot to them. They spend thousands of hours training their bodies and timing their gestures around this specific kind of bounce. Like all professional athletes, they develop an intimate knowledge of their instruments and environments of play because their fortunes are shaped by the kind of contact they do (or do not) make with the ball at key moments. Squash balls are industrial objects, technologies whose carefully calibrated specifications allow (or, are supposed to allow) players to count on their behavior. The World Squash Federation (WSF) specifications for a ball include narrow parameters for weight, diameter, stiffness, seam strength, rebound resilience, and percentage of allowable change under high and low temperature conditions. Around 90% of the squash balls sold around the world each year are made by Dunlop and the Dunlop Pro is the official ball for the women's and men's professional tours. While the national origins of today's top ranked squash players reflect the way the game's spread followed the British Empire, the true bounce that El Welily and so many other players around the world rely on depends in turn on the history of the transformation of rubber into an industrial colonial plantation crop and the massive role that Dunlop plays in that history. For the purposes of this chapter, I want to propose that the misshapen Dunlop squash balls in El Welily's photograph can stand in for all of the official balls of games played around the world. These small, hollow, just short of round rubber balls hold a sweeping story of the relationship between rubber and sport.

Vulcanized Play

Rubber is one of the foundational materials of modern sport. Indeed, it is a foundational material of modern life. Take a moment to consider the things that regularly carry you across any kind of distance: slippers, sandals, sneakers, shoes, boots, bicycles, motorbikes, wheelchairs, gurneys, cars, buses, planes. So many different kinds of movement rest on rubber. In the world of sports, there is an endless array of rubber. The wheels of almost any vehicle used in road racing are made of rubber. As are the vast majority of the solid, hollow, and inflated balls made for being hit with feet, heads, hips, hands, rackets, bats, clubs, sticks, and paddles. And of course, there are rubberized surfaces—gymnasium flooring, gymnastic tumbling mats, yoga mats, running tracks. Even some kinds of artificial grass are made with rubber backing and crumb rubber (chopped up tires) that sprays up onto player's bodies and makes for worse injuries than those that occur on grass (Litman 2014). It would be an exaggeration to say that the world is carpeted in rubber, but it is worth taking seriously the material effort that goes into cushioning impact, and the way this effort has shaped and reshaped landscapes and lives. Rubber has changed the ways we move and the ways we comport ourselves in movement.

When I say that rubber is a foundational material of modern sport and modern life, I use the word modern in part to emphasize the way the concept of sport is tied to the concept of modernity. The English word *sport* was derived from the French word *desport*, which meant both entertainment and comportment. These two meanings point toward the way forms of play and sport shape people as embodied subjects. *Sport* took on a new meaning of physical competition in the middle of the nineteenth century with the rise of organized sports such as football, rugby, cricket, and athletics (Oxford English Dictionary 2019). In the process, the concept became associated on the one hand with set of ideals around athleticism, masculinity, and imperialism that were fostered in the British public schools (Mangan 1981; Mangan and McKenzie 2010), and on the other hand it became the name for new professional kinds of competitions: spectacles that sold seats and merchandise to an emerging middle class equipped with new kinds of leisure (Tenner 2003). Modern sport is a form of institutionalized play and, as such, it contains the shape and form and material conditions of society. More specifically, it is a form of institutionalized play that conditions subject formation and is in turn conditioned by bounce: it is *vulcanized play*.

With the phrase *vulcanized play*, I aim to capture some key aspects of the relationship between rubber, sport, and technology by tying the history of play, and especially the formation we think of as modern sport, to the industrial and imperial projects that structure the production of truer (better, more reliable, more standard) forms of buffer and bounce primarily through the material technology of rubber. Vulcanization is the name given by Thomas Hancock, one of the founders of the British rubber industry, to the process of stabilizing, or curing, rubber through the use of high heat, mastication, and additives such as sulfur. The name, which invokes Vulcan, the Roman god of fire and technology, was suggested to Hancock by his friend William Brockedon, a painter, inventor, and author of books such as *Italy, Classical, Historical, and Picturesque* (Hancock 1857). Brockedon's suggestion reflects a common practice of the time of drawing on Greek and Latin roots to generate names for new technologies. (Think, for example, of the wealth of optical toys devised in Britain at this moment: the thaumatrope [wonder-turner], phenakistoscope [view- or eye-deceiver], daedaleum [in reference to Daedalus who built wings for his son Icarus], zoopraxiscope [life-by-practice viewer], and zoetrope [wheel of life]). This practice connects British culture to the Greek and Roman empires through the act of naming, often in the process papering over actual origins. In the case of rubber, the earliest technologies were developed by the Olmec (rubber people) and refined by the

Mixtec, Aztec, Maya, Tlaxcala, and other pre-Columbian civilizations in what is now named America (Loadman 2005; Tully 2011). Among other uses for the elastic material, these cultures organized spectacular ball games around rubber bounce (Whittington and Mint Museum of Art 2001; Wing 2015). Naming the process developed to cure rubber of its undesirable properties after the Roman god of technology dislocated the technology from its origins in Mesoamerican societies. The phrase *vulcanized play* carries forward and displays this trouble with names and asserts deep connections between our forms of play and sport, histories of rubber specifically, and histories of technology more broadly. If this volume aims to articulate relationships between sports, society, and technology, this chapter uses the multiple histories of Dunlop to claim material science, industrial manufacturing, and imperial power as underwriting partners of those three terms and to tell a set of stories about rubber and sport.

While for sport, rubber appears as a foundational material technology, for rubber, sport appears repeatedly at its sites of invention, incorporation, production, expansion, competition, and promotion. What follows are three stories of Dunlop. The first is a story of a person: John Boyd Dunlop Sr., inventor of the pneumatic tire and the co-founder of what would become the Dunlop Rubber Company. This is story about fathers and sons, the sport of cycling and its use as a testing ground for a new technology, the problem of antivibration, the power of names, and the massacres at the sites of rubber extraction at this time. The second is a story of a corporation. The Dunlop Rubber Company, built by the Du Cros family, was one of Britain's largest multinationals for much of the twentieth century and a top supplier of tires for car and cycling races and equipment for golf, cricket, and racket sports equipment. This is a story about a family of sportsmen and imperialists building a multinational company, transforming rubber into a plantation crop, and promoting what Arthur Du Cros calls "the playing fields of industry" (Du Cros 1938). The third is a story of a brand. Dunlop Sports and the Dunlop Sport brand were originally created under the umbrella of Dunlop Rubber but were sold off after the acquisition of the company by BTR (British Tyre and Rubber) in 1985. By the time Dunlop Pro squash balls began behaving erratically, the brand was owned by Mike Ashley's company Sports Direct. This is a story about a brand name, the problem of true and untrue bounce, and current conditions of global industrial production. Taken together, these Dunlop stories describe the everyday construction of patriarchy and empire. I call these stories following this understanding of storytelling as a form of thinking-with that enables a making-otherwise. In this, I am following Donna Haraway who writes, "Each time a story helps me remember what I thought I knew, or introduces me to new knowledge, a muscle critical for caring about flourishing gets some aerobic exercise" (Haraway 2016, p. 29). These stories are dense and take work to unwind. In exploring the overlaps of how sport has shaped the history of rubber, how rubber has shaped the history of sport, and how together they have shaped the histories of Dunlop, it becomes possible to say: sport runs the histories of Dunlop.

When the Rubber Hit the Road: The Story of John Boyd Dunlop and the Pneumatic Tire

> The solid tyred wheel from the tricycle went first. Rolled with an underarm movement, it ran along the paved yard, until all its energy, with which it had been propelled, had been used up, when it wobbled to a standstill and fell down. Next the wooden disc with the air tyre was rolled in the same way and with the same force. This bounded along the whole length of the yard, hit the closed doors at the far end, and rebounded, with energy still stored within it. This was the basic experiment. (Tompkins 1981, p. 7)

When I picture John Boyd Dunlop on that day in 1887 rolling his cobbled together "air tyre" across the yard and watching it bounce back with energy to spare, I wonder about all of the large and small histories that laid the ground for that moment, and about all of the ones that would follow from it. Dunlop was many things—a veterinary surgeon, a Scotsman, a father, a husband. But it was as the inventor of a pneumatic tire that his name became known to a larger public. If the squash ball is a minor object in history, the pneumatic tire is a major one. The combination of the automobile with the inflated tire fundamentally changed how people moved as well as the roads they traveled (Tully 2011). If you are a rider or racer of wheeled vehicles, mechanical or motorized, the story of the pneumatic tire has something to do with you.

Dunlop was not the first person, not even the first Scottish man, to make an inflated tire out of rubber. But the aerial wheels that Robert William Thompson had patented in 1845 failed to become established commodities. Thompson's wheels went the way of so many new technologies that are invented and then for any number of reasons forgotten, passed by, surpassed, or suppressed. They were only recalled to public attention in order to break the monopoly of Dunlop's 1888 patent for the air tire (Du Cros 1938, p. 102). In that patent, Dunlop identified "immunity from vibration" and "increased speed of travel" as the two ways in which his tire would improve the movement of "wheeled vehicles" over "roadways and paths, especially when these latter are of rough and uneven character" (Patent Specification No. 10,607 1888, p. 2). The patent singles out velocipedes (the name for early forms of bicycles), invalid chairs, and ambulances whose riders have a special interest in smoother and faster rides (Ibid).

Many accounts of Dunlop's invention tell it as a story of a father and son: in Belfast, in 1887, John Boyd Dunlop Sr. invented an air tire for his young son, John Boyd Dunlop Jr. (who was known as Johnnie), prompted by the boy's complaints of jarring rides across Belfast's cobblestoned streets on his tricycle. The father and son story is a common trope. And like most tropes, it hides as much as it reveals. There is no evidence that the invention was prompted by the boy's complaints. But Johnnie did take the first test ride on a tricycle outfitted with two air tires on the night of February 28, 1888 (Dunlop 1925, p. 15; Bijker 1997, p. 79). And after the first successful test, Dunlop recalls Johnnie repeatedly asking him to hurry up to make more tires so that he could use them to beat his bigger friends in their cycle races at the People's Park in Belfast—the first of an escalating series of cycling races that would convince people of the value of these new pneumatic rubber objects. Dunlop's own telling, completed and published posthumously by his daughter, Jean McClintock, situates the moment of invention not as a sudden inspiration provoked by Johnnie's tricycle rides but rather as the resolution of a lifelong interest in transportation and the problem of antivibration. Dunlop dates his interest in the shock of crossing uneven ground back to his early days as a child in Dreghorn, Ayrshire, where the Dunlop clan tended great swaths of land as tenant farmers, writing, "[a]s long as I can remember I have taken an interest in locomotion by road, rail, and sea" (Dunlop 1925, p. 10). In Belfast, Dunlop employed 16 horse-shoers in his veterinary practice, which was one of the largest in Ireland at the time (Cooke 2000, p. 6), and it is easy to imagine that his childhood interest in antivibration would have been animated and amplified by regularly tending to animals who were experiencing the full impact of the road.

Like many inventions, the air tire reflects the materials, objects, people, and practices of work and play that were immediately at hand. One of the most important of these was rubber. By 1887, the process of vulcanization had been in use for 40 years and rubber was being used in a wide range of contexts. Dunlop attributes his turn to rubber in part to his "experience in making rubber appliances which I had invented in connection with my veterinary work" (Dunlop 1925, p. 15). For the pneumatic component, he drew inspiration from a common play object, a football, borrowing his son's football pump to inflate the tire's rubber tube through a supply tube and tying "the little air supply tube in the same manner as one would tie a football" (Dunlop 1925, p. 13). He would also have been familiar with rubber from the solid rubber tires that were used on the carriages drawn by the horses he treated and on tricycles like Johnnie's. Cycling drove the story of the air tire. The nineteenth century had seen the rise of both road and track races in Northern Europe and North America (Tenner 2003, p. 80). With the advent of the cycling craze in the 1860s, production of bicycles, tricycles, and other velocipedes surged and clubs and organizations and newly minted cycling companies sponsored races to encourage the purchase of the vehicles and adoption of the practice. Although some women competed, and cycling would eventually play an important role in increasing women's mobility (Bijker 1997), most of the racers at the time were men.

On May 18, 1889, Willie Hume, captain of the Cruisers' Cycle Club, ran away with every event at the Belfast Queen's College Sporting Games on a racer fitted with Dunlop tires made by Edlin and Sinclair, bicycle makers who had partnered with Dunlop after witnessing an early test. Willie Hume was not known as an outstanding cyclist, so on that day in May people took note of his wins. Harvey Du Cros, a Dublin born businessman of French Hugenot descent and president of the Irish Cycling Association, paid special attention. Hume had beaten two of Du Cros' six sons in those races. Du Cros' sons were top cyclists and their father, a former competitive athlete himself, took winning, and losing, seriously. Du Cros was not the first person to approach Dunlop about creating a company, but he was the one who ended up purchasing Dunlop's patents and orchestrating the incorporation of the Pneumatic Tyre and Booths Cycle Agency in November of 1889. As the company grew, cycling races continued to do the work of creating desire and demand for the new tire, first across Ireland and then in England where the "Irish Brigade" won all of the championships (Cooke 2000, p. 15). While Dunlop himself may have been fascinated with antivibration, what sold the air tire was the pursuit of speed (Bijker 1997, p. 84). The race track was where speed was put on display and this allowed the new tire to make its mark.

The cycling races that served as a testing ground for this new pneumatic technology were one endpoint for a global supply chain. In the company's early days, before it purchased its own rubber mills, Dunlop personally ordered the rubber sheets and tubes from India rubber manufacturers such as Thornton and Co. of Edinburgh, Bates of Leicester, and Silverton and Co. (officially the India Rubber, Gutta Percha, and Telegraph Works Company) (Dunlop 1925, p. 31). In the 1890s, the companies that Dunlop was purchasing from would have still relied on "wild" rubber, collected from trees and vines scattered throughout forests by people who had been indentured, enslaved, or otherwise coerced into the work in Brazil (an independent nation under the control of a military dictatorship led by Deodoro da Fonseca) and the Congo Free State (a territory under the personal control of King Leopold II of Belgium). But the plantations in India, Ceylon, and Malaya were on the horizon and the coming transformation in the model of production promised to undercut the existing models of extraction in South America and Africa. As a result, those at the sites of wild rubber extraction faced systems of savage oppression and violence exacted under the cover of a discourse of efficiency and rationality (Hochschild 1998; Loadman 2005; Taussig 1980).

As the rubber industry grew and the market boomed based in large part on the demand for tires, the sites of rubber extraction became areas of mass death. There are two well-known cases of torture and mass murder. The first occurred in the Congo Basin from 1885 to 1908 under Leopold II of Belgium. The second took place in the Putumayo region from 1879 to 1912 under the control of Julio César Arana, the Peruvian head of the British-registered Anglo-Peruvian Amazon Rubber Company. These two sites of sustained murder became known to the broader British and American public in part through two reports written by Roger Casement, who was sent by the British Foreign Office to document, and report on each site. Others who played a significant role in witnessing, documenting, and writing about the massacres in Congo include Edmund Morel, Joseph Conrad, and George Washington Williams (Hochschild 1998). In *King Leopold's Ghost*, Adam Hochschild describes how in Congo, when people failed to meet rubber quotas, Belgian "Force Publique soldiers or rubber company 'sentries' often killed everyone they could find" (Hochschild 1998, p. 226). Casement's 1904 report details cases of Belgian soldiers cutting off and smoking hands and penises to send with the shipment of rubber as evidentiary explanation for why the load was light (Casement 1904). The best estimate of the number of people who died in the region due to murder, starvation or exhaustion, and disease during the period of rubber extraction alone is in the neighborhood of ten million, on par with the total number of causalities in World War I (Hochschild 1998). It is impossible to give an accurate number of deaths, let alone a complete list of names of those who died.

Dunlop's name was attached to the tires from the start, beginning the transformation of the Scottish clan name into a global brand. By 1891, the company was making tires with treads that "left a trail of DUNLOP DUNLOP DUNLOP along the road, in the soft mud on wet days and in the dust on dry ones" (Tompkins 1981, p. 27). But it was not John Boyd Dunlop Sr. and Johnnie Dunlop but Harvey Du Cros and his sons who built and ran the global multinational that would carry the name and brandish the image of Dunlop. Despite Dunlop's resignation from the board in 1895 due partly to tensions between him and Du Cros, the company still used his name when it was floated on the stock exchange as the Dunlop Pneumatic Company in 1896. And decades later, Dunlop would sue the company over an advertisement that presented "a new John Boyd Dunlop, a tall, handsome, stylishly dressed old man, with a shiny hat and boots with spats, who had all the airs of an old bean. A cane and an eyeglass added to the splendour of the figure who recommended Dunlop wares to the world" (Cooke 2000, p. 28). In her forward to her father's autobiography, Jean McClintock writes, "It was unfortunate that he considered it necessary to sever all connection with the Company, which bears his name" (McClintock in Dunlop 1925, p. 5) and in her appendix adds:

> I should here like to state clearly that my father has never at any time received money or compensation in any form from the Dunlop Pneumatic Tyre Co., either for the use of this name and bust or publication of the advertisement to which he objected … We all objected to the advertisement, not because it depicted a younger man than my father, but because it depicted a type, which is the antithesis of what my father really was. (McClintock in Dunlop 1925, p. 95)

The story of the invention of Dunlop's air tire is not, or not just, a story about a father and son and a set of cycling races. It is notable that Dunlop does not name his wife, Margaret Stevenson, or his daughter Jean in the text, while his son Johnnie is named and pictured as is Johnnie's son, John Boyd. There is a story to be told about a daughter representing a father, and another about wives and mothers who are hard to catch sight of in the accounts the fathers and sons have written. And there is a story to be told about the millions of others who participated in collecting, transporting, and processing the rubber that went into these new pneumatic objects. The story of Dunlop is a story about carrying on, covering up, casting off, and handing over names.

"The Playing Fields of Industry": Dunlop Rubber Becomes an "All-Up" Company

Arthur Du Cros, the third son and eventual managing director and deputy chairman of Dunlop Rubber, opens *Wheels of Fortune: A Salute to Pioneers*, his telling of the story of pneumatic tire with this: "Around this innocent invention clusters tales of sport and adventure, of fortune and misfortune, of bitter litigation, and high finance" (Du Cros 1938, p. 1). Throughout the book, Du Cros returns repeatedly to the central role sport played in the building and sustaining of the business. About the production sites, he writes:

> All forms of outdoor activity were encouraged, for we regarded sport in any form, with its community of feelings and friendships among all classes, an asset worthy even the attention of British statesmen. To-day 'the playing fields of Eton' and all they stand for are being out-rivalled by the playing fields of industry and the Nation, a valuable and significant feature of our modern commercial life. (Du Cros 1938, pp. 220–221)

The saying that Du Cros references is that "the battle of Waterloo was won on the playing fields of Eton." The remark is usually attributed to the Duke of Wellington although there is no evidence that the commander of that famous battle ever said these exact words. But the phrase has been picked up and passed down as a way of encapsulating the argument that the games that boys play in Britain's public schools train them to be good soldiers. In *The Games Ethic and Imperialism*, J. A. Mangan describes the "profound purpose" of game play: "the inculcation of manliness" (Mangan 1986, p. 18). The "games ethic" taught the public schoolboy "the basic tools of imperial command: courage, endurance, assertion, control and self-control ... it promoted not simply initiative and self-reliance but also loyalty and obedience. It was therefore a useful instrument of colonial purpose. At one and the same time it helped create the confidence to lead and the compulsion to follow" (Ibid.). Arthur Du Cros, who attended a national school rather than a more prestigious public school and entered the Civil Service at the lowest pay grade, turns the Duke of Wellington's phrase to make a counterargument: it is not the "playing fields of Eton" but "the playing fields of industry" that are training British men to be the workers and soldiers and leaders and shareholders that the empire requires (Du Cros 1938, p. 221) (Fig. 2).

Arthur learned the power of sport from his father. Almost every description of Harvey Du Cros highlights his athletic prowess. In his youth he was a champion in fencing, running, and boxing, "known to all

Fig. 2 "Play up, play up, and play the game," the refrain from Sir Henry Newbolt's 1892 poem "Vitaï Lampada," carved on the relief at the entrance to Lord's Cricket Ground, London (Photo by C. Wing, 2014)

Ireland mainly as the greatest athlete of his day" (T. P. O'Connor in Dunlop 1925, p. 99). Most accounts then go on to describe how he instilled a love of sport in his six sons and trained them into fearsome cyclists. As Dunlop grew into a giant multinational, Harvey Du Cros ran the company as its chairman and patriarch, carving out central roles for his sons and maintaining an emphasis on sport across the board. James McMillan describes how "the old man [Harvey] reveled in encouraging his work-force to take part in sports as once he had spurred his sons to the same endeavors. Rugby football remained a passion with the Du Cros' and each factory had its own team" (McMillan 1989, p. 37). The company also "sponsored cycle racing, arranged training facilities under a competent trainer, and organized a regiment of professional racing teams with multiple machines" (Bijker 1997, p. 84). Along with promoting sport within the company, there were also business relationships that were secured and solidified by the common ground shared by sporting men. Arthur Du Cros attributes the formation of a partnership with the Byrnes family's rubber goods business which would become Dunlop's first rubber mills, to a "kinship of sport and country" (Du Cros 1938, p. 208). The Du Cros used these "playing fields of industry" to promote the same game ethic that was fostered in the British public schools within the company as it expanded rapidly, creating and acquiring ever more subsidiaries in Europe, Africa, Asia, and the Americas, becoming its own empire.

From the early twentieth century on, Dunlop was an "all-up" company, "from raw rubber via cord to the finished tyre: manufactured worldwide and sold worldwide. Dunlop Rubber was now a multinational, perhaps the first of its kind on the face of the globe" (McMillan

1989, p. 37). To achieve this, the company had begun by purchasing patents and producing tires exclusively and worked backward from there to rubber mills and rubber manufacturers and finally to rubber trees and rubber plantations. Arthur Du Cros was part of the group that surveyed Ceylon and the Straits Settlements (the British name for what was in 1955 called Malaya and is now known as Malaysia). He chose the latter as the spot for the company to purchase plantations. In 1910, the company established its first rubber plantations in Malaysia and formed the Virginia Rubber Company in the US, which became Dunlop Plantations in 1915 (Dunlop Tire & Rubber Goods Co. 1953). At its peak in 1920, Dunlop had plantations with attached factories around the world, with especially large holdings in India and Malaysia. The company would continue to be the single largest private landholder in Malaysia through the 1970s.

Given the central role of sport, it is not surprising that when the company began to look beyond tires, they diversified by beginning to produce other kinds of sports equipment. The company's first sport product for ball games was the "Orange Spot" golf ball which arrived in 1910 followed by Dunlop tennis balls in 1922 (Dunlop Tire & Rubber Goods Co. 1953, p. 12). After the advent of vulcanized rubber, many balls began to be made with rubber bladders or rubber cores. Golf balls became inextricable from the rubber industry to such an extent that even today "half of the present market share in golf balls belongs to four manufacturers that emerged from the colonial rubber trade" (Brown 2015, p. 23), with Dunlop being one of these four. Dunlop's long-standing investment in sports was formalized with the creation of the Dunlop Sports subsidiary in 1928. This was just one of the company's many subsidiaries. The list of subsidiaries included in the Dunlop Rubber Company reports and balance sheets for the years 1901–1965 names 159 separate corporate entities (National Archives of the UK 2018). By 1946, the company had 90,000 shareholders and 70,000 employees around the world (Ibid). Each site and subsidiary had people with their own set of stories, people whose lives have been touched and torqued, made and unmade, by the making and moving and using of elastic things.

The company produced promotional materials for its customers and its workers. The media directed at its own workers included the publication of a romanticized and sanitized version of *The Story of Rubber* (31) and a similar film called *Dunlop in Malaya* (Dunlop 1955), which presented a picture of the first stop of the company's supply chain, Dunlop's rubber plantations in Malaysia. In *The Story of Rubber* (31), the transformation of rubber into a plantation crop is presented as necessary to ensure quality and volume. Describing the sites of wild rubber production, the text declares: "Not only were these areas unable to supply the quantities required, but because of a lack of care for the trees, the quality of the rubber was bad. To ensure the greatest production of high quality rubber, the areas selected for plantation were carefully chosen" (Dunlop Rubber Company 1957, p. 11). The description is striking. The claim that a lack of care for the trees made the quality of the rubber bad figures the plantation as a structure of care, a place where trees will be properly looked after. The phrasing reads as a displacement that tells us more about what the company did and did not care about than it tells us about how the trees and vines and people were treated. The film *Dunlop in Malaya* highlights the 20,000 person workforce made up of people of many different nationalities, religions and languages, the roads, hospitals, schools, religious buildings, recreational activities, and playing fields, before turning to the industrial processes and "security measures for the personnel on the estate" (Rice 2010). The film was screened at Dunlop sites in England, France, Germany, Australia, Brazil, Canada, India, Japan, New Zealand, South Africa, and the US. Neither the book nor the film name the history of mass deaths tied to rubber production, nor do they mention the Malaysian workers' strikes in 1940, which according to an exchange in the British Parliament in 1941 saw the arrests of two of the strike leaders, a march of 500 workers on the police station to protest these arrests, and police gunfire that killed 3 and injured many more (House of Commons and Lords Hansard 1941).

Three decades before *The Story of Rubber* and *Dunlop in Malaya* were produced, and a few years before Dunlop Sport was created, Arthur Du Cros and his brothers were pushed off the board largely because of Arthur's failure to separate his family's interests from the company's interests and his role in financial manipulation that left the company close to bankruptcy in 1921. Like the leaders of multinational companies then and now, Dunlop's leaders and representatives wielded multiple forms of authority. They were executives, employers, sponsors, patrons, patriarchs, overseers, leaders, political representatives. They did not always maintain clear or clean boundaries between the different kinds of authority and power that they wielded. The company was saved by F. A. Szarvasy of the British Foreign and Colonial Service (Jones 1984, p. 44) and the Du Cros family was ushered out. The expansion that followed was pursued in relation to the parallel growth of the other major rubber manufacturers and the relationships that each of these giant multinationals had to the nations that they claimed as homes and as territories. In 1985 Dunlop Rubber was acquired by its longtime competitor British Tyre and Rubber (BTR). BTR proceeded to spin off—sell—most of the company's subsidiaries and then renamed itself Invensys, as part of a transformation into a conglomerate of companies that focus on software, industrial automation, energy controls, and appliances. But the name Dunlop, which was first printed onto dirt roads in 1891, and the Flying D logo, which was launched in 1960, persist. Today, they are used by companies around the world that sell Dunlop tires, conveyor belts, golf balls, tennis rackets, mattresses, and footwear. In acquiring the right to use the Dunlop brand these disparate companies have acquired a common lineage while having no other necessary relation to each other. Their wielding of the brand can in turn render the lineages of the current companies (Goodyear, Sumitomo Rubber, the Ruia Group, Pacific Brands, Sports Direct) a little harder to see. We could think of this game of hide and seek as another kind of vulcanized play.

True Bounce and False Bounds: The Spinning Off of Dunlop Sport

The Dunlop Sport that Raneem El Welily directed her complaints toward in 2013 was Mike Ashley's Dunlop. When the World Squash Federation first partnered with Dunlop in 1991, the company had already been acquired by BTR. When BTR spun off a number of subsidiaries following the acquisition, Dunlop was sold to Cinven, a private equity fund backed by British Coal, the Railway Industry, and Barclay's Bank, in 1995. In 2002, Cinven closed the factory in Barnsley, England, that had produced the tennis balls for Wimbledon and most of the company's squash balls for many years. Production was moved to a factory in the Bataan Economic Zone in the Philippines, a move that included the machines from the Barnsley factory being shipped to Bataan. Cinven eventually turned the brand over to the Bank of Scotland who in turn sold the brand to Mike Ashley and his company Sports Direct in 2003. Before Ashley went into the sport retail business and became a billionaire by buying and selling brands, he was a county-level squash player and later a county-level squash coach. By the time he purchased the Dunlop Slazenger brand, Ashley was running the largest sport retail business in the UK. Sports Direct's business model is based on brands and bargain. The Channel 4 *Dispatches* episode, "The Secrets of Sports Direct," documented the company's misleading pricing policies including regular "slapping [brand logos] on anything they like," as well as their practice of keeping a majority of their employees on zero-hour contracts (Dowling 2015).

The balls in El Welily's photograph (see Fig. 1) are marked "Pro" and carry the stamp "WSF PSA WISPA" identifying the ball's standing as the official ball of the World Squash Federation (WSF), the Professional Squash Association (PSA), and the Women's International Squash Players Association (WISPA). But WISPA had been renamed the Women's Squash Association (WSA) in 2011 so the balls pictured are either two or more years old at the time of the photograph (and thus almost as old when El Welily used and discarded them) or the factory failed to change the stamp when the association changed its name. Was this a case of dumping factory seconds or old stock from recently defunct factories in England and South Africa? Or was there a problem at the factory in Bataan? Andrew Shelley, chief executive of the World Squash Organization, does not remember the specifics beyond some problem with quality control and that the balls were "losing nap" too quickly. (Nap being the name for the texture on the surface of the ball that lets players control the ball when it hits their rackets strings [A. Shelley, personal communication, Jan 7, 2019].) Some period of time after the professional squash organizations made an appeal to Dunlop, the balls began bouncing properly again. In 2017, Ashley sold the Dunlop Sports brand to Sumitomo Rubber, which already owned the rights to Dunlop Sport in Japan,

Taiwan, and Korea as well as the rights to Dunlop Tires and Dunlop Tyres in Asia and Africa.

True bounce is a quality that depends on regular objects, surfaces, and environments. The notion of true and false bounce appears in early twentieth-century American and British discussions of sport. A *New York Times* article from August 21, 1914, titled "No Cause for Worry: European War Will Have No Effect on American Sporting Implements," describes the difference in quality between English and American tennis balls as "a trifle in resiliency or 'true bounce' that only the most expert player can detect" (1914). Another article from the same year in the *London Times* details a dispute between the British and American Davis Cup tennis teams. The Americans were wearing steel points (what we would call cleats) that were tearing up Wimbledon's painstakingly pre-pared grass and of course impacting the bounce: "Steel points … produce false bounds, and the more false bounds the worse for the British Isles players, who allow the ball to bounce more often than the Americans do" (1913). The writer describes the difference as a difference in style of play, and says the Americans are understandably anxious about "their foot-hold, which depends upon wearing what they are accustomed to; and their foothold is as much to them as the true bounce is to us" (Ibid.). In this case the ball is true but the surface, marred with holes from the steel points, has become false. One way that true bounce is assured is through regular testing. Since the mid-twentieth century, Dunlop has used "robot players": machines that strike balls continuously with a racket such that they "rebound from concrete surfaces back again on to the machine which strikes them again. In this way the playing quality of the melton [fabric exterior] is measured in a very short time and special balls can be designed for use in parts of the world where different climatic conditions would affect their performance" (Dunlop Rubber Company 1957, pp. 58–59). Supplying true bounce is an important part of what sporting goods and tire manufacturers do.

While the World Squash Federation does not have the resources to regularly test the bounce of Dunlop's balls against their established specifications, better resourced ball sport organizations do. In the case of tennis, any company may submit balls to the International Tennis Federation (ITF) for testing and, if they pass, the balls from that particular production line are sanctioned by the ITF as proper. For big tournaments, samples of the already sanctioned balls are retested to ensure the quality of the batch. The bounce facility at the US Tennis Association (USTA), the American cousin of the ITF, exists for the sole purpose of testing balls and surfaces for "trueness" in the sense of consistency and reliability. The ITF is in charge of testing the balls that Dunlop makes for Wimbledon every year. Specifications are given in ranges rather than exact numbers: they name the degrees of difference that are considered tolerable or "true enough." Balls are strange objects to test for "truth." This is especially true of pressurized pneumatic objects. They are physically unable to stay constant to themselves. The tennis balls in the USTA bounce test facility are simply representative samples, standing in for all the others. Over 90,000 tennis balls are used during a single US Open tournament. The organizing bodies that set the rules and specifications of play and the global industrial supply chains that run from plantation and processing plant to factory and distribution center usually garner less attention than the spectacle of the players' performances. But these institutions produce the equipment and build the venues for sport that serve as the fixed ground that these athletes depend on and depart from. Athletes develop their highly channeled virtuosities around reliable objects and environments. At least in the case of ball sports, this kind of reliability makes possible their regular extraordinary demonstrations of the limits of human capacity.

True bounce continues to be achieved through standards, specifications, quality control, plantation agriculture, well-secured global supply chains, and dramatically unequal systems of labor and distribution. The Dunlop Pro squash ball is a small thing—a minor player in the ongoing story of globalization. But now picture all of the balls used for tennis, golf, basketball, volleyball, baseball, soccer, football, handball. Picture all of the ball pits, Walmart bins, and supermarket vending machines filled with bouncy balls. These ubiquitous objects connect our everyday gestures to global histories (Fig. 3). They are histories of children's play and organized sports spectacles, histories of the material technologies of rubbers and plastics, histories of industrial manufacturing including pneumatics systems and injection molding, and histories of colonialism,

Fig. 3 Balls collected by the author and Cuauhtli from the streets of Los Angeles (Photo by C. Wing, 2019)

postcolonialism, and the persistence of imperial power. These histories are the conditions of existence for so many seemingly simple objects that are so deeply embedded in our lives. I call this an era of vulcanized play rather than vulcanized sport, because it is not just our institutionalized forms of play that rest on rubber. What these histories of John Boyd Dunlop, Dunlop Rubber, Dunlop Sports, and the Dunlop Pro squash ball let us begin to understand is just how much of our formal and informal movements rest on and revolve around rubber, and what that material attachment ties us to. Rubber mediates contact and impact and, in doing so, structures both how we want to and how we are able to move.

Acknowledgments Thank you to all of the squash players who spoke with me about the behavior of the Dunlop Pro squash balls, to Mary McDonald and

Jennifer Sterling for running the sports and technology panels at the annual 4S conference and for inviting me to contribute to this volume, to Hannah Zeavin and Jessica Feldman for reading drafts of this chapter, and to Cuauhtli for collaborating with me in rescuing many abandoned balls from the streets of Los Angeles.

References

Bijker, W. E. (1997). *Of bicycles, bakelites, and bulbs: Toward a theory of sociotechnical change*. Cambridge, MA: MIT.

Brown, H. (2015). *Golf ball*. New York: Bloomsbury.

Casement, R. (1904). *Correspondence and report from his majesty's consul at Boma respecting the administration of the independent state of Congo*. Retrieved from https://archive.org/stream/CasementReport/CasementReportSmall_djvu.txt.

Cooke, J. (2000). *John Boyd Dunlop*. Dublin: Dreoilín Publications.

Dowling, T. (2015, April 15). The Secrets of Sports Direct review: Along with cheap trainers, Sports Direct is also known for its giant mugs – The customers. *The Guardian*. Retrieved from https://www.theguardian.com/tv-and-radio/2015/apr/28/the-secrets-of-sports-direct-review.

Du Cros, A. P. (1938). *Wheels of fortune. A salute to pioneers*. London: Chapman & Hall.

Dunlop. (1955). *Dunlop in Malaya* [35mm Film].

Dunlop, J. B. (1888). *10,607*. London: Patent Office.

Dunlop, J. B. (1925). *The history of the pneumatic tyre*. Dublin: A. Thom & Co.

Dunlop Tire & Rubber Goods Co. (1953). *The story of Dunlop through the reigns*. Toronto: Dunlop Tire and Goods Co. Ltd.

El Welily, R. (@RaneemElWelily). (2013, August 18). Dear @DunlopSport ur terrible squash balls r ruining my life. These'll all go to waste!! Not even round #BadQuality. Tweet. Retrieved from https://twitter.com/RaneemElWelily/status/369151620782649345.

Hancock, T. (1857). *Personal narrative of the origin and progress of the caoutchouc or India-rubber manufacture in England*. London: Longman, Brown, Green, Longmans, & Roberts.

Haraway, D. J. (2016). *Staying with the trouble: Making kin in the Chthulucene*. Durham, NC: Duke University Press.

Hochschild, A. (1998). *King Leopold's ghost: A story of greed, terror, and heroism in Colonial Africa*. Boston: Houghton Mifflin.

House of Commons and Lords Hansard. (1941, December 5). Malaya (rubber estate workers). HC vol 372 cc1022-5. Retrieved from https://api.parliament.uk/historic-hansard/index.html.

Jones, G. (1984). The growth and performance of British multinational firms before 1939: The case of Dunlop. *The Economic History Review, 37*(1), 35–53.

Litman, L. (2014, October 15). Alex Morgan on why artificial turf is tough for players. *USA Today*. Retrieved from https://www.usatoday.com/story/sports/soccer/2014/10/15/alex-morgan-us-women-artificial-turf-world-cup/17295011/.

Loadman, J. (2005). *Tears of the tree the story of rubber: A modern marvel.* Oxford: Oxford University Press.

Mangan, J. A. (1981). *Athleticism in the Victorian and Edwardian public school: The emergence and consolidation of an educational ideology.* Cambridge: Cambridge University Press.

Mangan, J. A. (1986). *The games ethic and imperialism: Aspects of the diffusion of an ideal.* New York: Viking.

Mangan, J. A., & McKenzie, C. C. (2010). *Militarism, hunting, imperialism: 'Blooding' the martial male.* London: Routledge.

McMillan, J. (1989). *The Dunlop story: The life, death, and re-birth of a multinational.* London: Weidenfeld and Nicolson.

New York Times. (1914, August 21). No cause for worry: European war will have no effect on American sporting implements.

Rice, T. (2010). Synopsis, context, and analysis of *Dunlop in Malaya.* Colonial Film: Moving Images of the British Empire. Retrieved from http://www.colonialfilm.org.uk/node/4440.

"sport, n.1". [Etymology and Def. 4a]. *Oxford English Dictionary.* 2019, March. Oxford University Press. Retrieved April 7, 2019, from http://www.oed.com/viewdictionaryentry/Entry/187476.

Taussig, M. T. (1980). *The devil and commodity fetishism in South America.* Chapel Hill, NC: University of North Carolina Press.

Tenner, E. (2003). *Our own devices: The past and future of body technology.* New York: Alfred A. Knopf.

The Story of Rubber. [With illustrations.]. (1957). London: Educational Productions in collaboration with Dunlop Rubber Co.

The Times (London). (1913, July 25). Lawn Tennis, p. 15.

Tompkins, E. (1981). *The history of the pneumatic tyre; produced by the Dunlop Archive Project.* Lavenham: Eastland.

Tully, J. A. (2011). *The devil's milk: A social history of rubber*. New York: Monthly Review Press.

Whittington, E. M., & Mint Museum of Art. (2001). *The sport of life and death: The Mesoamerican ballgame*. New York: Thames & Hudson.

Wing, C. (2015). Episodes in the Life of Bounce. *Cabinet*, (56). Retrieved from http://cabinetmagazine.org/issues/56/wing.php.

Manufacturing Invisibility in "the Field": Distributed Ethics, Wearable Technologies, and the Case of Exercise Physiology

Andi Johnson

On a cold, gloomy winter day in 2007, a team of British exercise physiologists set out to conduct a "field" study. The principal investigator, Andrew, aimed to investigate the physiological mechanisms of endurance.[1] This day, he and his team departed their laboratory carrying a clipboard, data-recording sheet, extra battery, stopwatch, and face mask. Their subject, Neil, a nationally ranked distance runner, wore several instruments that would measure his body while he ran outside. The instruments included a "K4" device to measure oxygen consumption (the face mask would hold a chamber into which Neil would breathe), another device to receive data transmitted from a "core temperature" pill Neil had ingested hours before and now resided somewhere in his gut, an "accelerometer" to measure his movement along three axes, and a GPS to track his position in time and space.

Andrew, his team, and Neil crossed a road, entered an undulating, urban park, and came to a halt at the bottom of a hill. Along the way,

A. Johnson (✉)
University of Pennsylvania, Philadelphia, PA, USA
e-mail: andria@sas.upenn.edu

© The Author(s) 2020

J. J. Sterling, M. G. McDonald (eds.), *Sports, Society, and Technology*,
https://doi.org/10.1007/978-981-32-9127-0_3

Fig. 1 Left: An exercise physiology field trial. Right: Subject wears the K4, core temperature pack, accelerometer, and GPS. A researcher puts on the face mask (Photos by A. Johnson)

they navigated people pushing prams (strollers), walking dogs, and cycling. Andrew smiled when those same passersby paused to stare at Neil, who looked as though he wore a jet pack (Fig. 1). Neil was to run 6.2 miles (10 km) in the park, three times around a route previously mapped out by Andrew. Two researchers on bicycles would accompany Neil, their task to guide him through the course and, Andrew only half-joked, to protect Neil from delinquent teenagers. Contemplating the dogs, babies, wind, and slick surfaces, one member of the team anticipated a crash.

Neil ran the first two loops of the course without event. Then, as he turned a tight downhill corner to enter some botanical gardens, Neil slipped. The fall looked serious, but Neil got up quickly and, unable to talk because of the face mask, gave a slight wave to signal he was okay. As Neil emerged from the last loop of the course, the research team cheered him into the finish, immediately removed his face mask, and rushed the sweat-drenched Neil back to the lab before he became too cold. Once inside, they detached the rest of the equipment, downloaded the data, and began reading the graphs generated by software programs. Exercise physiologists plot the individual data points generated by their instruments and rely upon "the graphical method" to represent physiological data (y-axis) over time (x-axis) (Brain 2015; Brain and Wise 1994; Hankins 1999). Crestfallen, Andrew explained to Neil that he would have to repeat this trial another day because, at $x = 20$ minutes, the curve of the oxygen consumption data "plummeted" in a way that suggested instrument error.

Cold, wind, pedestrians, dogs, prams, fear of falls, falls, extra batteries, data loss ... field studies, many scientists contend, are messy. To do science out in the world, away from the comfort and control of the laboratory, is, at best, hard; at worst, intellectually unreliable or physically dangerous. However, physiologists have regularly conducted field studies, including studies in far more extreme environments than this urban park, for over a century (Heggie 2013; Tracy 2012).

Drawing upon ethnographic data, this chapter follows exercise physiologists within and between the lab and "the field." In the mid-2000s, I spent seven months at three world-renowned exercise physiology "human performance" laboratories in South Africa, the UK, and the US. I lived near the laboratories, observed the daily routines of and talked informally to the scientists, took notes and photographs, and conducted 63 semi-structured, open-ended interviews with scientists and technicians. While employing standard techniques from "lab studies" (Dumit 2004; Knorr-Cetina 1999; Latour and Woolgar 1986; Traweek 1992), this research was not confined to the lab. I followed scientists within and between the lab and what *they* labeled "the field," documenting scientific practices, including scientist-subject relations. The sites of the field studies I witnessed were diverse, from spaces of athletic training (like the urban park described above or training camps for distance runners in the North Rift of Kenya) to spaces of racing (like the Comrades Marathon in South Africa).

In this chapter, I ask whether the practices of exercise physiology field studies differ from those of their lab studies, and, if so, how? I privilege the exercise physiologists' designations of which studies constituted "field studies" and "lab studies" and then my own observations as to what practices unified or differentiated their field from their lab. I pay particular attention to relationships between the scientists and their athlete-subjects. I argue that, in contrast to inhabiting a rather visible, palpable role in the laboratory, exercise physiologists manufacture their own invisibility in the field—to the point that athletes may not even *sense* that they are subjects of scientific research.[2]

Describing exercise physiologists' fieldwork as the "manufacturing of invisibility," I am repurposing an analytic from Science and Technology Studies (STS), that of "invisible labor." Most accounts of "invisible labor" in STS point toward work done by people who receive little to no credit for that work, either from the scientific community or from those of us who write the history or sociology of science and technology (Bangham and Kaplan 2016). These "invisible" laborers include different kinds of "erased" research subjects (Stark 2016); technicians, assistants, or other "hidden helpers" (who may themselves conduct and write up most or even all of an experiment or study) (von Oertzen 2016); and disempowered scientists (e.g., many twentieth-century women scientists) (Oreskes 1996; Shapin 1989). In this framing, where there is "invisible labor," social and political hierarchies are at play, and gender is a clear theme (Kohlstedt 2016). In their introduction to a recent volume on "invisible labor" Jenny Bangham and Judith Kaplan summarize this meaning of "invisibility" as follows: "For these authors invisibility connotes a lack of recognition or credit, so that the social and political marginalization of certain people and processes pose barriers to understanding how science operates" (Bangham and Kaplan 2016, p. 4). "Invisibility," then, in some STS scholarship, suggests a status—a vulnerable, oppressed, or exploited status—ascribed to and embodied by a person.

A different meaning of "invisible labor" emerges from this ethnographic account of exercise physiology laboratory and field studies. "Invisibility" here connotes not a form of work ascribed to and embodied by a *person* on a lower rung of a social or political hierarchy but rather as a form of scientific *practice* strategically desired and deployed by scientists. The claim that scientists may actually desire their own "invisibility" is not novel. Following Lorraine Daston's (1992) account of the rise of "aperspectival objectivity" in nineteenth-century sciences, STS scholars have described how nineteenth- and twentieth-century ideals of scientific "objectivity" involve a "detached" scientist who aims to minimize individual impact on experiment—and to write about research as such. With the rise of "aperspectival objectivity," natural scientists began avoiding the first-person "I," for example (Daston 1992). So it is not surprising that exercise physiologists may adopt practices that help them achieve "invisibility"—being inconsequential, unnoticeable, without any individual impact on the study—because that invisibility may enhance their credibility as "objective" researchers.[3] Three things about exercise physiologists' strategically deployed "invisible labor" are surprising, though. First, place matters. It is not in the lab, but in the field that exercise physiologists manufacture their own invisibility, in doing so reinforcing their own justifications that their field research, fraught and messy as those studies may be, captures phenomena even "more real" than in the lab. Second, *to whom* the scientists become invisible in the field matters (Star and Strauss 1999). The exercise physiologists become invisible to their athlete-subjects. Third, contrary to the scientists' characterizations of field sites as "more real" than the lab, that is, as places imagined as untouched or uncontrolled by scientists, exercise physiologists extend a great deal of effort to *manufacture* their own invisibility in the field. Documenting that effort is the goal of this chapter.

In the rest of this chapter, I first establish exercise physiology as an interesting case for both Sport Studies and STS scholars. Two sections then describe the exercise physiology lab and field, respectively, providing a backdrop for the argument to come. As I will show, in the "human performance laboratory," exercise physiologists unabashedly saturate trials with their own presence, with their hands-on, eyes-on, voices-on practices. In contrast, in "the field," the same exercise physiologists become "invisible" to their athlete-subjects; the scientist-subject relationship appears to dissolve. I then illustrate just *how* exercise physiologists manufacture their own invisibility in the field through two mechanisms, one ethical and the other technical. First, by taking advantage of the social heterogeneity of field sites, exercise physiologists distribute the ethical responsibility for their subjects' safety and consent. Second, by miniaturizing instruments, exercise physiologists study their subjects from a distance. The conclusion engages with recent Sport Studies and STS conversations about "wearable technologies" to consider the broader biopolitical implications of manufactured invisibility in exercise physiology field research.

Exercise Physiology at the Intersection of Sport Studies and STS

Exercise physiologists study bodies in motion. They investigate physiological systems (e.g., respiratory, cardiovascular, metabolic) under the condition of "exercise," or movement. Since the late nineteenth century, exercise physiologists have studied repetitive motions like running, walking, and cycling in laboratories, where these motions have been produced and measured using treadmills and stationary cycles (Gibson 2018; Heggie 2011; Johnson 2013a, b, 2015; Rabinbach 1990; Scheffler 2011, 2015; Wrynn 2010).[4] Outside of the laboratory, these physiologists have studied human movement in a range of environmental conditions. Through lab and field studies, exercise physiologists have aimed to elucidate mechanisms of human fatigue, metabolism, and endurance and to apply their findings to industry, the military, medicine, and sport (Heggie 2010, 2011, 2013; Hoberman 1992; Johnson 2015; Scheffler 2015; Svensson 2013; Svensson and Sörlin 2018; Tracy 2012).[5]

Some exercise physiologists use animal models in experiments. Others study human beings. Of the latter, some scientists, like Andrew, focus on the study of "well-trained" athletes, like Neil, because the scientists find athletes' familiarity with moving in repetitive ways (like running or cycling) helpful for particular research questions or protocols and because an athlete's familiarity with exercising means he or she will not experience a "training effect" or adaptation between experimental and control conditions (Hale 2008; Johnson 2013a).[6] Exercise physiology research involving "well-trained" athletes garners the label "human performance" research.

Exercise physiologists regularly confront questions fundamental to both Sport Studies and STS scholars: Which bodies do scientists define as "normal," "abnormal," or "supernormal"? How do scientists draw boundaries between "natural" and "unnatural" performances? In what ways do scientific facts succeed in capturing complex and dynamic relationships between biology, history, environment, and technology—in what ways do they fail? Definitions of sex, doping, and disability are some of the most controversial examples of the stakes of the knowledge produced by exercise physiologists (Fouché 2017; Henne 2015). Even more mundane aspects of exercise physiology—such as *where* to conduct research—raise questions about knowledge production intriguing to both Sport Studies and STS communities. Because scientists like Andrew move between their "human performance" laboratories and sporting spaces they call "the field," exercise physiology offers an exciting case to consider: Is the knowledge produced about human physiology in sporting spaces considered by scientists to be more or less "real" than their laboratory-generated data? (Did the cold, slippery, and somewhat crowded and hilly conditions make Neil's 10k respiratory, thermoregulatory, and running economy data more trustworthy than values he might produce on a treadmill back in Andrew's laboratory? Less?) How are sporting spaces transformed by exercise physiologists—ethically and technically—into sites of scientific field research? What are the consequences, if any, of this transformation, and for whom?

Historians and philosophers of science have long questioned whether scientists think about or practice research differently in "the lab" versus "the field," exploring scientists' own ideas about where and under what conditions facts are most reliably elicited (Gieryn 2006; Heggie 2013; Kingsland 2009; Kohler 2002, 2011; Kuklick 2011; Kuklick and Kohler 1996; Nielsen et al. 2012; Oreskes 2003; Rees 2006, 2007; Ries 2012; Vetter 2011). Important questions about scientific knowledge production are tackled in these studies: *Where* does scientific truth happen? How does *the place* of science affect what can be known, with what tools, and by whom? STS scholarship suggests that, on the one hand, the concept of "the field" is useful as an actors' category, a concept that "marks epistemological, temporal, and spatial boundaries" for scientists (Nielsen et al. 2012, p. 11). "The field" also marks scientists' moral boundaries. That is, scientists ascribe certain characteristics or values to field research and, in turn, to themselves (Heggie 2016b; Herzig 2005; Hevly 1996; Nielsen et al. 2012; Oreskes 1996; Ries 2012). Although "the field" may be an actors' category, STS scholarship demonstrates, on the other hand, that it is empirically untenable to assume a priori that the actual *practices* of research are different in places scientists label "the field" versus their laboratories (Kohler 2011, pp. 252–253; Latour 1999, pp. 24–79; Powell 2007, p. 3; Rees 2007, pp. 884–885). Moreover, examples of "lab-field hybrids" abound (Heggie 2016b; Henke 2000; Kingsland 2009; Kohler 2002, pp. 97–134), calling into question *any* analytical utility of the category of "the field" as distinct from "the lab" (Heggie 2016b). These two conclusions—that "the field" is a meaningful actor's category and yet the actual practices of lab and field sciences cannot be distinguished in advance by the analyst—suggest that what distinguishes field science, if anything, is an empirical question to be answered on a case-by-case basis.

Few *ethnographic* case studies of field research have been framed to contribute to our understanding of the lab and the field (though see Latour 1999; Henke 2000), and even fewer ethnographic studies of *human* science field research have been framed to do so. Not "human scientists" as traditionally defined—not, for example, anthropologists, sociologists, or psychologists—exercise physiologists who work with human subjects, nonetheless, consider their research subject, as one exercise physiologist wrote in 1990, "the intact human being in all the conditions in which he [*sic*] lives and breathes and has his [*sic*] being" (Chapman 1990, p. 30). Exercise physiologists regularly claim that they are not interested in understanding just one organ or just one physiological system but in understanding human beings as complex phenomena (Gibson 2018, p. 3). A student who worked with Andrew on the endurance physiology field study explained that Andrew's study was one of the few offered by his life sciences department that allowed him to study "whole people."

Visible Scientists and the Drama of the Human Performance Lab

Although they spanned three continents, the labs I studied shared many features of experimental practice (see Fig. 2), including the spaces of experiment, such as, rooms that contain treadmills or cycle ergometers, nearby biochemical labs, and environmental chambers; complex instruments, like gas analyzers, as well as simpler tools, such as Allen wrenches for adjusting a bike settings to an individual subject or paper towels for wiping a subject's sweat; and techniques such as anthropometry, normalizing instruments, drawing blood and taking muscle biopsies, getting informed consent, recording values in tables and representing data in graphs, and

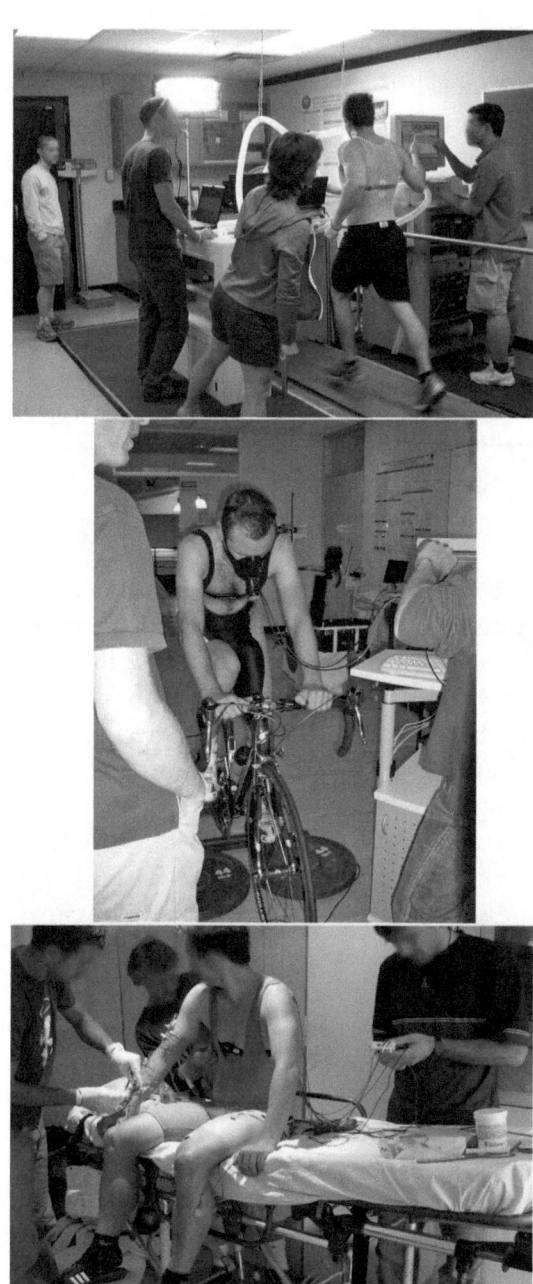

Fig. 2 Physiologists, instruments, and subjects in human performance laboratories (Photos by A. Johnson)

working in teams.[7] Although a full analysis of the colonial history of exercise physiology is outside the scope of this chapter, it is worth noting here that the three laboratories were all also gendered male and predominantly white.

The exclusivity of some field sites notwithstanding (e.g., getting to and up Mt. Everest, see Heggie 2016b, p. 822), laboratories, in particular, have long been characterized by STS scholars as spatial technologies of exclusion, an exclusion that promises control and discipline (Knorr-Cetina 1999; Kohler 2002). Gieryn (2006) observes, "Laboratory walls enable scientists to gain exquisite control over the objects of their analysis … Labs are designed to segregate out potential contaminants—both natural and human" (pp. 5–6). Together with scientists and their subjects, other people occupying the exercise physiology labs included custodians, technicians, visitors from funding agencies, and prospective graduate students. Nonetheless, all three exercise physiology laboratories constituted spatial technologies of exclusion. Entering the lab in South Africa required holding an institutional magnetic security card, being buzzed through an entrance gate by a security guard on the ground floor, moving through a controlled reception area, and having access to a particular key for the lab itself. The lab in the UK also restricted access to those with a building ID card, a key, and movement past a guard. In the US, while anyone could roam the building, the lab itself required a key for entry. All three labs were, in the words of historian Chris Henke, "cordoned off from the rest of the world, both physically and symbolically" (2000, p. 494).

Inside the walls of the human performance laboratory, exercise physiologists saturate trials with their own presence, that is, with their hands-on, eyes-on, voices-on practices. This dramatic role enables exercise physiologists to provoke the physiological processes of fatigue, metabolism, and endurance they aim to study—particularly during protocols that require a "max" effort. The century-old VO$_2$Max test is such a protocol. The VO$_2$Max test measures a person's ability to consume oxygen during "work" or exercise. A subject breathes into a face mask (that captures expired air to be analyzed) *while* running or biking at specified paces or watts designed to elicit fatigue (at "max") in a very short period of time (Hale 2008). Other protocols often require subjects to perform at their "peak" or "100%." Physiologists' knowledge claims about the causes of fatigue (as determined by these "max" tests) rest on their certainty that subjects are trying hard. One American researcher reminded his subject before a trial, "The effectiveness of my results depends upon you giving me a good effort." However, and this is the key point to understand about the drama of the human performance lab, exercise physiologists often do more than gently remind their human subjects about their expectations *before* the trial; the scientists also remind them—loudly—during the trial. During experiments, the scientists, well, they yell at their subjects.

One of the first times I experienced an exercise physiologist scream at a subject during a laboratory experiment, I was documenting an investigation of the brain's role in fatigue. The scientist's fatigue-inducing protocol required her subject to perform three "100%" bicep curls. That day, the scientist explained to her subject what she meant by 100%: Pull "as hard as you can. Like you're pulling someone out of the ocean who is drowning." After taking a baseline measurement during which the subject was still, the researcher said, "Ok. Are you ready? This is now the real one. 3 … 2 … 1 …" Suddenly she started screaming at him in the loudest voice I had heard since beginning my research. I jumped. My heart raced. Seeing this otherwise soft-spoken and nice person suddenly scream at another human being was jarring. She screamed, "Pull! Pull! C'mon, c'mon, pull harder! Pull harder, pull! Pull! And relax," with the word "relax" suddenly soft and quiet again. "That was very good," she said calmly. Then, "35 seconds left to rest, 25, 10 put your hand back up, 5, 4, 3, 2, 1, Pull! Pull! C'mon, C'mon, pull harder, pull harder, pull, pull, and relax … Perfect." And then everything was nice and calm, and she was talking in a normal voice. Then all of a sudden again this ear-splitting "Pull! Pull! Pull!" right in his face. I was shocked. Back in my corner of academia (history, sociology, anthropology), people did not normally scream at each other. Screaming was not an everyday thing. Yet, over the course of the next year of ethnographic research, I witnessed this screaming during many exercise physiology laboratory experiments involving human subjects. Scientists used different words: "You've got to go until you can't go anymore!" "Grit your teeth and hang on!" "Push! Push! Push!" "Keep going! Keep going as long as possible! Drive it. Drive it. Drive it. C'mon. Keep going!" But they all screamed. To summarize, then, exercise physiology human performance laboratories are relatively exclusive spaces where scientists outnumber their subjects and perform a loud, visible, and dramatic role to encourage their subjects to try their hardest.

"What's Actually Happening": Exercise Physiologists' Field

Beyond the lab, exercise physiologists interested in processes from thermoregulation to metabolism also study athletes while they are training or competing in "the field." Exercise physiologists define "the field" as sites of human movement in the "real world," that is, *any place other* than the laboratory. This definition echoes constructions of "the field" in other disciplines. In the 2002 volume *Landscapes and Labscapes*, historian Robert Kohler takes up the basic question, "What is the field?" He remarks that twentieth-century American biologists came to define the field "as not-lab." "If the definition is not exactly true," Kohler suggests, "it is at least an actors' category" (2002, p. 6). Indeed, the variety of exercise physiology field studies I witnessed (set in an urban park, marathon medical tent, and rural region of Kenya) might seem wide-ranging and disparate, but this was precisely an artifact of the *scientists'* definition of the field as "not-lab."

Exercise physiologists conduct field studies because they value an assessment of what "actually happens" in human beings who are moving. One physiologist, who conducts both lab and field studies, pointed out to me in an interview that lab studies are the "gold standard" in terms of being able to "control for everything," which "as scientists that is what we should be striving for." However, he added, "I do like the field studies, because the benefit of them is that you're looking at, it's one thing to see what happens in the lab, it's another thing to look at what actually happens on the road." Field studies are useful, he repeated, "because that *represents what's actually happening*" (italics added). This physiologist's definition of "the field" echoes scientists who contend that field sites are more "real" or "natural" than the laboratory. In his analysis of manuscripts written by members of the Chicago School of the 1920s and

1930s, historian Thomas Gieryn (2006) notes how sociologists described Chicago as a field site where they encountered "reality before it has been made artificial via laboratory interventions" (Gieryn 2006, p. 6). Similarly, historian Amanda Rees describes the importance placed on the "naturalness" of the field by mid-twentieth-century primatologists. "The challenge [of field research]," Rees summarizes, "was thus to produce information that could bear comparison with that produced according to laboratory standards *without compromising the 'natural' state of the structures under study*" (2006, p. 311, italics added). "The field," then, is where some scientists feel they learn about "reality," "nature," or, in exercise physiology, "what actually happens" when human beings move.

What does the study of exercise physiology as it is "actually happening" involve in practice? Out in "the field," scientists appear much less concerned with eliciting, provoking even, their subjects' movements and efforts. Andrew's team cheered Neil into the finish, but they were not screaming at him the whole time, telling him how fast to go, nor really too concerned (for the trial) when he slipped and fell in the park. This is not surprising. Kohler (2002) notes that early twentieth-century American biologists appreciated that the environments of their field studies varied across time and place and were unpredictable, unrepeatable, and outside of the scientist's control. This "realness" of the studies is part of what made them valuable.

Nonetheless, some degree of control remains vital to exercise physiologists' knowledge production in the field. In fact, while field studies may be messy, exercise physiologists who conduct field studies do so because these sites are thought to provide *more* control than the laboratory when it comes to one particular variable of study: the subject's effort. During studies of competitions, in particular, scientists assume that athletes are moving at "max"—the key physiological event necessary for exercise physiologists to study the fatigue process. And herein lies one reason exercise physiologists in the field become "invisible." Gone is the physiologists' need (in the laboratory) to yell at their subjects in an attempt to elicit a "max" performance. In the field, actual coaches, supportive teammates, screaming fans, eager managers, and any number of nearby competitors, not to mention an athlete's anticipation of potentially breaking personal records or winning prize money, provide motivation enough.

At this point in my account, Sport Studies and STS scholars may find this comparison of the lab and "the field" in exercise physiology not particularly surprising. However, what is most interesting about the invisibility of exercise physiologists in "the field" is just how much social and technical work the physiologists have to do to successfully "detach" themselves from their subjects, even though the scientists' individual voices and relationships are no longer necessary to produce "max." In other words, ethnographic data suggests that exercise physiologists in the field do not passively observe "what actually happens." Rather, in the field, exercise physiologists actively work to render themselves less visible and dominant than in the laboratory. The next two sections describe two ways exercise physiologists manufacture invisibility in the field. First, they distribute the ethics of research across a socially heterogeneous space. Second, exercise physiologists abrogate control to miniaturized instruments.

Social Heterogeneity and Distributed Ethics

Many more kinds of people, all in different ethical relationships with one another, occupy the space of an exercise physiologist's "field." As a result, working in a far more socially heterogeneous space than their walled-off, keyed-in laboratories, exercise physiologists in the field distribute the ethical responsibility for human subjects' research to actors outside the scientist-subject relationship. This is not to say that scientists in the field deny any responsibility for the well-being of their human subjects, only that scientists may consider that responsibility shared across a more diverse array of actors, from sporting event directors and coaches, who solicit athletes' consent to participate in competition or training and who provide physical or emotional care to athletes, to others who use, share, or maintain the space of the field site, to the subjects themselves. (Sure, Neil fell during Andrew's field study, but both Andrew and Neil attributed the fall to a wet spot in the park and Neil's attempt to take the turn too quickly.) The social heterogeneity of the field enables the ethical relationship between the scientist and subject to be much more diffuse, at times even invisible. While Neil knew he was being studied by Andrew, in other field studies the subject does not even know the scientist is there.

I now take you into the "not-lab" of the Comrades Marathon. The Comrades Marathon is an 89-km (56 mile) race between the cities of Pietermaritzburg and Durban in the KwaZulu Natal province of South Africa. Initiated in 1921 as a living tribute to soldiers who died in World War I, the Comrades Marathon attracts participants from all over the world. For many South African runners, the race is something of a pilgrimage, with women and non-white men first officially allowed to participate in 1975. All participants who finish the race within a cut-off time (12 hours) earn a nationally recognized medal. Each year, teams of South African exercise physiologists travel to the Comrades Marathon to study participants' performances and to track various factors that might lead to or prevent fatigue. I had been documenting one team's laboratory studies when the opportunity arose to accompany a physiologist, whom I will call Kara, on her field study of hydration. Kara's goal was to document the serum sodium levels of fatigued (collapsed) runners as they received intravenous (IV) fluids. Over a span of about ten hours on race day, Kara's field study unfolded in the Comrades medical tent, a space roughly 50–60 meters × 25 meters enclosed by parachute material (Fig. 3). Located at the end of the race in Pietermaritzburg, by the end of the day this field site appeared more like a military clinic than a road race. Messy, indeed.

Kara spent a great deal of time and effort during the day coordinating her field research with the activities of many kinds of people who had as much or more claim to the space as she did. In fact, there were so many different kinds of people that they wore different color T-shirts. Green meant "runner" (not in the athlete sense of the word, but in the "gofer" sense of the word); yellow, doctor; gray, specialist; blue, nurses, sisters, or anyone who could take blood samples and blood pressure; orange, stretcher-bearers; yellow with black trim, massage therapists; red, physiotherapists. Kara's research team did not have its own color, though they all wore a shirt with the logo of their institution. Other people occupying the tent over the course of the day included a drug enforcement officer, grocery store clerks who "checked in" the athletes, high school volunteers, and family members looking for missing runners.

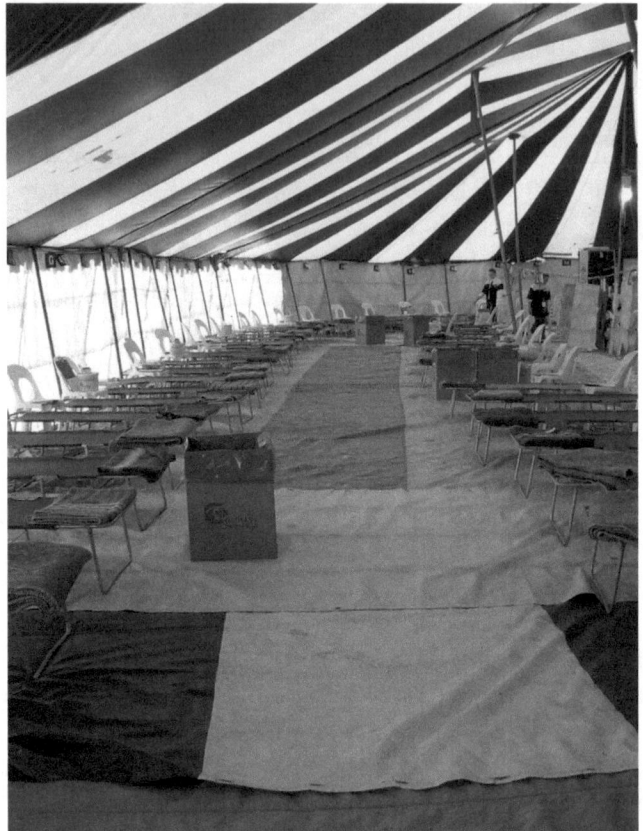

Fig. 3 The empty tent (Photo by A. Johnson)

Social heterogeneity is a distinguishing feature of field science. STS scholars have noted the ways in which twentieth-century high-altitude physiologists collaborated with alpinists, royalty, artists, soldiers, and guides (Heggie 2016b, p. 815); wildlife ecologists integrated their work with the lives of local farmers and hunters (Kohler 2002); primatologists navigated amongst the activities of tourists and backpackers, hunters, people who needed wood, other scientists, local field assistants, local administrators, park wardens and managers, and journalists (Rees 2006); and scientists conducting agricultural field trials articulated their experiments with inspectors from the county agricultural commissioner's office, migrant workers, Immigration and Naturalization Service agents, and thieves (Henke 2000).[8] STS scholarship on field science reveals how, in the words of historian Lynette Schumaker, "scientists in the field develop methods in response to political, social, cultural, and material conditions, which include the preexisting practices of others who share the field" (1996, p. 258). Adding to these studies of non-human sciences, this ethnographic account of exercise physiology field studies reveals the effect social heterogeneity has on scientist-subject relations.

First, as described above, exercise physiologists rely upon "the field" to elicit fatigue "naturally," allowing scientists to move to the shadows or the sidelines of the human performance. In a sea of other people, the scientists no longer occupy center stage, no longer need to dominate the research encounter. Second, the social heterogeneity of "the field" demands that exercise physiologists modify the ways they care for their research subjects and their data. Medical anthropologist Adriana Petryna has documented and critiqued flexible and therefore suspect applications of international ethics standards in global pharmaceutical research. She has showed how ethics are "used variably and tactically by all actors in a chain of interests involved in human subjects research" (2006, p. 53). In exercise physiology field studies, ethics are *distributed* across different relationships, often removing the scientist from the view of the subject. The consequence of this mechanism of invisibility, distributed ethics, is that, even though the athlete may sign different forms of consent (or waivers of liability) for different actors in the field, the athlete may not be aware of his or her participation in the exercise physiologist's specific study.

Several moments from Kara's field study exemplify how, in navigating socially heterogeneous spaces in the field, scientists distribute the ethical responsibility for the care of their research subjects and data and in so doing make their own presence less evident to their subjects. About 10 a.m. (over four hours after the start of the race), while still waiting for collapsed runners to be brought into the tent, Kara reviewed her protocol with the head doctor. Kara and the doctor agreed to abandon her proposed rehydration protocol and instead to ask the medical personnel to administer a liter of fluid, tracked over time and, if necessary, another liter. Kara emphasized that what she really needed were the athletes' blood sodium values over time (which would require the doctors to take discharge blood samples). The medical director assented. They agreed that each person on her team would partner with a particular doctor and area of the tent. Finally, when Kara began describing her process for getting informed consent from individual collapsed runners, the medical director steadfastly refused, asserting, "This is a privileged area" and reminding her that she is "not doing anything." Kara explained that she needed informed consent to publish the data. He shrugged, "Nonsense," offering to take full responsibility if any runners objected to having the amalgamated data published down the road. Kara acquiesced, partially distributing the research ethics of both care and consent through this medical authority.[9]

Throughout the day, Kara's team of physiologists maintained control over the athlete's blood, for the most part unbeknownst to the runners themselves, by working with and through other people who occupied the field site. By 2:30 in the afternoon, the orange-shirted stretcher-bearers (mostly high school rugby players) entered the tent regularly, carrying collapsed runners. Over the next four hours, the medical tent buzzed with activity. The gray-shirted specialists roamed. Kara's team of physiologists occasionally chatted with their runner-subjects, checked clipboards, and walked blood samples over to the folks at the radiometer.

By 6 p.m., over 12 hours since the race itself began, the scientists and others in the tent were still working, the tent full and busy (Fig. 4). With the sun setting and temperature plummeting, people layered on sweaters and coats. The runner-subjects laid on cots under wool blankets, making friends with the runners lying to their right and left, sometimes holding hands and telling each other it will be okay—another example of distributed care. When Kara offered to go to the hospital to follow up on three cases of hyponatremia, the medical director did not think this was appropriate and went alone. In total, 237 cases of collapse—maximum performances that "actually happened"—were seen in the medical tent that day, and Kara went on to publish the results from her field study in a peer-reviewed article about the relationship between serum sodium values, IV fluid administration, and recovery in collapsed runners. Kara remains one of the world experts on the physiology of hydration and fatigue.

Fig. 4 The full tent, with different color T-shirts indicating different kinds of actors. The figures under gray blankets are fatigued (collapsed) runners (Photo by A. Johnson)

What does an ethnographic perspective on Kara's field study reveal about how *the place* of science affects knowledge production or about differences between the lab and the field at the level of practice? All field scientists—regardless of their object of study, regardless of whether they are interested in bobwhite quail in Wisconsin, celery in California, sex workers in Chicago, or blood sodium values in Pietermaritzburg—navigate the social heterogeneity of their field sites. They work to understand a local culture, negotiate with others, and gain trust. Indeed, at the level of practice, Kara's field study required different skills of her than in the laboratory: She had to talk to different kinds of people, smile, help others out, sit back and be patient, compromise, strategize, and vigilantly watch over the actions of people who were *not* her research subjects. In fact, her research subjects hardly knew she was there.

Miniaturization of Instruments

Along with the distribution of ethics, a second element of exercise physiology field studies renders the scientist's presence less visible: mobile instruments to measure an array of physiological variables. Exercise physiologists need instruments of precision measurement to assess athletes' performances, and they need a way to record those measurements in real time. In the case of the Comrades medical tent, Kara's team took advantage of the radiometer that had been brought from a laboratory into the space of the tent. In other studies, field scientists deploy mobile instruments (Bourguet et al. 2002; Latour 1999, pp. 24–79; Kohler, 2002, pp. 97–134). Here, I call attention to reliance upon *miniaturized*, mobile technologies because of the impact they have upon the scientist-subject relationship in exercise physiology research. One exercise physiologist praised new mobile technologies in an interview, explaining, "With technology these days becoming more and more accessible you can do things like have people exercise with data loggers that don't represent any hindrance to them, and you can have them, you can record different physiology, physiological parameters for hours at a time, actually look at what's happening." It is as though, in this exercise physiologist's ideal field study, he would disappear altogether from the trial itself, receding from the presence of his subject by abrogating control to unnoticeable mobile technologies. No longer screaming, perhaps no longer perceptibly "there," but leaving behind an army of mobile instruments to record physiological data—like Neil's K4, GPS, accelerometer, core temperature pill, and heart rate monitor.

Exercise physiologists' acquisition or application of these mobile instruments is not easy. Not only does a data measuring instrument need to be small and mobile, so too does a data-recording device. Furthermore, what counts as mobile is relative. In the process of getting a muscle recruitment study up and running, one junior exercise physiologist shared with her colleague that she was without a halter for her subjects to wear while running (the halter could hold a electromyography [EMG] data-recording box). The colleague asked why she did not just use his muscle physiology instrument, the "BioPac," and his leads. "[The leads] are so light," he explained. She asked, "Is it portable?" He assured her it was. "Can someone run with it around a track?" she clarified. "No." Laughing at the misunderstanding of what she meant by "portable," they imaged her pushing a cart with the BioPac, running around the track trying to keep up with the subject. (BioPac developed a more mobile unit, the BioNomadix, in 2011.)

If the portability of mobile instruments is one issue, reliability in a range of environmental conditions is another. One goal of Andrew's study in the urban park was to validate a mobile instrument used to measure oxygen consumption, the "K4." Manufactured by the Italian medical technology company, COSMED, since the late 1990s, the $K4b^2$, or simply "K4" as it is known in human performance research, was the first entirely mobile instrument capable of recording the volumes of oxygen and carbon dioxide exchanged on a breath-by-breath basis. The K4 unit stores this data. According to Andrew and other researchers, one problem with the K4 was that it worked perfectly well in the lab, but once they tried to use it out in the field, the results were terrible.[10] Another problem with the K4 was that, while it was mobile, it was not comfortable. None of their elite athlete-subjects were willing to wear the K4 during competition.

Interestingly, the GPS unit worn by Neil contained within it a "triaxial accelerometer," meaning it could detect movement in three directions. Exercise physiologists are interested in the data generated by accelerometers when studying how a subject's efficiency of movement contributes to fatigue. However, Andrew's team had not managed to get the accelerometer feature of the GPS unit to work *indoors*, and so they continued to use both GPS and accelerometer units as they moved between the lab and the field.

Along with the K4, GPS, and accelerometer, two other mobile technologies played a key role in Andrew's study: the core temperature pill and the heart rate monitor. Designed by NASA and Johns Hopkins University in the late 1980s to monitor the health of astronauts remotely, the "CorTemp" core temperature pill transmits data telemetrically to a receiver pack that is worn on the lower back of a person.[11] It must be ingested a certain amount of time before a trial so that it can travel to the appropriate place in the subject's gut in order for its signal to be detected and recorded by the unit worn on the subject's back. According to Andrew, each core temperature pill cost £60 (or $120 at the time), and every trial for every athlete required a new pill (although, in theory, one could retrieve it after it had been passed.) The core temperature pill can be *too* mobile. If the researchers wait too long after the subject consumes a pill to start the study, or if the subject's metabolism is unusually fast, the pill passes through the subject before the study even begins. Andrew explained that for some subjects, the pill "went through" in 3–4 hours. "For some people with crap diets," he noted, "it can take days."

Unlike the core temperature pill, by the mid-2000s the heart rate monitor was not prohibitively expensive for many exercise scientists and relatively well-off athletes (Gibson 2018, p. 10). By the mid-2000s, a basic heart rate monitor started at $60 (and, unlike the core temperature pill, was reusable, both in theory *and* in practice). In 1983, the Finnish company Polar developed the first wireless ECG-accurate heart rate monitor to record skiers' heart rates. The heart rate monitor quickly became a fixture in exercise physiology field studies of both training and competition. By the early 2000s several teams of exercise scientists had published studies documenting the heart rates (and other variables) of elite cyclists *while* the cyclists competed in the Tour de France and other professional endurance races. Both the core temperature pill and the heart rate monitor represented the ideal of a mobile technology in exercise physiology field research: for instruments to be light enough and mobile enough that the athlete-subjects would not even notice them.

In contrast to their visible, loud role in the lab, exercise physiologists in "the field" do not dominate the script. Scientists leave in their stead an army of mobile instruments to record physiological data. The heart rate monitor is worn like a second skin. The core temperature pill is literally ingested. The instruments, too, ideally recede from view until they are one with the human subject himself, what sociologist Elizabeth Wissinger calls "a disappearing technology" (2017, p. 4). In the case of exercise physiology, scientists manufacture their own invisibility in "the field" with miniaturized, mobile, ideally imperceptible technologies.

Conclusion: All the World's a Field?

Exercise physiologists—those who study "whole people"—interact with their research subjects in ways rarely described in STS scholarship about laboratory research. In the lab, the scientists care for their subjects—wiping sweat, dabbing blood, helping a fatigued or sweaty cyclist to lie down—and they also motivate their subjects. Exercise physiologists in the lab scream and cheer. Human performance laboratories are just that—human performances, with the exercise physiologist co-starring with the subject. The scientist's visible, dramatic role does not seem to interfere with the validity of the knowledge produced. Quite the contrary, because these scientist-subject interactions help produce "max" experiences that can be measured, they help constitute reliable scientific facts about human fatigue, endurance, metabolism. In striking contrast, exercise physiologists aim to minimize their presence in "the field." They work through human and non-human surrogates to manage the ethics and logistics of data collection and to interact with their research subjects. On the one hand, it may seem that scientists do not want to intervene as much with their subjects when they are doing "field" research. And yet, what I have tried to show is that the scientists *are* in fact intervening, just not always in ways that are perceptible to their human subjects.

Interestingly, the lab-field distinction may soon prove untenable for a new reason. Well-trained athletes continue to be studied in exercise physiology laboratories, cheered and poked and prodded by scientists as athlete-subjects sweat and "dig" and fatigue. However, in the past decade, elite sporting competitions as "field" sites have become even easier to study.[12] Growing numbers of national and international sporting organizations have partnered with technology companies to produce real-time biometric data of competing athletes. (So far accelerometers and heart rate monitors have gained the most traction.) In addition, used in conjunction with "lifestyle" or health apps, mobile, wearable devices (biometric data-tracking and sensing wristbands, socks, jewelry, and more) are more ubiquitous than ever amongst lay consumers.

As mobile technologies (wearable, ingestible!) continue to penetrate elite sporting events and mass consumer markets, exercise physiologists' ability to study "what actually happens" may appear vast, perhaps total. For sciences that study "whole people," the laboratory—that twentieth-century achievement of exclusion, standardization, and control—may become passé. Why bring subjects into a laboratory if "what's actually happening" can be studied reliably through mobile, miniaturized instruments? Why bring subjects into a laboratory if physiologists can navigate socially heterogeneous spaces to ensure that research subjects and data are cared for and that the ethical demands of human subjects research are attended to by *someone*, if not themselves? Most STS and Sport Studies scholarship on wearable technology highlights the surveillance potential for governments, schools, workplaces, and entrepreneurs (Lupton 2013; Rich and Miah 2017). An ethnographic account of how exercise physiologists manufacture their own invisibility—how scientists in the field move to the sidelines of their subjects' experiences and senses—suggests that exercise physiologists will be there as well, if mostly invisible. New questions will arise about how the logics of digital algorithms intersect with the racial, classed, aged, abled, gendered, and national logics of sports participation and tech consumption to shape physiologists' facts about human fatigue and endurance. Although, at that point, the more interesting research question may be, not how do exercise physiologists practice their research, but how do athlete-subjects avoid it?

Acknowledgments I thank the scientists, physicians, and subjects who permitted me to enter the laboratory—and field!—with them and to observe their work. I am particularly grateful to "Kara," who gave helpful feedback on previous versions of this chapter, as did Rob Kohler, Mary Mitchell, Taylor Dysart, and Jon Johnson. Thank you to Mary McDonald and Jennifer Sterling for organizing the 4S panel, editing this book, and helping to bring the worlds of Science and Technology Studies and Sport Studies together. I am also extraordinarily grateful for the way they pushed me to clarify the argument and writing in this chapter. A Doctoral Dissertation Improvement Research Grant from the National Science Foundation and a Helfand Graduate Fellowship in the History of Medicine and Health helped support the research.

Notes

1. All names have been changed to preserve the anonymity of the scientists and their research subjects. Faces in images have been obscured for the same reason.

2. Only the phases of exercise physiology research that involve human subjects have this quality of being "dramatic." There are different kinds of exercise physiology research. As mentioned, some exercise physiologists work with animal models, others with human subjects. My own fieldwork only involved documenting the research practices of physiologists who work with human subjects. While all exercise physiologists are concerned in some way with elucidating physiological mechanisms, exercise physiologists also work at different and overlapping scales, from the molecule to the "performance." Here I am describing the phases of laboratory and field studies of exercise physiologists during which the scientists were "capturing" the performances of human subjects. After the trials, when the same physiologists analyzed the *parts* of their subjects, for example, blood samples, muscle biopsies, or saliva, their work practices were not "dramatic."

3. To be clear, here, I am not concerned with and not contrasting the ways the physiologists write about their research and communicate "aperspectival objectivity" to their peers. Rather, I am contrasting how laboratory and field studies unfold over real time.

4. Late nineteenth- and early twentieth-century physiological studies of running or cycling might have been called "the physiology of exercise," "work physiology," and/or "industrial physiology."

5. Sport historians have been studying physiologists' contributions to the histories of physical education and sports medicine for decades, for example, Berryman (1995, 2010), Berryman and Park (1992), Delheye (2014), Heggie (2010, 2011), Hoberman (1992), Park (2007, 2011, 2012), and Wrynn (2010). The role of exercise physiology or exercise/ sport science in the history of science is less well-established, but growing, for example, Heggie (2013, 2016a, b), Henne (2015), Kasperowski (2009), Johnson (2013b, 2015), Oakes (2015), Scheffler (2011, 2015), Svensson (2013), and Tracy (2012). Massengale and Swanson (1997) and Tipton (ed.) (2011, 2014) provide practitioner histories of exercise and sport science.

6. Heggie (2016a) points out that what or who constitutes "well-trained" athletes—and whether physiologists implicitly or explicitly consider such folks "normal"—is historically contingent. "Athletes" (by twenty-first-century standards of physical activity) may have in fact been the unmarked "invisible participants of scientific work" in much of nineteenth- and early twentieth-century physiological research (p. 187).

7. For an ethnographic perspective on exercise physiology laboratory research, see Gibson (2018) and Johnson (2013a, b).

8. Beyond describing the social heterogeneity of field research during the data-acquisition, or what physiologists would call the "testing," phase, other STS scholars document how field scientists interact with non-scientists before and after gathering data, taking up issues of funding and controversy, respectively. See Kuklick (2011), Oreskes (2003), and Bonneuil et al. (2008, pp. 217–223).

9. I distributed ethics in my fieldwork, too. After Kara's meeting with the race medical director, I introduced myself, explained my research, and asked if it was okay if I took notes and photographs. He said it was fine, but that if I took photographs, either they had to be wide panoramic, anonymous shots or I needed to ask permission from individual runners to do a close-up. He explained those were his instructions to the camera crews as well.

10. They had noted a plateau in the results after a certain speed that the subject ran, whereas the results should continue to rise. They had talked to other research groups, and other scientists had had similar problems working with the K4 outside, but, in the mid-2000s, no one had published these results. The K4 had been advertised to exercise scientists as a mobile instrument capable of bringing the precision of the lab to the field, while the validation studies of the K4 were performed in the lab (against other devices or techniques for measuring gas exchange), not the field.

11. On the Cold War pressure for NASA to develop telemetric tracking devices, see Benson (2010).

12. Describing the history of the standardization of sporting spaces is outside the scope of this chapter but crucial to the construction of the sporting competitions as "field" sites. See Bale (1994), Bale and Vertinsky (2004), and Guttmann (1978), and see Heggie (2016a) for more on the historical relationship between modern sport and modern science.

References

Bale, J. (1994). *Landscapes of modern sport*. New York: St. Martin's Press.

Bale, J., & Vertinsky, P. (Eds.). (2004). *Sites of sport: Space, place, and experience*. New York: Routledge.

Bangham, J., & Kaplan, J. (2016). Editorial: (In)visibility and labour in the human sciences. In J. Bangham & J. Kaplan (Eds.), *Invisibility and labour in the human sciences* (pp. 3–9). Berlin: Max-Planck-Institut für Wissenschaftsgeschichte.

Benson, E. (2010). *Wired wilderness: Technologies of tracking and the making of modern wildlife*. Baltimore: Johns Hopkins University Press.

Berryman, J. W. (1995). *Out of many, one: A history of the American College of Sports Medicine*. Champaign, IL: Human Kinetics Press.

Berryman, J. (2010). Exercise is medicine: A historical perspective. *Current Sports Medicine Reports, 9*(4), 195–201.

Berryman, J. W., & Park, R. J. (Eds.). (1992). *Sport and exercise science: Essays in the history of sports medicine*. Urbana: University of Illinois Press.

Bonneuil, C., Joly, P.-B., & Marris, C. (2008). Disentrenching experiment: The construction of GM-crop field trials as a social problem. *Science, Technology, & Human Values, 33*(2), 201–229.

Bourguet, M.-N., Licoppe, C., & Sibum, H. O. (Eds.). (2002). *Instruments, travel, and science: Itineraries of precision from the seventeenth to the twentieth century*. New York: Routledge.

Brain, R. (2015). *The pulse of modernism. Physiological aesthetics in fin-de-siècle Europe*. Seattle: University of Washington Press.

Brain, R. M., & Wise, M. N. (1994). Muscles and engines: Indicator diagrams and Helmholtz's graphical methods. In L. Krüger (Ed.), *Universalgenie Helmholtz – rückblick naar 100 jahren* (pp. 124–149). Berlin: Akademie Verlag.

Chapman, C. B. (1990). The long reach of Harvard's Fatigue Laboratory, 1926–1947. *Perspectives in Biology and Medicine, 34*(1), 17–33.

Daston, L. (1992). Objectivity and the escape from perspective. *Social Studies of Science, 22*(4), 597–618.

Delheye, P. (2014). Statistics, gymnastics and the origins of sport science in Belgium (and Europe). *European Journal of Sport Sciences, 14*(7), 652–660.

Dumit, J. (2004). *Picturing personhood: Brain scans and biomedical identity*. Princeton, NJ: Princeton University Press.

Fouché, R. (2017). *Game changer: The technoscientific revolution in sports*. Baltimore: Johns Hopkins University Press.

Gibson, K. (2018). Laboratory production of health and performance: An ethnographic investigation of an exercise physiology laboratory. *Sport in Society.* https://doi.org/10.1080/17430437.2018.1435002.

Gieryn, T. F. (2006). City as truth-spot: Laboratories and field-sites in urban studies. *Social Studies of Science, 36*(1), 5–38.

Guttmann, A. (1978). *From ritual to record.* New York: Columbia University Press.

Hale, T. (2008). History of developments in sport and exercise physiology: A.V. Hill, maximal oxygen uptake, and oxygen debt. *Journal of Sports Sciences, 26*(4), 365–400.

Hankins, T. (1999). Blood, dirt, and nomograms: A particular history of graphs. *Isis, 90*(1), 50–80.

Heggie, V. (2010). A century of cardiomythology: Exercise and the heart c. 1880–1980. *Social History of Medicine, 23*(2), 280–298.

Heggie, V. (2011). *A history of British sports medicine.* Manchester: Manchester University Press.

Heggie, V. (2013). Experimental physiology, Everest and oxygen: From the ghastly kitchens to the gasping lung. *British Journal for the History of Science, 46*(1), 123–147.

Heggie, V. (2016a). Bodies, sport and science in the nineteenth century. *Past and Present, 231*(1), 169–200.

Heggie, V. (2016b). Higher and colder: The success and failure of boundaries in high altitude and Antarctic research stations. *Social Studies of Science, 46*(6), 809–832.

Henke, C. R. (2000). Making a place for science: The field trial. *Social Studies of Science, 30*(4), 483–511.

Henne, K. E. (2015). *Testing for athlete citizenship: Regulating doping and sex in sport.* New Brunswick, NJ: Rutgers University Press.

Herzig, R. (2005). *Suffering for science: Reason and sacrifice in modern America.* New Brunswick, NJ: Rutgers University Press.

Hevly, B. (1996). The heroic science of glacier motion. *Osiris, 11*, 66–86.

Hoberman, J. (1992). *Mortal engines: The science of performance and the dehumanization of sport.* New York: Free Press.

Johnson, A. (2013a). The athlete as model organism: The everyday practice of the science of human performance. *Social Studies of Science, 43*(6), 878–904.

Johnson, A. (2013b). Measuring fatigue: The politics of innovation and standardization in a South African lab. *Biosocieties, 8*(3), 289–310.

Johnson, A. (2015). 'They sweat for science': The Harvard Fatigue Laboratory and self-experimentation in American exercise physiology. *Journal of the History of Biology, 48*(3), 425–454.

Kasperowski, D. (2009). Constructing altitude training for the 1968 Mexico Olympics: The impacts of ideals of certainty and uncertainty. *The International Journal of the History of Sport, 26*, 1–29.

Kingsland, S. E. (2009). Frits Went's atomic age greenhouse: The changing labscape on the lab-field border. *Journal of the History of Biology, 42*(2), 289–324.

Knorr-Cetina, K. (1999). *Epistemic cultures: How the sciences make knowledge.* Cambridge: Harvard University Press.

Kohler, R. E. (2002). *Landscapes and labscapes: Exploring the lab-field border in biology.* Chicago: University of Chicago Press.

Kohler, R. E. (2011). Paul Errington, Aldo Leopold, and wildlife ecology: Residential science. *Historical Studies in the Natural Sciences, 41*(2), 216–254.

Kohlstedt, S. G. (2016). Accounting for knowledge production. In J. Bangham & J. Kaplan (Eds.), *Invisibility and labour in the human sciences* (pp. 137–141). Berlin: Max-Planck-Institut für Wissenschaftsgeschichte.

Kuklick, H. (2011). Personal equations: Reflections on the history of fieldwork, with special reference to sociocultural anthropology. *Isis, 102*(1), 1–33.

Kuklick, H., & Kohler, R. E. (1996). Introduction. *Osiris, 11*, 585–610.

Latour, B. (1999). *Pandora's hope: Essays on the reality of science studies.* Cambridge: Harvard University Press.

Latour, B., & Woolgar, S. (1986). *Laboratory life: The construction of scientific facts.* Princeton, NJ: Princeton University Press.

Lupton, D. (2013). Understanding the human machine. *IEEE Technology and Society Magazine, 32*(4), 25–30.

Massengale, J. D., & Swanson, R. A. (Eds.). (1997). *The history of exercise and sport science.* Champaign, IL: Human Kinetics Press.

Nielsen, K. H., Harbsmeier, M., & Ries, C. J. (2012). Studying scientists and scholars in the field: An introduction. In K. H. Nielsen, M. Harbsmeier, & C. J. Ries (Eds.), *Scientists and scholars in the field: Studies in the history of fieldwork and expeditions* (pp. 9–28). Aarhus: Aarhus University Press.

Oakes, J. (2015). Alliances in human biology: The Harvard Committee on Industrial Physiology, 1929–1939. *Journal of the History of Biology, 48*(3), 365–390.

Oreskes, N. (1996). Objectivity or heroism? On the invisibility of women in science. *Osiris, 11*, 87–113.

Oreskes, N. (2003). A context of motivation: US Navy oceanographic research and the discovery of sea-floor hydrothermal vents. *Social Studies of Science, 33*(5), 697–742.

Park, R. J. (2007). Physiologists, physicians, and physical educators. *The International Journal of the History of Sport, 24*(12), 1637–1673.

Park, R. J. (2011). Physicians, scientists, exercise and athletics in Britain and America from the 1867 boat race to the four-minute mile. *Sport in History, 31*(1), 1–31.

Park, R. J. (2012). Soldiers may fall but athletes never!: Sport as an antidote to nervous diseases and national decline in America, 1865–1905. *Journal of the History of Sport, 29*(6), 792–812.

Petryna, A. (2006). Globalizing human subjects research. In A. Petryna, A. Lakoff, & A. Kleinman (Eds.), *Global pharmaceuticals: Ethics, markets, practices* (pp. 33–60). Durham: Duke University Press.

Powell, R. C. (2007). "The rigours of an Arctic experiment": The precarious authority of field practices in the Canadian high Arctic, 1958–1970. *Environment and Planning A, 39*(8), 1794–1811.

Rabinbach, A. (1990). *Human motor: Energy, fatigue, and the origins of modernity*. New York: Basic Books.

Rees, A. (2006). A place that answers questions: Primatological field sites and the making of authentic observations. *Studies in the History and Philosophy of the Biological and Biomedical Sciences, 37*(2), 311–333.

Rees, A. (2007). Reflections on the field: Primatology, popular science, and the politics of personhood. *Social Studies of Science, 37*(6), 881–907.

Rich, E., & Miah, A. (2017). Mobile, wearable, and ingestible health technologies: Towards a critical research agenda. *Health Sociology Review, 26*(1), 84–97.

Ries, C. J. (2012). Armchairs, dogsleds, ships, and airplanes: Field access, scientific credibility, and geological mapping in northern and north-eastern Greenland 1900–1939. In K. H. Nielsen, M. Harbsmeier, & C. J. Ries (Eds.), *Scientists and scholars in the field: Studies in the history of fieldwork and expeditions* (pp. 329–361). Aarhus: Aarhus University Press.

Scheffler, R. W. (2011). The fate of a Progressive science: The Harvard Fatigue Laboratory, athletes, the science of work, and the politics of reform. *Endeavor, 35*(2), 48–54.

Scheffler, R. W. (2015). The power of exercise and the exercise of power: The Harvard Fatigue Laboratory, distance running, and the disappearance of work, 1919–1947. *Journal of the History of Biology, 48*(3), 391–423.

Schumaker, L. (1996). A tent with a view: Colonial officers, anthropologists, and the making of the field of northern Rhodesia, 1937–1960. *Osiris, 11*, 237–258.

Shapin, S. (1989). The invisible technician. *American Scientist, 77*(6), 554–563.

Star, S. L., & Strauss, A. (1999). Layers of silence, arenas of voice: The ecology of visible and invisible work. *Computer-Supported Cooperative Work, 8*, 9–30.

Stark, L. (2016). The bureaucratic ethic and the spirit of bio-capitalism. In J. Bangham & J. Kaplan (Eds.), *Invisibility and labour in the human sciences* (pp. 13–23). Berlin: Max-Planck-Institut für Wissenschaftsgeschichte.

Svensson, D. (2013). How much sport is there in sport physiology? Practice and ideas in the Stockholm School of Physiology at GCI, 1941–1969. *The International Journal of the History of Sport, 20*(8), 892–913.

Svensson, D., & Sörlin, S. (2018). The 'physiologization' of skiing: The lab as an obligatory passage point for elite athletes. *Sport in Society*. https://doi.org/10.1080/17430437.2018.1435031.

Tipton, C. (Ed.). (2011). *Exercise physiology: People and ideas*. Oxford: Elsevier Science.

Tipton, C. (Ed.). (2014). *History of exercise physiology*. Champaign, IL: Human Kinetics Press.

Tracy, S. W. (2012). The physiology of extremes: Ancel keys and the international high altitude expedition of 1935. *Bulletin of the History of Medicine, 86*(4), 627–660.

Traweek, S. (1992). *Beamtimes and lifetimes: The world of high-energy physicists*. Cambridge: Harvard University Press.

Vetter, J. (2011). Labs in the field? Rocky Mountain biological stations in the early twentieth century. *Journal of the History of Biology, 45*(4), 587–611.

von Oertzen, C. (2016). Hidden helpers: Gender, skill, and the politics of workforce management for census compilation in late nineteenth-century Prussia. In J. Bangham & J. Kaplan (Eds.), *Invisibility and labour in the human sciences* (pp. 47–50). Berlin: Max-Planck-Institut für Wissenschaftsgeschichte.

Wissinger, E. (2017). Wearable tech, bodies, and gender. *Sociology Compass, 11*. https://doi.org/10.1111/soc4.12514.

Wrynn, A. (2010). The athlete in the making: The scientific study of American athletic performance, 1920–1932. *Sport in History, 30*(1), 121–137.

The Tangled Multiplicities of CTE: Scientific Uncertainty and the Infrastructures of Traumatic Brain Injury

Matt Ventresca

Chronic traumatic encephalopathy—better known by its acronym, CTE—is a medical diagnosis that has largely come to define sports' "concussion crisis." Scientific definitions typically describe CTE as a neurodegenerative condition associated with repeated exposure to traumatic brain injury (TBI) (e.g. Asken et al. 2017; McKee et al. 2015).[1] Although the exact neuropathological characteristics of CTE are thoroughly contested within the ever-expanding literature on the topic, prevailing neuroscientific definitions tend to conceptualize the condition as a progressive disease linked to abnormal production of tau protein within the brain. The crux of CTE diagnoses is the suggestion that tangles of tau protein induce gradual degeneration of brain tissue associated with symptoms including cognitive decline, emotional or behavioral changes, and motor impairment (e.g. Montenigro et al. 2014). While scholars have demonstrated that victims of intimate partner violence and military veterans previously exposed to high-impact blasts are also high-risk populations, the bulk of scientific and public interest has revolved around prevalence of CTE

M. Ventresca (✉)
University of Calgary, Calgary, AB, Canada
e-mail: matthew.ventresca@ucalgary.ca

© The Author(s) 2020   **73**
J. J. Sterling, M. G. McDonald (eds.), *Sports, Society, and Technology*,
https://doi.org/10.1007/978-981-32-9127-0_4

among male athletes from violent, collision sports such as gridiron football and ice hockey (Morrison and Casper 2016).

Concern about the long-term consequences of brain trauma among athletes is historically well-documented in the medical literature, especially regarding patterns of psychological decline in boxers (Casper 2018a, b). Yet CTE largely emerged as a scientific and cultural phenomenon following high-profile investigative reports detailing how small numbers of National Football League (NFL) players had been diagnosed with the condition and exposing the league's strategic involvement in neuroscientific studies concealing the long-term effects of traumatic brain injury among football players (Fainaru-Wada and Fainaru 2013). CTE has subsequently become a topic of controversy within other sports such as ice hockey, rugby, mixed martial arts, professional wrestling, and soccer, with sports organizations often being forced to revise their injury protocols. Scientists and advocates have since made calls to broaden the scope of CTE research to include female athletes (Kindelan 2018).

Controversies around CTE have been punctuated by the suicides of well-known athletes such as NFL players Junior Seau and Aaron Hernandez and National Hockey League (NHL) players Wade Belak and Rick Rypien, all of whom were diagnosed with CTE postmortem. These and similar deaths received extensive media coverage and raise harrowing questions about the connections between violent sports, CTE, and suicide (Brayton and Helstein in press). Unsettling accounts of athletes' cognitive and emotional decline have become fixtures of media coverage, with many athletes describing their lived experiences of brain trauma and expressing fears about how CTE might impact their lives (Ventresca 2019). CTE has similarly been a focal point of athlete advocacy in the form of legal action against the NFL, National Hockey League (NHL), and National Collegiate Athletics Association (NCAA), as well as proposed legislation to ban tackling in youth gridiron football in parts of the United States (Standen 2017). Yet many commentators have responded to this growth in media coverage and advocacy by asserting that intensified public concern is fueled by exaggerated representations of the prevalence of CTE and the condition's connection to brain trauma (e.g. Asken and Bauer 2018; Iverson et al. 2018; Solomon 2018).

Despite the public attention afforded CTE, scientific conceptions of the condition are characterized by much uncertainty. Patterns of CTE symptoms are highly variable in type, onset, and severity; some symptoms appear indistinguishable from those related to other neurological or psychiatric conditions potentially unrelated to brain trauma (Asken et al. 2016; Iverson et al. 2018; Montenigro et al. 2014). Some researchers have proposed traumatic encephalopathy syndrome as a clinical diagnosis identifying patterns of CTE symptoms; yet scientists generally regard clinical symptoms as insufficient indicators of CTE onset (Montenigro et al. 2014). Medical diagnoses of CTE are therefore exclusively produced after a person dies, through sophisticated neuroscientific study of brain tissue rendering abnormal tangles of tau protein visible through the lens of a microscope (McKee et al. 2016). The reliance on postmortem diagnoses has enabled two related developments: first, the growing trend for athletes' brains to be preserved after death and donated to laboratories for scientific study; and, second, the emergence of neuroscience (and neuropathology more specifically) as the preeminent source of "definitive" knowledge about CTE.

Yet the neuroscientific literature around CTE and the long-term effects of TBI more broadly is characterized by polarizing debates. On the one hand, neuropathological analyses from high-profile "brain banks" have produced alarming results. A well-publicized 2017 study by Mez and colleagues reported that 110 out of 111 brains from deceased NFL players showed evidence of CTE pathology (Mez et al. 2017). This research continued the series of studies from Boston University demonstrating a high prevalence of postmortem CTE diagnoses among participants in collision sports (e.g. McKee et al. 2013). These troubling findings have informed calls to define the risk of CTE among athletes as an urgent public health problem (Bachynski and Goldberg 2014; Finkel and Bieniek 2018; Goldberg 2012). On the other hand, the legitimacy of well-known CTE studies has been widely criticized for perceived methodological shortcomings. These critiques often revolve around the limited representativeness of convenience samples of donated brains, often from athletes who had displayed CTE symptoms (Maroon et al. 2015; Randolph 2018; Schwab and Hazrati 2018; Solomon 2018). Critics also argue that these results are based on inadequate standards for what constitutes a CTE diagnosis. Questioning the validity of the diagnostic criteria used in CTE research, neuropsychologist Christopher Randolph (2018) went so far as to conclude that "chronic traumatic encephalopathy is not a real disease."[2] Scientific conclusions about the implications of CTE research, moreover, tend to foreground the persistence of unanswered etiological and epistemological questions: does any materialization of abnormal tau protein in the brain automatically represent CTE? How does the presence of CTE pathology translate into lived symptoms? How can this relationship be adequately measured? What is the statistical prevalence and calculable risk of CTE among athletes and across broader populations of non-athletes?

These and similar questions illustrate how scientists depict current knowledge about CTE as incomplete and beset by a variety of "unknowns." Not knowing, of course, is very much the basis of scientific inquiry; part of the scientific process is to systematically identify knowledge gaps and craft research questions designed to address gaps in knowledge. Yet, following scholarship explaining how socioeconomic contexts and power hierarchies shape the production of scientific knowledge, critical theories of *ignorance* resist understanding gaps in knowledge as "natural" aspects of the scientific process or as the steadily retreating terrain of what is "not yet known" (Proctor 2008; Stocking and Holtstein 1993; Sullivan and Tuana 2007; Zehr 2017). Despite sophisticated "objective" methods designed to ensure (or undermine) confidence in scientific results, boundaries between known and unknown are highly subjective, remaining open to redrawing by scientists as they frame the significance of their findings (Zehr 2017). Scientific ignorance—like scientific knowledge—is socially constructed through a process of claims-making about what is known and unknown. In other words, scientists actively negotiate when something can be identified as unknown (or unknowable), just as they debate when a piece of information can be considered scientific "fact." Accordingly, as much as scientists can claim to produce "new" knowledge about a phenomenon, scientific results can also highlight how much is *not known* about something (Stocking and Holtstein 1993). Scientists frequently acknowledge the production of partial or imperfect knowledge by making mundane statements about study limitations or methodological caveats, yet repeated claims about what remains unknown about an area of scientific study can cumulatively cast doubt on the certainty of existing knowledge claims.

In this chapter, I explain how CTE has become a condition defined by *scientific uncertainty*. By "cracking open" (Murphy 2006, p. 13) the ever-expanding archive of neuroscientific literature about the long-term consequences of TBI, I examine how scientists articulate what is unknown about CTE and construct the condition as a domain of uncertainty. I describe how the growing neuroscientific inventory of unknowns surrounding CTE shapes, and is shaped by, what about the condition is sayable, perceptible, tangible, natural, and normal. Following scholars who have sought to delineate theoretical differences between ignorance and uncertainty (Pinto 2015; Smithson 1989; Zehr 2017), I use the language of uncertainty throughout this chapter to highlight how negotiating the boundaries between known and unknown is not exclusively an intellectual process but an emotive, affective one (Nicholson et al. 2019). The production of uncertainty not only influences the perceived strength of scientific evidence but also generates impressions about how we should *feel* about bodies of scientific knowledge. The distinctiveness of uncertainty as an affective state is crucial for exploring how scientific knowledge confronts social values and areas of public concern (Zehr 2017). As Zehr (2017) writes, "Scientific uncertainty may emerge as a consequence of social conflict rather than being its cause." Collective anger or confusion can be generated by a lack of certainty around a scientific problem, but social conflict may also influence how scientists take up the notion of uncertainty in their work. The cultural, legal, and political stakes hinging on scientific investigations into CTE have unavoidably intensified the impact of statements representing knowledge about the condition as incomplete or uncertain. Scientific uncertainty, moreover, is not neatly divisible from the lives of athletes experiencing long-term symptoms of brain injury and facing uncertain futures of their own (Ventresca 2019).

My analysis uncovers the multiple, competing ways in which uncertainty around CTE is produced. Pinto (2015) outlines how scientific actors can construct uncertainty through two related, but distinct, processes. First, scientists (and oftentimes industry or political stakeholders) can strategically seek to manage and manipulate public opinion by making scientific consensus appear uncertain or controversial (e.g. Oreskes and Conway 2010; Proctor 2008). Second, Pinto also explains how the production of uncertainty can be enabled by institutional and disciplinary mechanisms that support the validation of some types of knowledge and not others. Scientists' adherence to dominant theoretical or methodological paradigms can also facilitate scientific uncertainty by enacting standards for what counts as conclusive evidence. Thus, while uncertainty around CTE materializes in part through scientists' active framing of existing bodies of knowledge as incomplete or inconclusive, I argue that critical attention to institutional and disciplinary conventions governing neuroscientific research can reveal how uncertainty also stems from the limits of neuroscience in representing the material complexity of the brain and its connection to human experience. The production of uncertainty around CTE involves processes extending far beyond the actions and investments of individual scientists, but emerges through connections between ideas, bodies, objects, environments, and technologies (Murphy 2006). What we know (and do not know) about CTE is not simply made up of ideas and words, but through complex arrangements of "words, things, practices, and people" (Murphy 2006, p. 12).

I contend, therefore, that scientific uncertainty should not be mobilized to demonstrate that CTE is not "real," but should instead represent evidence that repetitive brain trauma is embodied in ways defying neuroscientific frameworks of cause and effect. Building upon Michelle Murphy's (2006, 2013) analyses of sick building syndrome and chemical toxicity, I resist citing scientific uncertainty around CTE as "proof" that collision sports do not inflict damage on athletes' brains. Rather, I affirm that the neuroscientific paradigms driving most CTE research offer narrow parameters for conceptualizing how brain trauma occurs through sport and shapes athletes' experiences. Given the multifaceted and overlapping ways in which athletes experience harm, identifying the sources of these harms should not revolve around isolating individual causes and effects but instead interrogating the varied *assemblages* (Deleuze and Guattari 1987) of practices, values, and environments—the *infrastructures of harm*—that together facilitate contexts in which athletes sustain and endure damage. Athletes' firsthand experiences of navigating these infrastructures, then, should be valued as embodied counter-knowledge to scientific uncertainties around CTE. In sum, this examination of onto-epistemological groundings offers alternative ways of knowing as pathways to understanding the multifaceted assemblages constituting repetitive brain trauma.

CTE and the Uncertainty of Causality

Neuroscientific studies of CTE articulate the boundaries between certainty and uncertainty through carefully constructed, sometimes competing, claims. Tagge et al. (2018) state that "while the pathogenesis of CTE is unknown, emerging evidence points to a putative causal association with neurotrauma" (p. 424). Asken et al. (2017) similarly write that "exposure to [repetitive brain trauma] represents the greatest risk factor for CTE pathological features, although clinicopathological correlates and the nature of onset and progression of symptoms are largely unknown" (p. 1261). Maroon et al. (2015) make similar claims, closing their review by asserting, "there is no credible data with which to establish the incidence or prevalence of CTE in former contact sport participants" (p. 12). Scientific uncertainty functions differently through each statement about what is *not known* about CTE. Each claim identifies substantial knowledge gaps in the study of CTE, through which the authors offer varying assessments of how much is known about the condition. Most vividly, whereas Tagge and colleagues assert that unknowns around CTE onset should not discount evidence of the condition's "putative causal relationship with neurotrauma," Maroon and colleagues cite the same uncertainty around CTE risk factors but declare that "no credible data" exists linking the condition to collision sports.

The production of uncertainty is even more striking in the predominance of causation as a scientific benchmark for conceptualizing how and why CTE develops. In a review of the existing scientific evidence on CTE, Solomon (2018) assesses and interprets an extensive list of CTE-related studies, concluding, "despite anecdotal and case series reports, it is my opinion that there is no compelling empirical evidence to indicate that sport-related concussion or subconcussive impacts are *the sole and direct cause* of psychiatric illness, suicide, mild cognitive impairment, or neurodegenerative disease/CTE" (p. 303, italics in original). The 2016

Berlin Consensus Statement on Sport-Related Concussion similarly declares, "A cause-and-effect relationship has not yet been demonstrated between CTE and SRCs [sport-related concussion] or exposure to contact sports. As such, the notion that repeated concussion or subconcussive impacts cause CTE remains unknown" (McCrory et al. 2017, p. 7). Both Solomon and the Berlin Consensus Statement dictate that scientific uncertainty around CTE stems from inadequate evidence of a causal link between the condition and brain trauma. Their matter-of-fact statements of uncertainty are not "false" and cannot be easily rebutted with the irrefutable proof of causation these authors seek; indeed, similar claims pervade the neuroscientific CTE literature (e.g. Iverson et al. 2018; Schwab and Hazrati 2018). Such reliance on causal explanations is complicated by how philosophers of science contest the meaning of "causation" as a scientific and epistemological construct (e.g. Cartwright 2004). Yet the symbolic power of cause-and-effect relationships (or lack thereof), however, remains central to the production of scientific uncertainty around CTE.

The very act of declaring and repeating these uncertain "truths" as part of the scientific record performs substantial political work in the production of uncertainty. These claims establish CTE causation as the scientific benchmark for conclusive "proof" of the long-term consequences of sport-related brain injury. The aforementioned statements about causation (and similar examples) explicitly foreground the existence of "unknowns" around CTE and can be cited in response to public concern about the risks of brain injury in collision sports. Unsurprisingly, uncertainty around CTE causation is a central theme of sports organizations' efforts to deflect public criticism or avoid legal responsibility for the long-term effects of brain trauma (Benson 2017; Finkel and Bieniek 2018; Goldberg 2012; Ventresca 2019).

The potential for sports stakeholders to opportunistically generate and exploit uncertainty as a public relations tactic is an example of how those in positions of power (e.g. governments, military, or corporations) can strategically construct scientific uncertainty for economic or political gain (Oreskes and Conway 2010; Pinto 2015; Proctor 2008; Zehr 2017). Most commonly, this strategy involves employing compliant researchers to produce results casting doubt on prevailing scientific thinking around a controversial issue (such as climate change or smoking) to sway public opinion or delay political action. Scholars have highlighted how sports organizations have mobilized the production of scientific uncertainty as a tactic to "manufacture doubt" about the relationship between repetitive brain trauma and CTE (Bachynski and Goldberg 2014; Benson 2017; Casper 2018a; Goldberg 2012; Ventresca 2019). Historian Stephen Casper (2018a) writes that the contemporary emphasis on CTE causation conflicts with the lineage of research that, despite acknowledging a multitude of unanswered questions, decisively identified brain trauma as the source of neurodegenerative processes in athletes. Current uncertainty, according to Casper, is a recent invention of scientific and industry actors strategically neglecting this history of research in the interest of manufacturing doubt around the long-term effects of TBI. Skepticism around the role of the sports industry in shaping scientific results has been bolstered by studies uncovering conflicts of interest pervading research partnerships involving corporations such as the NFL (Bachynski and Goldberg 2018).

Yet uncertainty around CTE has also been enabled by shifting onto-epistemological foundations within neuroscience. Innovations in brain sensing and imaging technologies throughout the 1980s ushered in a "neuroscientific turn" across the life sciences (Pitts-Taylor 2016). The concurrent emergence of a "neuromolecular style of thought" popularized the notion that all mental states and cognitive processes could be directly linked to activity within the brain detectable through neuroscientific techniques (Rose and Abi-Rached 2013). Yet new potentials for neuroscientific precision also facilitate discursive space for uncertainty structured around the promise of determining exact causes and effects. Put simply, belief in neuroscientific capacities to *know more* widens the field of what is not yet known. Scientists can represent the unhealthy brain as a site of uncertainty if precise neurophysiological processes elude the grasp of neuroscientific methods (Rose and Abi-Rached 2013). In doing so, the production of uncertainty around perceived neuroscientific capacities to reveal specific causes and effect reproduces evidence hierarchies in which experiential knowledge is actively marginalized (Pitts-Taylor 2016).

CTE and the Lessons of Sick Building Syndrome

There are clear parallels between the prominence of uncertainty as a defining characteristic of CTE and the phenomenon known as *sick building syndrome*. Michelle Murphy (2006) details how office workers in the 1970s and 1980s began complaining about a litany of symptoms, ranging from headaches and runny noses to scratchy throats and skin rashes. These workers, typically women, collectively concluded that their experiences were linked to a type of "indoor pollution" that circulated through modern office buildings. Scientists, however, could not trace workers' symptoms to specific physical, chemical, or molecular causes. Their problems did not fit standard models of disease causality, having no perceptible origin or predictable effects. Sick building syndrome could not be rendered scientifically as a knowable disease with identifiable causal pathways between acute exposure and corresponding physiological expression; yet the symptoms were very much "real" for those experiencing them.

Murphy explains how sick building syndrome was only intelligible as an outcome of the very conditions of office work: the standardized ecosystem of chemicals, technologies, and corporate practices that together generated a health hazard for people inside these buildings. The primary risk factor for sick building syndrome was nothing more than being an office worker. Responding to the groundswell of worker activism, employers and public health officials were forced to formally recognize the materiality of symptoms even though their cause could not be reliably traced. Sick building syndrome, then, became formalized as a phenomenon *defined by its very uncertainty*.

The history of sick building syndrome provides important lessons regarding the limits of science in representing human experience. When toxicological studies were unable to detect harmful chemicals in office environments, industry officials sought to delegitimize complaints by claiming that workers were merely under the influence of "mass hysteria" triggered by job-related stress and psychosomatic delusion. Yet Murphy explains how the materiality of symptoms associated with sick building syndrome defied attempts by industry scientists and health officials to undermine the legitimacy of workers' experiences. Scientific uncertainty around the cause of symptoms stood in vivid contrast to the persistence with which office employees asserted the authority of their experiences. Sick building syndrome revealed the inability of science—in this case, toxicological models—to adequately represent the complex relationships between office workers and their environment.

Following the lessons of sick building syndrome, it is important to critically interrogate the material processes making CTE both an embodied experience and an elusive object of scientific knowledge-making. The production of uncertainty around CTE grows out of the assumption that more precise research will eventually reveal the "truth" about whether repetitive brain trauma causes CTE pathology and symptoms. Such an assurance, however, ignores how the brain supports, complicates, and resists the production of knowledge in ways contingent on specific material processes, which may or may not be perceptible via dominant neuroscientific practices. There is no guarantee that brain processes will neatly coincide with scientific paradigms (such as dose-response curves or threshold limit values[3]) that expect bodies to react predictably and consistently to harm. The inherent challenge in conceptualizing CTE lies in the recognition that neural matter itself often refuses to be fully knowable or predictable (Pitts-Taylor 2016).

In this way, the major dilemma emerging from my analysis so far is that the context of uncertainty in which we come to know (and not know) CTE did not emerge from a cosmic void and is not manufactured out of thin air. While actively structured by human actors invested one way or another in the outcome of neuroscientific findings, uncertainty around CTE still *comes from somewhere*. The brain is not a blank slate on which scientists can project uncertainty about CTE to suit their interests; nor do objective neuroscientific practices discover matter and processes that are "already there," passively waiting to be captured by the scientific gaze (Pitts-Taylor 2016). Uncertainty emerges through the active structuring of what is known and knowable, but also through the brain's material complexity that resists coherence or standardization.

CTE is, therefore, a phenomenon encapsulating the intersections of the discursive and the material: on the one hand, scientists shape "what CTE is" by establishing diagnostic criteria and applying neuroscientific techniques; on the other hand, brain matter has the capacity to continually transform and shape experiences in ways defying neuroscientific classification. Like sick building syndrome, CTE is defined by the tensions between how imperfect systems of scientific knowledge can inscribe meaning onto the body and the unpredictable, unrelenting materiality of human experience. These tensions are illustrated through defining characteristics of CTE that both support and resist uncertainty: latency, imperceptibility, and multiplicity.

Latency and Imperceptibility

If CTE materializes as a progressive condition, this means that associated neurodegenerative processes occur gradually with symptoms typically presenting years or decades after exposure to brain trauma (Montenigro et al. 2014). Such a conception requires that CTE, both in its neuropathological development and in its diagnosis, takes time. There is considerable lag between exposure to injury and emergence of symptoms, but also between the onset of lived symptoms and postmortem diagnoses. The temporal dimensions of CTE reflect what Murphy (2013) calls the politics of *latency*. In medicine, latency can be conceived as a period of incubation through which illness and disease gradually materialize in the body and become perceptible over time. Yet latency is not a guarantee: any potential state of being can emerge, remain unrealized, or escape scientific classification. As such, latency induces a crucial gap in knowledge-making practices that influence neuroscientific conceptions of CTE. The temporal variability with which CTE materializes in the brain and potentially impacts athletes' everyday experience complicates the creation of reliable timescales of cause and effect. The inability for neuroscience to detect or measure abnormal production of tau protein in real time facilitates uncertainty regarding the temporal relationships between injury exposure, symptoms, and pathology onset.

The production of uncertainty around CTE is similarly enabled by domains of *imperceptibility*. Imperceptibility and uncertainty are related phenomena; that which lies outside the boundaries of perceptibility can be represented as non-existent or uncertain. CTE exemplifies important distinctions between what material relationships might exist within and between bodies and what can be perceived via technoscientific practice. The condition's proposed link to asymptomatic, subconcussive brain impacts by definition constitutes a domain of imperceptibility. These impacts are not substantial enough to induce acute symptoms, but some studies suggest that they might contribute to cumulative neurophysiological damage associated with CTE (Montenigro et al. 2017; Tagge et al. 2018). If subconcussive impacts are linked to the gradual development of CTE, then the material consequences of these injuries are initially imperceptible and lie latent until they reemerge years later as perceivable symptoms and/or brain pathology.

Multiplicity

Scientific debates about CTE causality often revolve around multiplicity, specifically in determining why some athletes exposed to repetitive brain trauma develop CTE, while others do not or do not experience symptoms. As Montenigro et al. (2015) write, "while head trauma is a necessary variable for developing CTE, it is not sufficient. That is, not everyone who experiences repetitive impacts will get the disease" (p. 314). This supposition is substantiated by reports of athletes with documented neurocognitive decline who were not diagnosed with CTE postmortem (e.g. Hazrati et al. 2013). Thus, a key aspect of contemporary CTE research involves determining how exposure to repetitive brain trauma combines with other variables to induce the neuropathological changes associated with the condition. The scientific literature on CTE identifies genetic predispositions, preexisting psychiatric conditions, drug and alcohol abuse, and sleep disturbances, as potential factors that might prompt or intensify the production of abnormal tau in some people and not others (McCrory et al. 2017; Montenigro et al. 2015; Solomon 2018).

The potential influence of contemporaneous variables has, predictably, been a focal point of neuroscientific arguments highlighting the perceived tenuousness of causal links between repetitive brain trauma and CTE. Isolating the influence of factors that contribute to CTE onset is a difficult task for scientists, exacerbated by the latency and imperceptibility of the condition's defining characteristics. There are numerous complicating factors beyond repetitive brain impacts that can be alluded to as "unknowns" in neuroscientific theorizing around why CTE materializes in the brains and lives of some athletes and not others. These unknowns emerge through the material complexity of the brain, but also the neuroscientific emphasis on parsing the effects of brain trauma within the vast array of human experiences that shape, and are shaped by, the brain. Multiplicity, then, like latency and imperceptibility, serves as a renewable resource in the production of uncertainty around CTE.

CTE and the Dangers of Multiplicity

The inability for neuroscientists to demonstrate a causal link between repetitive brain trauma and CTE, in the face of the chorus of athletes publically conveying their day-to-day struggles and fears, provides an opportunity to confront the limits of neuroscientific definitions of causation. These limits require reflection on what alternative knowledge practices might more adequately capture the social and material complexities of human experience. Malcolm (2009) and Hardes (2017) explain how the authority of biomedical and neuroscientific knowledge about sport-related TBI comes at the expense of athletes' non-specialist knowledge about their own embodied experiences. As such, decision-making about the diagnosis, treatment, and legal ramifications of TBI is based on narrowly defined ways of knowing and states of being. The presumed authority of empirical, often quantitative research allows critics to discredit media reports and athlete accounts as anecdotal or merely "folk wisdom" (Malcolm 2009, p. 136). Such skepticism is especially directed at journalists for producing overly negative stories exaggerating the effects of brain trauma and the conclusiveness of CTE research (Asken and Bauer 2018; Kuhn et al. 2017; Schwab and Hazrati 2018; Solomon 2018). Through these critiques, stories and narrative accounts are largely written off as subjective and politicized "non-science" inseparable from the values and motives of knowledge producers (Moore and Stilgoe 2009). This embodied and often contradictory knowledge, however, challenges scientific domains of uncertainty by providing rich, intimate details of specific experiences and social conditions.

The revaluing of experience as evidence was a crucial aspect of the formalization of sick building syndrome (Murphy 2006). The scientific response to the ambiguity of chemical exposures was to examine the human body and office environment with more precise and sophisticated toxicological techniques, hoping to map the effects of smaller degrees of chemical exposure and more minute physiological or molecular changes. Yet these methods could still not adequately conceptualize the imperceptibilities and multiplicities that characterized what office workers were experiencing; the inability to detect a definitive biochemical cause for sick building syndrome left the shared experience of working in an office building as the most valuable lens for understanding associated symptoms.

The histories of sick building syndrome illustrate the power of communicating shared experiences of illness, even when experts declare underlying causal relationships untenable. As such, sick building syndrome offers important lessons regarding how athletes' experiences are treated as evidence of the long-term effects of brain trauma. Experiences of memory loss, confusion, aggressive behavior, or emotional distress reported by athletes and their families exist irrespective of neuroscientific knowledge of distinct causal roots; their struggles are embodied and, indeed, "real." The lived experiences of athletes, expressed through interviews, memoirs, and legal proceedings, should be valued even when they cannot be explained through dominant neuroscientific frameworks. Unlike medicalized diagnoses such as traumatic encephalopathy syndrome, athletes' portrayal of their own struggles represent potent "materializations from below" (Murphy 2006, p. 58) through which experiences of CTE are articulated outside the narrow confines of institutionalized science.

Similarly, the political power of sick building syndrome came not from definitive proof of causation, but rather the sheer density of complaints describing the tangible perils of office work. As Murphy (2006) concludes, it was precisely scientists' inability to detect specific causes of ailments that enabled worker movements to articulate a broader critique of corporate capitalism. In other words, the uncertainty of sick building syndrome shifted the concern from finding and eliminating identifiable hazards to reassessing the corporate systems through which modern office buildings were designed and operated. The neuroscientific emphasis on the uncertainty around CTE causation has in many ways delayed or constrained large-scale critiques of corporate or industry practices that structure collision sports. Yet controversies around CTE can indeed reveal how elite sports operate as industries benefiting from the physical work of athletes and the multiple harms they incur (Benson 2017; Brayton et al. 2019).

Media stories offer a platform for athletes to detail their day-to-day struggles and express emotions within a hyper-masculine, profit-driven milieu rarely affording opportunities to do so (Ventresca 2019). These communicative acts, moreover, offer intimate details of an athlete's quality of life and challenge the drive for neuroscientific certainty and generalizability. The recent groundswell of athlete stories can therefore resist dominant knowledge-making practices and unequal relations of socio-economic power. An emphasis on athlete experiences as important counter-knowledge to dominant neuroscientific paradigms can also build further recognition of how elite collision sports are a site of inherently dangerous and precarious working conditions. A greater focus on lived experiences of CTE rather than the search for its root neurophysiological causes can also help foster empathy for athletes in a labor context increasingly characterized by exploitation and expendability (Brayton et al. 2019).

Valuing experience as counter-knowledge forces us to confront the social conditions through which repetitive brain trauma materializes in the embodied experiences of athletes. Morrison and Casper (2016) define CTE as the co-production of "masculinity and money, bodies and brutality, spectacle and showmanship, health and self-image—all speaking to the multiple positions of men in terms of corporeal, social, and economic capital" (p. 165). The lessons of sick building syndrome illuminate the multiplicity of CTE and the corresponding dangers of this multiplicity: the sources of harm represented in Morrison and Casper's definition coalesce through the practices, policies, and values enabling the occurrence of repetitive brain trauma in collision sports. Yet these factors are not exclusively associated with repetitive brain trauma; they also simultaneously support manifestations of other forms of harm beyond head impacts. Instead of examining the biomechanical or chemical specificity of different forms of harm, emphasizing the shared social conditions underlying these processes challenges the notion that multiplicity unavoidably generates uncertainty. Rather, multiplicity can offer alternative knowledges that reveal how uncertainty is actively constructed through the production and classification of scientific evidence.

Some scientists have indeed highlighted how behaviors with no apparent connection to TBI such as substance abuse may be at play in the materialization of tau proteins characteristic of CTE (Asken et al. 2017; Solomon 2018). These hypotheses, however, fail to consider how the use of such substances, such as anabolic steroids, prescription painkillers, or alcohol, are practices related to the same assemblage of bodies, violence, and hyper-masculine spectacle around which repetitive brain impacts are normalized as intrinsic to collision sports (Holstein et al. 2016; King 2014; King et al. 2014). As steroids are technologies designed to produce bigger, more powerful bodies to inflict harm on opponents, painkillers offer (temporary) relief from embodied responses of such violence. Holstein, Jones, and Koonce (2016) similarly highlight the trend for NFL players to also use alcohol as a means to cope with the physical and psychical damage of a life in football. Popular biographies of NHL enforcers who were diagnosed with CTE postmortem, such as Derek Boogaard and Steve Montador, detail how their struggles with symptoms of TBI were dangerously entangled with their extensive use of painkillers and use of alcohol or other drugs (Branch 2014; Dryden 2017). As many neuroscientists seek to isolate how factors beyond repetitive brain trauma contribute to the onset of CTE, high-profile studies such as those detailed above typically neglect to examine how these elements become entangled within the cultures of collision sports.

Mapping Infrastructures of Harm

Commentators often cite neuroscientific uncertainty surrounding CTE when assessing potential risk of brain trauma alongside the perceived benefits of sport participation (e.g. Asken and Bauer 2018; Hardes 2017). Asken and Bauer (2018) write that although it is "no longer possible to ignore the potential risks of extended involvement in sports that involve repetitive head impacts," discussions about CTE risk should not over-shadow how "the physical and mental benefits of sport participation are undeniable" (p. 674). While involvement in sports can most definitively facilitate positive experiences for some athletes, overly idealistic portray-als of sport participation often obscure how many of the potential bene-fits and harms associated with (collision) sports inhere to the same sets of values and practices. Celebrated masculine virtues such as determination, toughness, and aggression support contexts in which violent collisions are normalized as "part of the game" despite their capacity to inflict immediate and long-term damage to athletes' bodies (Young 2011). Neuroscientific paradigms typically require conceptualizing these colli-sions as isolated injury events with measurable effects on the brain. Yet the experience of brain injury is not an isolated event, but one conse-quence of contexts in which athletes are put in positions to collide with other bodies or objects, then react to these impacts in conjunction with configurations of medical and neuroscientific practice. Thus, understand-ing athletes' experiences of brain trauma must move beyond determining the "cause" of CTE pathology or its specific role in the emergence of physical, cognitive, and emotional struggles. Instead, it is most useful to conceptualize these struggles as materializing through the social condi-tions in which athletes encounter and endure damage to their brains.

When theorizing the roots and legacies of environmental toxicity, Murphy (2013) describes the workings of "chemical infrastructures," the varied pathways through which industrial chemicals permeate and struc-ture life. Murphy defines chemical infrastructures as

> the spatial and temporal distributions of industrially produced chemicals as they are produced and consumed, and as they become mobile in the atmo-sphere, settle into landscapes, travel in water ways, leach from commodi-ties, are regulated (or not) by states, monitored by experts, engineered by industries, absorbed by bodies, metabolized physiologically, and as they bioaccumulate in food changes, break down over time, or persist. (p. 3)

Exposure to harmful chemicals, then, is not a discrete process, but one that materializes through an assemblage of extensive infrastructures—social, ecological, industrial, economic, regulatory, administrative, and architectural. While industrial chemicals are the source of harm to bodies and ecologies, they need not be conceptualized in terms of cause and effect. Like sick building syndrome, the dangers of environmental toxicity are embedded within the very practices, structures, and ecosystems through which multiple chemicals interact with bodies and the world around them.

Repetitive brain trauma is also not a discrete process. These injuries are themselves part of wider *infrastructures of harm* that permeate the cultures of collision sports: the varied elements that together produce a context in which an athlete becomes exposed to and embodies repetitive brain trauma. While the onset of CTE pathology or noticeable cognitive or emotional decline is not inevitable for athletes in collision sports, how their bodies respond to the damage accumulated throughout their career is contingent on specific social conditions and material processes. In other words, an athlete's brain encounters trauma under a particular set of circumstances. The athlete then embodies this trauma through neurophysiological changes that are shaped, managed, and (sometimes) become perceptible through neuroscientific practice and/or subjective experiences. Mapping infrastructures of harm is a way to consider both the contextual specificity of an athlete's struggles *and* the materiality of their experience.

This approach also engages with important aspects of Morrison and Casper's definition of CTE: how bodies react to violent collisions and how athletes (and medical professionals) manage the embodied aftermaths of these impacts, using various techniques, technologies, and practices of self-medication; cultural norms that celebrate masculine toughness and facilitate the successful commodification of violence; economic and social incentives for athletes to enact these norms and play through injury; medical procedures designed to mask pain, hasten recovery, and improve athlete productivity; policies and protocols intended to improve safety and well-being, but can otherwise insulate sports organizations from challenges to their value systems and business models; the implications of overreliance on protective equipment and other medicalized technologies; scientific investigations that create new knowledge, but also highlight uncertainty. This expansive network of infrastructures are experienced by athletes in collision sports, not as isolated occurrences with identifiable effects, but together as an assemblage that continually enables the systematic production of harm.

Acknowledging the influence of broader infrastructures of harm challenges the tendency for scientists and sports organizations to hold up the number of postmortem CTE diagnoses as the only definitive evidence of the dangers of repetitive brain trauma. A growing number of studies have raised questions about how neuroscientific focus on CTE might overshadow other harmful neuropathological outcomes of repetitive brain trauma. Recent studies have identified possible associations between histories of repetitive brain trauma and other forms of neurodegeneration, some of which may co-occur with CTE (e.g. Adams et al. 2018; Moszczynski et al. 2018). In fact, disability claims for Parkinson's disease and amyotrophic lateral sclerosis (ALS) under the NFL player's concussion settlement have far exceeded the payout projections established when the agreement took effect in 2017 (Hruby 2018). These ambiguities not only reflect the multiplicity of sport-related harms, but more importantly may also guide how we value accounts from athletes that might not comply with neuroscientific frameworks or have yet to be confirmed through postmortem diagnosis. Even in the absence of conclusive diagnoses or clinical criteria, the rise of CTE as a cultural phenomenon has enabled athletes to describe complex experiences in terms invested with neuroscientific authority; indeed, the notoriety of CTE offers athletes a provocative vocabulary for articulating a multiplicity of struggles that are bound up with—even if not directly caused by—harms associated with violent sports (Ventresca 2019).

Focusing on broader infrastructures of harm, rather than specific causal mechanisms, can work to combat the strategic mobilization of uncertainty by scientists and sport organizations that can disempower athletes. Documenting uncertainty surrounding a phenomenon and advocating for more thorough or sophisticated science can (intentionally or not) protect the status quo and the socioeconomic relations supporting existing states of affairs (Stocking and Holtstein 1993; Zehr 2017). Decisions made in the interest of "good science" and methodological rigor can do little to engage broader social conditions (Jasanoff 1987). Re-centering athletes' firsthand accounts as valuable knowledge of the daily intricacies of their struggles and uncertainties, rather than unconvincing anecdotes requiring verification through objective science, can shift scientific priorities away from questions of causation toward ways to dignify experience and alleviate suffering. Such an analysis must be informed by attention to the contextual specificity of TBI, but also by an acceptance of the potential limitations of neuroscience to map the material legacies of these injuries. These tensions highlight the importance of valuing subjective experience as counter-knowledge supplementary to, rather than hostile toward, scientific ways of knowing. Instead of scientific skepticism toward the stories and self-reported ailments of athletes, placing greater value on the embodied experiences of athletes could re-align scientific priorities in the interest of dignity and quality of life. First and foremost, the multiplicity and messiness of an athlete's experience should be embraced as producing valuable knowledge that can combat uncertainty rather than undermine the validity of their struggles.

Notes

1. In this chapter, I use the terms traumatic brain injury and brain trauma to encompass a broad spectrum of damage to the brain that may occur in sports contexts. This spectrum includes injuries that may be clinically diagnosed as concussion, but also types of brain trauma that are not formally diagnosed by medical professionals.
2. Randolph argues that, while repetitive brain trauma may facilitate the production of abnormal deposits of tau protein, it is possible that these proteins are benign and not amenable to the toxic, damaging processes from which CTE is defined as a neurodegenerative disease.
3. Dose-response curves are statistical representations of changes to an organism following exposure to a stimulus or stressor, whereas threshold limit values is a calculation of how much an organism can be exposed to a stimulus or stressor before experiencing adverse effects.

References

Adams, J. W., Alvarez, V. E., Mez, J., Huber, B. R., Tripodis, Y., Xia, W., et al. (2018). Lewy body pathology and Chronic Traumatic Encephalopathy associated with contact sports. *Journal of Neuropathology & Experimental Neurology, 77*(9), 757–768.

Asken, B. M., & Bauer, R. M. (2018). Chronic Traumatic Encephalopathy: The horse is still chasing the cart. *Journal of Orthopedics Sports Physical Therapy, 48*(9), 672–676.

Asken, B. M., Sullan, M. J., DeKosky, S. T., Jaffee, M. S., & Bauer, R. M. (2017). Research gaps and controversies in Chronic Traumatic Encephalopathy: A review. *JAMA Neurology, 74*(10), 1255–1262.

Asken, B. M., Sullan, M. J., Snyder, A. R., Houck, Z. M., Bryant, V. E., Hizel, L. P., et al. (2016). Factors influencing clinical correlates of Chronic Traumatic Encephalopathy (CTE): A review. *Neuropsychology Review, 26*(4), 340–363.

Bachynski, K. E., & Goldberg, D. S. (2014, Fall). Youth sports and public health: Framing risks of mild traumatic brain injury in American football and ice hockey. *Journal of Law, Medicine, and Ethics, 42*, 323–333.

Bachynski, K. E., & Goldberg, D. S. (2018). Time out: NFL conflicts of interest with public health efforts to prevent TBI. *Injury Prevention, 24*(3), 180–184.

Benson, P. (2017). Big football: Corporate social responsibility and the culture and color of injury in America's most popular sport. *Journal of Sport and Social Issues, 41*(4), 307–334.

Branch, J. (2014). *Boy on ice: The life and death of Derek Boogaard.* Toronto: HarperCollins Publishers.

Brayton, S., & Helstein, M. (in press). The athlete's body and the social text of suicide. In M. Ventresca & M. G. McDonald (Eds.), *Sociocultural Examinations of Sports Concussions.* New York: Routledge.

Brayton, S., Helstein, M. T., Ramsey, M., & Rickards, N. (2019). Exploring the missing link between the concussion "crisis" and labor politics in professional sports. *Communication & Sport, 7*(1), 110–131.

Cartwright, N. (2004). Causation: One word, many things. *Philosophy of Science, 71*(5), 805–819.

Casper, S. T. (2018a). Concussion: A history of science and medicine, 1870–2005. *Headache*, March.

Casper, S. T. (2018b). How the 1950s changed our understanding of traumatic encephalopathy and its sequelae. *CMAJ, 190*(5), E140–E142.

Deleuze, G., & Guattari, F. (1987). *A thousand plateaus: Capitalism and schizophrenia*. Minneapolis: University of Minnesota Press.

Dryden, K. (2017). *Game change: The life and death of Steve Montador, and the future of hockey*. Toronto: Signal.

Fainaru-Wada, M., & Fainaru, S. (2013). *League of denial: The NFL, concussions, and the battle for truth*. New York: Crown-Archetype.

Finkel, A. M. & Bieniek, K. F. (2018). A quantitative risk assessment for chronic traumatic encephalopathy (CTE) in football: How public health science evaluates evidence. *Human and Ecological Risk Assessment: An International Journal, 25*(3), 564–589.

Goldberg, D. S. (2012). Mild traumatic brain injury, the US National Football League, and the manufacture of doubt: An ethical, legal, and historical analysis. *Journal of Legal Medicine, 34*(2), 157–191.

Hardes, J. (2017). Governing sporting brains: Concussion, neuroscience, and the biopolitical regulation of sport. *Sport, Ethics and Philosophy, 11*(3), 1–13.

Hazrati, L.-N., Tartaglia, M., Diamandis, P., Davis, K., Green, R., Wennberg, R., et al. (2013). Absence of chronic traumatic encephalopathy in retired football players with multiple concussions and neurological symptomatology. *Frontiers in Human Neuroscience, 7*, 222.

Holstein, J. A., Jones, R. S., & Koonce, G. E., Jr. (2016). *Is there life after football? Surviving the NFL*. New York: NYU Press.

Hruby, P. (2018, August 8). Startling jump in NFL player claims for Parkinson's and ALS pushes payout projections past 65-year total in 18 months. *Los Angeles Times*. Retrieved from http://www.latimes.com/sports/nfl/la-sp-nfl-medical-payouts-20180808-story.html.

Iverson, G. L., Keene, C. D., Perry, G., & Castellani, R. J. (2018). The need to separate Chronic Traumatic Encephalopathy neuropathology from clinical features. *Journal of Alzheimer's Disease: JAD, 61*, 17–28.

Jasanoff, S. S. (1987). Contested boundaries in policy-relevant science. *Social Studies of Science, 17*(2), 195–230.

Kindelan, K. (2018). 3 female Olympians pledge to donate brains for concussion research. *ABC News*. Retrieved from https://abcnews.go.com/GMA/Wellness/female-olympians-pledge-donate-brains-concussion-research/story?id=52878103.

King, S. (2014). Beyond the war on drugs? Notes on prescription opioids and the NFL. *Journal of Sport and Social Issues, 38*(2), 184–193.

King, S., Carey, R. S., Jinnah, N., Millington, R., Phillipson, A., Prouse, C., & Ventresca, M. (2014). When is a drug not a drug? Troubling silence and unsettling painkillers in the National Football League. *Sociology of Sport Journal, 31*(3), 249–266.

Kuhn, A. W., Yengo-Kahn, A. M., Kerr, Z. Y., & Zuckerman, S. L. (2017). Sports concussion research, chronic traumatic encephalopathy and the media: repairing the disconnect. *British Journal of Sports Medicine, 51*(24), 1732 LP–1731733.

Malcolm, D. (2009). Medical uncertainty and clinician-athlete relations of concussion injuries in rugby union. *Sociology of Sport Journal, 26*(2), 191–210.

Maroon, J. C., Winkelman, R., Bost, J., Amos, A., & Mathyssek, C. (2015). Chronic Traumatic Encephalopathy in contact sports: A systematic review of all reported pathological cases. *PLoS ONE, 10*(2), 1–16.

McCrory, P., Meeuwisse, W., Dvorak, J., Aubry, M., Bailes, J., Broglio, S., et al. (2017). Consensus statement on concussion in sport – the 5th international conference on concussion in sport held in Berlin, October 2016. *British Journal of Sports Medicine, 51*(11), 1–10.

McKee, A. C., Cairns, N. J., Dickson, D. W., Folkerth, R. D., Dirk Keene, C., Litvan, I., et al. (2016). The first NINDS/NIBIB consensus meeting to define neuropathological criteria for the diagnosis of chronic traumatic encephalopathy. *Acta Neuropathologica, 131*(1), 75–86.

McKee, A. C., Stein, T. D., Kiernan, P. T., & Alvarez, V. E. (2015). The neuropathology of chronic traumatic encephalopathy. *Brain Pathology, 25*(3), 350–364.

McKee, A. C., Stein, T. D., Nowinski, C. J., Stern, R. A., Daneshvar, D. H., Alvarez, V. E., et al. (2013). The spectrum of disease in chronic traumatic encephalopathy. *Brain, 136*(1), 43–64.

Mez, J., Daneshvar, D., Kiernan, P., et al. (2017). Clinicopathological evaluation of chronic traumatic encephalopathy in players of American football. *JAMA, 318*(4), 360–370.

Montenigro, P. H., Alosco, M. L., Martin, B. M., Daneshvar, D. H., Mez, J., Chaisson, C. E., et al. (2017). Cumulative head impact exposure predicts later-life depression, apathy, executive dysfunction, and cognitive impairment in former high school and college football players. *Journal of Neurotrauma, 34*, 328–340.

Montenigro, P. H., Corp, D. T., Stein, T. D., Cantu, R. C., & Stern, R. A. (2015). Chronic Traumatic Encephalopathy: Historical origins and current perspective. *Annual Review Clinical Psychology, 11*, 309–330.

Montenigro, P. H., Baugh, C. M., Daneshvar, D. H., Mez, J., Budson, A. E., Au, R., et al. (2014). Clinical subtypes of chronic traumatic encephalopathy:

Literature review and proposed research diagnostic criteria for traumatic encephalopathy syndrome. *Alzheimer's Research & Therapy, 6*(68), 1–17.

Moore, A., & Stilgoe, J. (2009). Experts and anecdotes. *Science, Technology, & Human Values, 34*(5), 654–677.

Morrison, D. R., & Casper, M. J. (2016). Gender, violence, and brain injury in and out of the NFL: What counts as harm? In D. Leonard, K. B. George, & W. Davis (Eds.), *Football, culture, and power* (pp. 156–175). New York: Routledge.

Moszczynski, A. J., Strong, W., Xu, K., McKee, A., Brown, A., & Strong, M. J. (2018). Pathologic Thr175 tau phosphorylation in CTE and CTE with ALS. *Neurology, 90,* 1–9.

Murphy, M. (2006). *Sick building syndrome and the problem of uncertainty.* Raleigh, NC: Duke University Press.

Murphy, M. (2013). Distributed reproduction, chemical violence, and latency. *The Scholar and Feminist Online, 11*(3), 1–9.

Nicholson, P. J., Dixon, D., Pullanikkatil, D., Moyo, B., Long, H., & Barrett, B. (2019). Malawi stories: Mapping an art-science collaborative process. *Journal of Maps, 0*(0), 1–9. https://doi.org/10.1080/17445647.2 019.1582440.

Oreskes, N., & Conway, E. M. (2010). *Merchants of doubt: How a handful of scientists obscured the truth on issues from tobacco smoke to global warming.* New York: Bloomsbury Press.

Pinto, M. F. (2015). Tensions in agnotology: Normativity in the studies of commercially driven ignorance. *Social Studies of Science, 45*(2), 294–315.

Pitts-Taylor, V. (2016). *The brain's body: Neuroscience and corporeal politics.* Durham, NC: Duke University Press.

Proctor, R. N. (2008). Agnotology: A missing term to describe the cultural production of ignorance. In R. N. Proctor & L. Schiebinger (Eds.), *Agnotology: The making and unmaking of ignorance.* Stanford, CA: Stanford University Press.

Randolph, C. (2018). Chronic traumatic encephalopathy is not a real disease. *Archives of Clinical Neuropsychology, 33*(5), 644–648.

Rose, N., & Abi-Rached, J. M. (2013). *Neuro: The new brain sciences and the management of the mind.* Princeton, NJ: Princeton University Press.

Schwab, N., & Hazrati, L.-N. (2018). Assessing the limitations and biases in the current understanding of Chronic Traumatic Encephalopathy. *Journal of Alzheimer's Disease: JAD, 64*(4), 1067–1076.

Smithson, M. (1989). *Ignorance and uncertainty: Emerging paradigms.* New York: Springer-Verlag.

Solomon, G. (2018). Chronic traumatic encephalopathy in sports: A historical and narrative review. *Developmental Neuropsychology, 43*(4), 279–311.

Standen, J. (2017). Blood sports in an age of liability. In M. A. McCann (Ed.), *The Oxford handbook of American sports law* (pp. 139–160). New York: Oxford University Press.

Stocking, H. S., & Holtstein, L. W. (1993). Constructing and reconstructing scientific ignorance. *Knowledge: Creation, Diffusion, Utilization, 15*(2), 186–210.

Sullivan, S., & Tuana, N. (2007). Introduction. In S. Sullivan & N. Tuana (Eds.), *Race and epistemologies of ignorance* (pp. 1–10). New York: SUNY Press.

Tagge, C. A., Fisher, A. M., Minaeva, O. V., Gaudreau-, A., Moncaster, J. A., Zhang, X., et al. (2018, February). Concussion, microvascular injury, and early tauopathy in young athletes after impact head injury and an impact concussion mouse model. *Brain, 141*, 422–458.

Ventresca, M. (2019). The curious case of CTE: Mediating materialities of traumatic brain injury. *Communication & Sport, 7*(2), 135–156. https://doi.org/10.1177/2167479518761636.

Young, K. (2011). *Sport, violence and society*. New York: Routledge.

Zehr, S. (2017). Scientific uncertainty in health and risk messaging. *Oxford Research Encyclopedia of Communication*. https://doi.org/10.1093/acrefore/9780190228613.013.215.

The Agency of Numbers: The Role of Metrics in Influencing the Valuation of Athletes

Roslyn Kerr, Christopher Rosin, and Mark Cooper

One of the most significant changes that new technologies have brought to sport is the increasing use of, and in some cases, reliance on, technologically generated numeric data. The importance of numbers in sport was perhaps most famously identified by Allen Guttmann in 1978, when he deemed 'quantification' and 'records' to be two of the seven characteristics of modern sporting practice. In Guttmann's time, he was referring primarily to the use of numbers in rules and as a mechanism for determining winners. Both remain important today, but the use of quantitative data has also been extended owing to the proliferation of measuring technologies, which mean that more data is available than ever before (Gerrard 2017; Millington and Millington 2015). The prominence of data increased with the growth of the discipline of sports science, particularly favoured by nationally centralised systems such as those of the Eastern bloc and later Australia (Collins and Bailey 2013), which emerged

R. Kerr (✉) • C. Rosin
Lincoln University, Christchurch, New Zealand
e-mail: Roslyn.Kerr@lincoln.ac.nz; christopher.rosin@lincoln.ac.nz

M. Cooper
University of California, Davis, Davis, CA, USA

© The Author(s) 2020
J. J. Sterling, M. G. McDonald (eds.), *Sports, Society, and Technology*,
https://doi.org/10.1007/978-981-32-9127-0_5

99

in the 1970s and 1980s as a significant outgrowth of increasingly accurate and repeatable data collection.

In this chapter, we focus more specifically on the role of numbers, or metrics, in changing the workings of sport. In a review of literature related to metrics and sports, we identify an emphasis on the active role of metrics as an external influence that changes the performance, organisation and experience of sport. We extend this analysis by arguing that the embracing of numeric data in sport represents an effort to impose a sheen of uniformity across an otherwise complex and context-rich activity for the purposes of facilitating objective assessment of both performance and athletic potential. We draw on two theoretical devices to develop our argument. First, we use Latour's concept of the 'immutable mobile' to demonstrate the logic and desirability of a tool (in this case, measurement and application of numeric data) that can be applied irrespective of circumstance (it is mobile) with the expectation of an objective and comparable (it is immutable) assessment. In addition to examining the capacities of numeric data, we also turn to Deleuze and Guattari's concept of territorialisation to examine the dynamics through which the effort to achieve uniformity alters the workings of sport as well as those dynamics that eventuate as uniformity is contested.

The empirical basis for our argument involves an examination of three distinct contexts. In the first of these—athletics and gymnastics—we examine the tension between the numbers or scores that represent particular sporting performances. Through the examples of the 10-second 100 m sprint and the perfect-10 routine, we demonstrate the potential for numbers to hold agency by generating unanticipated or unintended consequences of designing the sport or determining the score. Second, we focus on the role of metrics in the context of talent identification and question whether an athlete's talent and/or potential can be reduced to a numeric form. In this case, we explore the U.S. National Football League (NFL) 'combine' system as a rather different context where the reduction of an athlete's abilities to a numeric form is more contested. Together, these examples indicate the extent to which the workings of sport, and our experience of the performance, is as much the product of the numbers as it is that of athletes' actions.

Numbers in Sport

Throughout human history, measurement has been a common means of building knowledge and allowing for the evaluation of the physical world (Kuhn 1961; Mari 2003), with the advantage of generating forms of information that facilitate shared interpretation (Rossi 2007). Although systems of measurement often appear natural and incontestable, rendering a complex phenomenon into numbers involves an authoritative declaration of what is to be valued and what the essence of an activity is. The translation of qualities into quantities requires abstracting from context and assigning a numerical value that can be communicated to distant places and people (Porter 1994; Power 2004). These characteristics of measurement have given the numbers it generates an important role in sports. In what follows, we outline how previous research has focused on the way metrics have perpetuated or widened already existing power relationships: first, in the context of management and governance; second, as the quantification of movement; third, in the coaching environment; and finally, through the sport-media nexus.

As a range of authors have observed, the use of scientific data or metrics as a management mechanism has become commonplace in sport and viewed as a form of managerialism with national or international governing bodies demanding high levels of accountability from sports organisations who report to them (see Baerg 2017; Hutchins 2016; Macris and Sam 2014; Williams and Manley 2016). In this context, the quantitative component allows for the definitive measuring of success. For example, in many countries, the number of Olympic medals won, or the numeric placing of an athlete, determines the amount of government funding that the sport or athlete will receive (Grix and Carmichael 2012). As Sam and Macris (2014) outline, these tactics can result in problematic behaviours from sports organisations as they adopt practices purely to acquire money rather than promoting sport.

Indeed, a potential threat of the value of sport being overshadowed by the emphasis on numbers was identified by Colás (2017), who traces the history of quantification in the sport of basketball and questions the dominance of numbers both as an analytic tool and for keeping score. He notes that in the past, it had been argued that basketball may be improved without the score, since the sport is essentially about physical movement prowess. He suggests that by focusing on the score so strongly, the more important dimensions of the game, such as the quality of movement performed, are de-emphasised. Konoval (2018) makes the same observation in the context of endurance running training, where numbers in the form of athletes' times become the focus of attention to a far greater extent than the physical act of running. A similar argument has been applied in the talent identification literature by social scientists who have examined the appropriateness of such a strong quantitative emphasis. In this context, physical ability testing has traditionally been used as a method to quantifiably measure an athlete's talent (Lidor et al. 2009). Quantitative psychology or psychometric tests have also been used (Collins and Cruickshank 2017). However, recently, a range of authors have questioned the dominance of quantified tests in talent identification and development, arguing that these have poor predictive ability in comparison to the subjective views of experienced coaches who are able to account for a far wider number of variables than those that can be quantitatively measured (Christensen 2009; Lidor et al. 2009; Miller et al. 2015).

At the same time, studies have found that coaches too are increasingly relying on quantitative data for their decision-making processes. Both Williams and Manley (2016) and Denison and Mills (2014) argue that quantitative data can work as a control mechanism within the coaching context. It works in a similar way to the previously discussed managerial mechanism; it occurs at the individual level and has been found to produce some problematic outcomes for athlete welfare. While Denison and Mills (2014) utilise Foucault, Williams and Manley (2016) draw on the work of Gilles Deleuze, who in *Postscript on the Societies of Control* (1992) focused on the role of numeric data in the twenty-first century as contributing to a new form of society of control. In their study of the use of quantitative data in a rugby club, Williams and Manley (2016) argue that the data was used by coaches to survey and discipline the athletes, and that as a result of the reliance on the data, each athlete was reduced to nothing more than a data set. In their critique of Williams and Manley's (2016)[1] work, Collins et al. (2015)

claim that while they disagree with Williams and Manley's (2016) overall interpretation, they agree that quantification can be detrimental when it is solely relied upon. Specifically, they point out the risk when coaches focus only on variables that can be quantified, even though sporting success relies on many facets that cannot be quantified. For example, they note that the sport of rugby union involves mastering a range of complexities, including quick decision-making, which is not easily quantifiable. Baerg (2017) agrees that the monitoring of athletes through data, by coaches and others is a troubling development as it creates a digital divide where the athletes are unempowered due to their lack of access to digital data. He suggests that athletes could potentially overcome this scenario if they were to collect their own health data and use it for their own ends, or if they were to resist the collection of data for reasons of privacy.

Continuing the theme of access and inequalities, in the sport media context, Hutchins (2016) notes how the prizing of big data in sport has opened up considerable new commercial opportunities. He identifies how the increasing use of data has exacerbated already wide inequalities between lucrative team sports that dominate the media and other, less visible, men's teams or women's sports (Hutchins 2016, 495). By contrast, Baerg (2013) notes how analytics can reveal unexpected results that provide opportunities for less-celebrated athletes. Using the work of Latour, Baerg (2013) focuses on the agentic role of numbers in being able to reveal what is not apparent to the human eye. For example, he argues that while individuals directly observe what is happening at the game, surprises can be revealed through numeric analysis. For example, Baerg refers to a case where a player who has not performed in a spectacular way and therefore may have gone unnoticed by fans, may in fact end up with the best ratings of the season due to consistently good performances. Baerg (2013) also notes the way that analytics can allow the detection of flaws in a team's performance that otherwise would not be seen. Clashes between quantitative-focused analysts and those who observe with more traditional qualitative eyes have also been found to arise (Baerg 2013).

The Agency of Numbers

With the exception of the work of Baerg (2013), the role of metrics in sport has most often been understood as maintaining existing power arrangements. In the above discussions, the focus is strongly on the human relationships, such as coaches surveying athletes (e.g. see Williams and Manley 2016) or organisations holding others accountable (e.g. see Sam and Macris 2014). In such contexts, metrics are recognised as tools used by the individuals in those relationships. By contrast, in this chapter, we instead utilise a similar perspective to Baerg (2013) in noting that metrics can hold agency in and of themselves. This line of argument has been commonly used in Science and Technology Studies (STS), where numerous authors have pointed out that technologies have agency—that they have particular physical or other properties that create particular effects. One of the theorists most famous for noting the agentic role of technologies or other non-humans is Bruno Latour, and in this chapter, we draw on his concept of non-humans being 'immutable mobiles' (Latour 1987, 1990).

An immutable mobile refers to a relatively stable assemblage that can be displaced yet still holds its shape. The displacement refers to the way a certain set of ideas, or ways of doing things, can be moved or utilised across contexts or geographical locations, while the idea of holding shape refers to the concept that it is stable enough to continue functioning regardless of its movement (Law and Mol 2001). Cooren et al. (2007, p. 157) explain the concept: 'By immutable mobile, Latour means an entity that can travel from one point to the other without suffering from distortion, loss, or corruption'. The appeal of metrics as an immutable mobile in the sports context lies in the hope of creating a definitive assessment of athletic performance that transcends vagaries of time, variation in assessment preferences and the variegated capabilities of individual athletes. These are crucial for the identification of talent or winners, and for distributing information between athletes, coaches, administrators and sports fans.

While Latour (1990) did not specifically refer to metrics or sports, he did write extensively on graphs as a unique form of immutable mobile and an essential feature of Western science. He argued that graphs allow abstract or 'invisible' information to become clearly visible, and then to be transported and communicated. In this chapter, we argue that these phenomena are apparent in sport through numbers and metrics.

Additional theoretical insight is drawn from the concept of territorialisation as introduced by Deleuze and Guattari in *A Thousand Plateaus* (1987). In this work, they represent the world as an assemblage, that is as a joining together of disparate elements (human and non-human) that interact in a manner through which a reality is manifest without being distinguished by hierarchical and purposive action. The definition and explanation of the assemblage is contested as its emergent (ever-evolving) structure, components and relations defy any claims to a definitive characterisation. They also acknowledge the tendency for assemblages to cohere as observable, explainable and manageable through a process of territorialisation that 'fixes' elements and features of the assemblage in conceptual space. For example, the agreement to rules governing the practice of sport territorialises specific activities by distinguishing football from rugby, badminton from tennis. Territorialisation is, however, always ephemeral, being subject to de-territorialisation via the contestation of its parameters and a subsequent re-territorialisation as the assemblage stabilises and coheres within a new conceptual space. Thinking in terms of the (de-)(re-)territorialisation of the 100 m sprint, gymnastics and the evaluation of athletic potential in the NFL Combine, we investigate not only the agency of the metrics but also the social, material and conceptual dynamics that ensue in response to the involvement of metrics in sports.

Immutable Excellence

Perhaps the most obvious application of metrics to sport involves their use in determining the competitive performance in a specific event that occurs across diverse contexts. For example, whereas assessing the winner of a given heat of the 100 m sprint can be determined visually by noting the *order* in which participants cross the finish line, it becomes necessary to measure the *time* required to facilitate comparison of performance across heats (for seeding purposes) or across time (for record times). In this context, ten seconds has assumed the role of a seemingly immutable signifier of excellence across time and space (except in the case of 'excessive' tailwind or altitude). Despite Usain Bolt having established a world record time of 9.58 seconds, no more than 25 athletes have been timed under the 10-second mark during any year since 2010.[2] Even the least interested of observers is likely to acknowledge the achievement of an individual who runs the 100 m in less than 10 seconds. In fact, this measure has become the criteria for assessing the potential of sprinters, as future champions are expected to be approaching the barrier by their late teenage years.

In this case, these numbers come to act as an immutable mobile, an inscription that stabilises in a particular form and can therefore travel. The metric of finishing time means that, without observing the race or the athlete, we can instantly understand that the runner is successful. Just as in Latour's (1990) example of the graph, the numbers provide the information that allows the athlete's performance—even if not seen—to become immediately visible, easily understandable and globally transportable. This example additionally relates to Colás' (2017) argument that focusing on the numeric score obscures the performance itself. The metric of finishing time means that it is not necessary to see the physical performance; its excellence can be appreciated without any mention of the actual movements being performed.

Because the 10-second mark arguably remains an immutable metric of excellence, it has also altered the manner in which the sport is practised—in other words, re-territorialising the practice of sprinting. Over time, training for the event has evolved to include attention to discrete elements of the sprint, including more scientific assessment of the positioning and foot placement in the starting blocks, improved reactive response to the starting gun and selective muscle development for turnover rate and strength (Majumdar and Robergs 2011; Simperingham et al. 2016; Slawinski et al. 2012). The improvement of human performance has been further enhanced through technological advances in the shoes, uniforms and track materials focused on shaving tenths or hundredths of seconds from sprinting times. These changes have also initiated efforts to enhance observational capabilities and to limit cheating. In order to ensure the accuracy of timing, electronic sensors have replaced handheld stopwatches and there is increasing use of sport imaging technologies in order to determine placings (Finn 2016). Because the shift to electronic technology occurred at the time the 10-second mark was first being broken, sprinters who have broken the mark according to handheld timings fail to gain official recognition of their achievement. More recently, analyses of human reaction time (indicating a 0.1 second delay) have led to the introduction of new rulings on false starts, whereby electronic sensors on the starting blocks are used to measure whether a sprinter is legally responding to the starting gun as opposed to anticipating the starter's actions (Pain and Hibbs 2007). One result of these advances in timing technology has been a greater emphasis on high-speed photographic stills and slow-motion video of the start and finish of races, especially when close finishes exceed the capacity of the human eye to distinguish a winner. In addition, the timing for preliminary heats (and associated measurements of wind speed and direction) in larger meets become as important as the actual placements in each heat. In athletics, therefore, the 10-second mark has contributed to enacting a more reductionist approach to performing, observing and assessing the 100 m sprint.

The Translation of Movement to Score

In the 100 m sprint, timing developments have occurred due to the requirement that sporting events include a mechanism for determining the winner. As illustrated above, in 'race'-like events, the winner is the athlete who completes the required distance in the fastest numeric time, while in many team sports, the winner is the team who accumulates the most points. Yet beyond these ranking systems, other numeric forms also come into play when certain athletic performances become defined by their relationship to a particular number.

One of the most memorable performers at the 1976 Olympic Games was the gymnast Nadia Comaneci. Comaneci most certainly performed amazing feats, but so too did her Russian rival, Nellie Kim. What rocketed Comaneci to incredible fame was her being the first person to achieve the score of a perfect 10 (Kerr 2006).

The significance of Comaneci's achievement was that the number 10 served as a symbol of perfection and, once awarded, de-territorialised the stable order of scoring under which gymnastic performance was experienced. Prior to 1976, scores had been awarded out of a maximum of 10 points, serving as a ranking mechanism in order to determine the winner. The awarding of the 10 indicated a new possibility: the disappearance of relativity. The gymnast awarded a 10 was guaranteed to be in first place, regardless of the performances of remaining competitors. It did not matter if another gymnast performed a routine that was more difficult or better executed than a gymnast who had been awarded a 10, as it was impossible to award a higher mark.

The agency of the 10 was also apparent in the asymmetry between the framing of Comaneci's achievement and the thinking of the judges who awarded the score. According to the judges, Comaneci was not awarded a 10 because her routines were entirely perfect, but because they had already awarded other gymnasts scores very close to 10; therefore, when Comaneci performed a superior routine, they felt they had no choice but to award her a 10 (Kerr 2006). However, this was not well known, and the media and fans assumed that Comaneci had achieved perfection. Indeed, Comaneci was dubbed 'Little Miss Perfect' by the media. This example demonstrates how, although scores or numbers may be the result of human decision-making, their impact can be greater or different from what those humans intended. This is an excellent example of Latour's argument that non-humans can hold agency. In this case, the fact that the number awarded was a 10, rather than a 9.9, meant that an impression was created that was not the intention of the judges; but due to the scoring system being what it was, the number spoke for itself.

By the time the next un-boycotted Olympic Games occurred in 1988, the situation had changed. Where 10s had been awarded occasionally during the previous 12 years, at the 1988 Games, 41 perfect 10s were awarded, creating two significant issues. First, the nature of the 10 meant that there was no possibility of awarding extra marks to those who performed more difficult movements, leading to doubts about whether the gymnasts who were awarded 10s truly were the best. Second, gymnasts were at times awarded 10s when there were questions about whether the gymnast deserved it. For example, a media report from the Games stated:

In the uneven bars, East Germany's Dagmar Kirsten ended an otherwise fine routine with a little jump on her landing. The gymnast herself appeared downcast, and reacted with disbelief when her score was posted—looking as though even she didn't really want such an "imperfect 10," as one commentator described it. (Eldridge 1988, para. 7, https://www.csmonitor.com/1988/1004/prom.html)

By 1988 then, an interesting situation had developed where the numeric nature of the 10 meant that no extra marks could be awarded in relative terms, but at the same time, due to this facet, it resulted in an overuse of the 10. The capacity of the 10 to act as an immutable symbol of perfection was therefore challenged, at least to educated fans of the sport.

Essentially, the 10 had held significant power to determine the outcome of the competition, and indeed it was the de-territorialising power of the 10 that led the International Gymnastics Federation (FIG) to eradicate it in 2006 (Kerr and Obel 2015). In the new scoring system, the 10 ceiling was replaced with an open-ended scoring system, because of the desire to increase gymnasts' agency rather than agency of numbers. By re-territorialising gymnastics performance with the new system, the FIG argued that a gymnast could focus either on performing higher difficulty elements or on executing each move with perfection (Kerr and Obel 2015). In other words, it would eliminate the power of the 10 to determine the winner before the competition was complete. It also provided more visible assessment criteria for observers.

Territorialising the Mutable

We can also see the agency of numbers at work in the context of physical ability testing. The overall concept of physical ability testing, within the talent identification context, is that an athlete is tested in a variety of ways and then the results of the testing are converted into metrics of some form, whether an absolute score or a ranking, with the metrics then used as a method to determine the talent level of the athlete (Kerr 2018; Lidor et al. 2009). Sports scientists, coaches or others analysing the testing results receive quantitative accounts of replicable assessments of skills or abilities, which are used to determine the athlete's level of talent. Thus, even more than competitive performances which are at least recorded and televised, the results of the tests come to represent sporting talent. In many talent identification scenarios, the quantification is seen as final and objective, and athletes have no opportunity to negotiate the assessment of their results. In this context, the metric is expected to act as an immutable mobile (Latour 1987, 1990), by again becoming a way for the details of the movements performed at the test to be distributed in a stable form. It also provides the mechanism to territorialise what can be a highly diverse set of abilities conducted outside the actual practice of a given sport.

There is a large amount of literature critiquing the efficacy of these kinds of quantitative talent identification methods (e.g. see Anshel and Lidor 2012; Collins and Cruickshank 2017; Lidor et al. 2009); but here, we suggest that the overall difficulty lies in the assumption that talent identification can be reduced to a numeric form. Studies have found a very large number of factors that contribute to sporting success, including physical, physiological, psychological and sociological factors (Lidor et al. 2009). Additionally, these vary over time due to athletes' maturation (Malina et al. 2004) and are complicated by the role of deliberate practice (Ericsson et al. 1993), coaching and other environmental concerns. Given this high level of complexity, there are substantial challenges in determining which metrics best represent the relevant abilities and skills, which metrics might sufficiently predict the abilities of an individual and therefore which metrics merit data collection. This complexity would appear to belie attempts to reduce physical ability to numbers. However, the necessity of metrics in this context is usually understood, or justified, on the grounds that sports governing bodies have limited funds and so must identify the athletes to support in order to achieve elite sporting success (Grix and Carmichael 2012). However, as Sam and Macris (2014) argued in a wider national policy context, these kinds of funding practices can lead to organisations undertaking behaviours designed to ensure that athletes or organisational bodies are scored with the appropriate metrics, as opposed to producing the best outcome for the country. For example, in the talent identification environment, it could easily lead to athletes training purely to achieve good scores on the talent identification tests which do not necessarily translate to successful results in elite sport more generally (Muller 2018). Nonetheless, metrics continue to be used to both select and de-select athletes for many elite teams and programmes due to the belief that they are fair, objective and unbiased measures (Collins and Bailey 2013; Kerr 2018).

In the very different, professionalised context of the NFL draft, the process of selecting athletes for teams has become a sporting event of its own. For many observers, a key moment in this process is the League-hosted 'combine', where invited athletes are measured across a suite of performance indicators, including speed (e.g. 40 and 100 m sprints), agility (shuttle runs) and strength (bench press, standing jumps) as well as position-specific skills (throwing, catching). The combine also includes the Wonderlic intelligence test to estimate cognitive ability. The value of the combine lies in the ability for evaluators to assess measurable skills in a more objective manner, given that all participants are facing the same conditions and without the influence of varying levels of competition that are characteristic of the collegiate game. Moreover, as in the case of the 100 m sprint, it is possible to set performance criteria that indicate NFL potential relevant to positional skillsets.

Within the context of the NFL, the success (or failure) of individual players can have significant consequences for the team, both in terms of winning games and in relation to the financial implications of a player's relative location in the draft.[3] Furthermore, draft selections can have a substantial impact (positive for good picks, extremely negative for 'busts') on a team's public standing. As a result, each team employs a dedicated scouting staff in addition to the coaches and senior management to contribute to the process of selecting future players on potential. This staff follows the on-field performance and training habits of players at the collegiate level developing an assessment informed by attendance at live games, extensive review of tape and interaction with collegiate level coaching staffs. Despite this extensive research, concerns regarding the risks and rewards of player selection reinforce the value of the combine.[4] The relative performance of the participants at the event can influence not only draft preferences but also decisions regarding the desirability of current team members and available free agents.

For both the casual and more interested fan, the combine results draw much attention by providing an insight into the evaluation process. This is particularly true given that access to the results for individuals, let alone the actual performance, has recently been publicly accessible. In this context, the importance of combine performance to the ranking of players on each team's draft board is likely overstated. It is possible for the value of an individual athlete to drop as a result of poor performance—for example, the precipitous fall of Orlando Brown, an offensive lineman, due to slow timings in sprint and agility tests as well as a lower than expected number of repetitions in the bench lift.[5] Similarly, a less vaunted prospect can overcome relative obscurity through a good performance—as evident in the increased recognition of NFL potential attributed to Shaquem Griffin whose top of category numbers among linebackers helped overcome concerns about a missing hand.[6] Such examples are, however, more the exceptional cases that challenge expectations developed through more traditional scouting or other preconceptions based on physical characteristics such as size and weight. Thus, such situations do not limit discussions in media and among fans that definitively peg the participants' performance in the combine to their expected NFL potential.

The expectations that potential can be forecast based on the accumulated metrics—or that the combine results act as an immutable mobile—are increasingly questioned (Lyons et al. 2011). Despite the increased awareness of player capabilities associated with the publication of combine results, the draft remains a risky process littered with the proverbial busts and the unrecognised late-round stars. Furthermore, the draft selections of individual teams seldom correspond directly to the ranking of prospects based on the combine results. Rather, increasingly reference is made to such factors as leadership potential, willingness to learn and self-confidence. Assessment of such factors is once again shrouded in the activities and expertise of specialist scouts who are in the employ of specific teams. Thus, metrics may still perform as an immutable mobile, but these are most likely to exert significant influence (beyond the more qualitative and subjective assessments of players in context) when exposing extremely high or low abilities. In this role, the metrics act to alert interested teams to additional risk or potential that may be obscured through other assessment methods.

Discussion

The power of metrics used in sports can be found in their capacities as immutable mobiles, similar to examples identified by Latour, Law and Callon (and others) in the context of the practice of science. Both the 10-second 100 m and the perfect 10 in gymnastics demonstrate the capacity of metrics to facilitate comparison of performance (as first noted by Guttmann (1978) with regard to records) and to act as immutable indicators of excellence. Furthermore, both physical ability testing and the NFL 'combine' show that metrics can also act to assess performance, although in both cases, their influence is reduced owing to the significance of less measurable attributes in projections of athletic potential. The difficulty of reducing performance predictors to metrics suggests that immutability decreases as complexity increases. When a single measure such as a single time—10 seconds—is used, then immutability is almost guaranteed owing to the ease of understanding and to the discrete outcome of focus (the first to cross the finish line). By contrast, in a case like the 'combine', the greater number of measures and the complexity of the assessed outcome (potential to contribute to victories in a team sport) reduce the potential for achieving immutability. This reflects Latour's (1987) argument that stability is required for immutability, which explains the importance of ensuring consistency, and therefore stability, in more complex settings.

The use of metrics has also changed the manner in which sport is practised and observed. The excellence of an individual 100 m performance is no longer possible to appreciate without the addition of electronic timing to produce a sufficiently accurate time. A gymnast's routine is now similarly impossible to value without the complex arrangement of metric-dominated rules of the new scoring system that set out the numeric value of each skill performed, and its quality. Athletes being selected for talent identification programmes or professional teams are reduced to numeric forms, a potentially paradoxical development given the increasingly thorough understanding of the complexity of factors that produce athletic performance.

At the same time, it remains possible for metrics to be outdone or overcome through particular athletic performances causing the metrics to be questioned or even rewritten. In other words, the immutability of metrics is subject to performances that belie the simplicity and stability of the resulting measures. We suggest that the emergent nature of the engagements between humans, the materiality of sports performance and metrics could be understood through Deleuze and Guattari's (1987) concept of territorialisation.

As this chapter emphasises, any given sporting performance defies human capacity to comprehensively and unerringly assess it. In an effort to place boundaries on that complexity—to territorialise it as a shared form of interpretation and designation—humans increasingly turn to metrics that are presumed to offer objective and unbiased assessment. Deleuze and Guattari note, however, that any territorialisation is subject to disruption (de-territorialisation) and efforts to rebound the complexity (re-territorialisation). In the context of the case studies presented in the chapter, it is possible to identify distinct processes of territorialisation that reflect not only the particularities of each sport and the individuality of participants but the agency of the metrics as well. In the 100 m sprint, the metric of '10 seconds' territorialised the physical performance of sprinting, reducing its assessment to measurement via electronic devices at the start and finish. This territorialisation has been subject to minor disruptions as means to defy the metrics' objectivity (tailwind, anticipation of starting gun, performance-enhancing drugs) required further sets of measures to bound the participants' actions and the material context of performance. More recently, we argue, the extraordinary performance of Usain Bolt in recording times tenths of a second faster than his closest opponents (allowing him to look back at his competitors and celebrate before crossing the line) re-oriented the focus from the time back to the spectacle of the running. The potential to de-territorialise the 100 m sprint appears to be dissipating, however, with the lack of equally capable sprinters. The emergence of the extraordinary performer in gymnastics, by contrast, initiated a significant re-territorialisation of that sport. Valuation of performance in gymnastics bounded by the concept of

10-point scoring reinforced perceptions of the relative value of athleticism and grace under which the preferences of the judges might obscure the basis for distinguishing among participants. By contrast, when the proliferation of perfect 10s disrupted the validity of these assessments, the sport was re-territorialised according to dual metrics involving both a score for difficulty and a judged score for the execution of the routine. Finally, the intense interest in the NFL 'combine' shows the desire to impose boundaries on a poorly defined selection process through an effort to standardise the criteria applied to the prospective 'draftees'. Whereas initial access to the combine performance data territorialised the process in the minds of observers, it has become increasingly apparent that the metrics have only moderate predictive capacity in terms of future performance (Lyons et al. 2011). Despite the resulting re-territorialisation of the assessment process, the agency of the metrics is evident in the strategic use of the combine by prospects who engage in test-directed training, selective or non-participation and even limiting participation in post-season football competitions to avoid injury and increase training time for the combine.

Conclusion

With the proliferation of data generated by new technologies, it is increasingly important to consider the role of metrics in our understanding of today's sporting practice. As this chapter has shown, and despite the intention behind their application, metrics are far from simplistic and benign. Rather, they offer ways to assess, understand and disrupt—to territorialise and re-territorialise—the way athletic performance is watched and performed. Through three very different cases, we have emphasised both the difficulty of assessing sporting performance solely on the basis of metrics, and the complex relationships between metrics, scoring, future prediction and rankings.

In theoretical terms, we offer two related conceptual possibilities to explore metrics. In order to emphasise the way metrics can encapsulate particular notions such as excellence, we note how certain numbers have become immutable mobiles; signifiers of a particular standard of performance that mean it is unnecessary to see the performance to appreciate its excellence. However, we also note how immutability is more easily achieved through less complex measures, such as the 10-second 100 m, whereas it becomes more challenging for contexts such as predicting future athletic ability or success.

At the same time, it is necessary to account for the diverse elements that unsettle the stability imposed on sporting performance by immutable metrics. Immutability provides a useful theoretical device for explaining the temporal uniformity of timings in sprints, gymnastics scoring and assessments of potential. When the focus of analysis shifts to the emergent practices through which various components engage with one another to produce particular outcomes, Deleuze and Guattari's metaphor of territorialisation proves more valuable. In this chapter, territorialisation allowed us to track the changes in the use of metrics as related to unexpectedly strong performances or other disruptions, while simultaneously offering a theoretical argument for the efforts to re-establish stability, often via new metrics or measures. What both immutability and territorialisation emphasise, however, is the significant agentic role played by metrics in the production of sport.

Notes

1. William and Manley's article was published as an Advance Online Publication in 2014 and hence the publication of a critique of the article in 2015.
2. Based on data reported by the International Association of Athletics Federations   (www.iaaf.org/records/toplists/sprints/100-metres/men/senior, accessed 29 June 2018).
3. For example, in 2017, the player selected first signed a US$30+ million contract; the 11th selection received approximately half of that. Contract values ranged from 2–7 million through the remaining selections (data from www.sportrac.com/nfl/draft/2017/, accessed 29 June 2018).
4. https://operations.nfl.com/the-players/getting-into-the-game/national-scouting-combine/ (accessed 29 June 2018).
5. https://thebiglead.com/2018/03/02/orlando-brown-nfl-combine-performance-40-bench-vertical/ (accessed 29 June 2018).

6. https://thebiglead.com/2018/03/06/2018-nfl-combine-draft-winners-losers/ (accessed 29 June 2018).

References

Anshel, M., & Lidor, R. (2012). Talent detection programs in sport: The questionable use of psychological measures. *Journal of Sport Behavior, 35*, 239.

Baerg, A. (2013). Sport, analytics, and the number as a communication medium. In P. Pedersen (Ed.), *The Routledge handbook of sport communication* (pp. 75–83). London: Routledge.

Baerg, A. (2017). Big data, sport, and the digital divide: Theorizing how athletes might respond to big data monitoring. *Journal of Sport and Social Issues, 41*(1), 3–20.

Christensen, M. K. (2009). An eye for talent: Talent identification and the 'practical sense' of top-level soccer coaches. *Sociology of Sport Journal, 26*(3), 365–382.

Colás, Y. (2017). The culture of moving dots: Toward a history of counting and of what counts in basketball. *The Journal of Sport History, 44*(2), 336–349.

Collins, D., & Bailey, R. (2013). 'Scienciness' and the allure of second-hand strategy in talent identification and development. *International Journal of Sport Policy and Politics, 5*(2), 183–191.

Collins, D., & Cruickshank, A. (2017). Psychometrics in sport: The good, the bad and the ugly. In *Psychometric testing: Critical perspectives* (pp. 145–156). Hoboken, NJ: John Wiley & Sons, Ltd.

Collins, D., Carson, H. J., & Cruickshank, A. (2015). Blaming Bill Gates AGAIN! Misuse, overuse and misunderstanding of performance data in sport. *Sport, Education and Society, 20*(8), 1088–1099.

Cooren, F., Matte, F., Taylor, J., & Vasquez, C. (2007). A humanitarian organization in action: Organizational discourse as an immutable mobile. *Discourse & Communication, 1*(2), 153–190.

Deleuze, G. (1992). Postscript on the societies of control. *October, 59*, 3–7.

Deleuze, G., & Guattari, F. (1987). *A thousand plateaus: Capitalism and schizophrenia*. London: Athlone Press.

Denison, J., & Mills, J. (2014). Planning for distance running: Coaching with Foucault. *Sports Coaching Review, 3*(1), 1–16.

Eldridge, L. (1988, October 4). Too many 'perfect' scores of 10 distort Olympic gymnastics results. *Christian Science Monitor*. Retrieved June 21, 2018, from https://www.csmonitor.com/1988/1004/prom.html.

Ericsson, K. A., Krampe, R. T., & Tesch-Römer, C. (1993). The role of deliberate practice in the acquisition of expert performance. *Psychological Review, 100*(3), 363.

Finn, J. (2016). Timing and imaging evidence in sport: Objectivity, intervention, and the limits of technology. *Journal of Sport and Social Issues, 40*(6), 459–476.

Gerrard, B. (2017). Analytics, technology and high performance sport. In N. Schulenkorf & S. Frawley (Eds.), *Critical issues in global sport management*. London: Routledge.

Grix, J., & Carmichael, F. (2012). Why do governments invest in elite sport? A polemic. *International Journal of Sport Policy and Politics, 4*(1), 73–90.

Guttmann, A. (1978). *From ritual to record*. New York: Columbia University Press.

Hutchins, B. (2016). Tales of the digital sublime: Tracing the relationship between big data and professional sport. *Convergence I, 22*(5), 494–509.

Kerr, R. (2006). The impact of Nadia Comaneci on the sport of women's artistic gymnastics. *Sporting Traditions I, 23*(1), 87–102.

Kerr, R. (2018). The role of science in the practice of talent identification: A case study from gymnastics in New Zealand. *Sport in Society, 22*(9), 1–15.

Kerr, R., & Obel, C. (2015). The disappearance of the perfect 10: Evaluating rule changes in women's artistic gymnastics. *The International Journal of the History of Sport I, 32*(2), 318–331.

Konoval, T. S. (2018). *Moving on to practice: Exploring the impact of a Foucauldian-informed coach development collaboration*. PhD thesis, Faculty of Kinesiology, Sport, and Recreation, University of Alberta.

Kuhn, T. (1961). The function of measurement in modern physical science. *Isis, 52*(2), 161–193.

Latour, B. (1987). *Science in action: How to follow scientists and engineers through society*. Cambridge, MA: Harvard University Press.

Latour, B. (1990). Drawing things together. In M. Lynch & S. Woolgar (Eds.), *Representation in scientific practice* (pp. 19–68). Cambridge, MA: MIT Press.

Law, J., & Mol, A. (2001). Situating technoscience: An inquiry into spatialities. *Society and Space, 19*, 609–621.

Lidor, R., Côté, J., & Hackfort, D. (2009). ISSP position stand: To test or not to test? The use of physical skill tests in talent detection and in early phases of sport development. *International Journal of Sport and Exercise Psychology, 7*(2), 131–146.

Lyons, B. D., Hoffman, B. J., Michel, J. W., & Williams, K. J. (2011). On the predictive efficiency of past performance and physical ability: The case of the National Football League. *Human Performance, 24*(2), 158–172.

Macris, L. I., & Sam, M. P. (2014). Belief, doubt, and legitimacy in a performance system: National sport organization perspectives. *Journal of Sport Management, 28*(5), 529–550.

Majumdar, A. S., & Robergs, R. A. (2011). The science of speed: Determinants of performance in the 100m sprint. *International Journal of Sports Science & Coaching, 6*(3), 479–493.

Malina, R. M., Bouchard, C., & Bar-Or, O. (2004). *Growth, maturation, and physical activity* (2nd ed.). Champaign, IL: Human Kinetics.

Mari, L. (2003). Epistemology of measurement. *Measurement, 34*, 17–30.

Miller, P. K., Cronin, C., & Baker, G. (2015). Nurture, nature and some very dubious social skills: An interpretative phenomenological analysis of talent identification practices in elite English youth soccer. *Qualitative Research in Sport, Exercise and Health, 7*(5), 642–662.

Millington, B., & Millington, R. (2015). 'The datafication of everything': Toward a sociology of sport and Big Data. *Sociology of Sport Journal, 32*(2), 140–160.

Muller, J. (2018). *The tyranny of metrics*. Princeton, NJ: Princeton University Press.

Pain, M. T. G., & Hibbs, A. (2007). Sprint starts and the minimum auditory reaction time. *Journal of Sports Sciences, 25*(1), 79–86.

Porter, T. (1994). Making things quantitative. *Science in Context, 7*(3), 389–407.

Power, M. (2004). Counting, control and calculation: Reflections on measuring and management. *Human Relations, 57*(6), 765–783.

Rossi, G. B. (2007). Measurability. *Measurement, 40*, 545–562.

Sam, M. P., & Macris, L. I. (2014). Performance regimes in sport policy: Exploring consequences, vulnerabilities and politics. *International Journal of Sport Policy and Politics, 6*(3), 513–532.

Simperingham, K. D., Cronin, J. B., & Ross, A. (2016). Advances in sprint acceleration profiling for field-based team-sport athletes: Utility, reliability, validity and limitations. *Sports Medicine, 46*(11), 1619–1645.

Slawinski, J., Dumas, R., Cheze, L., Ontanon, G., Miller, C., & Mazure-Bonnefoy, A. (2012). 3D kinematic of bunched, medium and elongated sprint start. *International Journal of Sports Medicine, 33*(7), 555–560.

Williams, S., & Manley, A. (2016). Elite coaching and the technocratic engineer: Thanking the boys at Microsoft! *Sport, Education and Society, 21*, 828–850.

The Numbers Game: Collegiate Esports and the Instrumentation of Movement Performance

Nicholas Taylor

This chapter examines how data is conceptualized, gathered, and put to work by a team of competitive video game players at North Carolina State University (NCSU). This team is part of a burgeoning collegiate electronic sports (esports) scene in the United States and Canada, consisting of multiple leagues, organizations, tournaments, and increasingly, scholarship and athletics programs, centered on playing and watching competitive video games between university-based teams.[1] In exploring how this team uses statistical and video data to improve their *League of Legends* (LoL) play in an increasingly crowded collegiate esports system, I offer a theorization of the relationship between esports and conventional competitive sports[2] that sidesteps predictable, if somewhat limiting questions over whether and how competitive gaming constitutes a legitimate sport. Such questions are rooted in romanticized notions of sport as a domain of "pure" physicality or of athleticism involving major muscle groups: from this perspective, competitive gaming is not a sport because

N. Taylor (✉)
North Carolina State University, Raleigh, NC, USA
e-mail: nttaylor@ncsu.edu

© The Author(s) 2020
J. J. Sterling, M. G. McDonald (eds.), *Sports, Society, and Technology*,
https://doi.org/10.1007/978-981-32-9127-0_6

players do not move (they do), do not sweat (they do), or do not train their bodies (they do). These arguments have been refuted elsewhere, primarily through the groundbreaking work of TL Taylor (2012) and Emma Witkowski (2012); my goal is not to rehash these arguments, but to build from them.

The account I offer here draws equally from Science and Technology Studies (STS) research on sports and from posthumanist media theory. The former acknowledges the agency of non-humans in contemporary sport, including the increasing role of statistical data in transforming the ways elite athletic performance is measured, assessed, and consumed. The latter provides a robust set of concepts for articulating the role of various media in these transformations, specifically via the notion of media technologies as "instruments" which do not simply record and measure, but shape the conditions of possibility, for the phenomena with which they are associated. I entwine these together as theoretical grounding for an ethnographic study of a highly competitive collegiate LoL team, showing how the team's activities are enabled by a game that is built, from the ground up, to record data—data which is made freely available to players of all skill levels.

In offering this account, I hope to both extend and problematize the recent interest in esports on the part of researchers and practitioners in the growing field of sports analytics. This interest is indicated by the attention given to esports at the 2017 MIT Sloan Sports Analytics Conference (McMahan 2017), "the" gathering for those whose stock in trade is the quantification of athletic performance—the scouts, managers, owners, technicians, analysts, coaches, trainers, and (occasionally) athletes who "perceive their professional assignment as intimately bound up with fine-grained statistical knowledge of athletic performance" (Yarrow and Kranke 2016, p. 445). It is not at all coincidental that esports is surging in popularity at the same time as major sports leagues and organizations are intensifying their efforts at "datafication", defined here as the conversion of social action into quantitative information (van Dijck 2014). Likewise, consumers of conventional sport increasingly do so through statistically driven platforms, including video games and fantasy leagues. And of course, a vibrant subset of sports scholarship considers the social implications of datafication in sport—which, while it precedes the widespread advent of digital media (Guttmann 1978), is becoming far more widespread and agential via new technologies for the *automated* storage, processing, and transmission of digital data (Colás 2017; Millington and Millington 2015; Puerzer 2002; Yarrow and Kranke 2016). In light of the transformations wrought by this "big league" push into automated datafication, esports offers sports scholars a compelling glimpse of what athletic performance looks like when it unfolds in digital environments that are already instrumented for data collection, from the ground up; if anything comes natural to esports, it is data.

I begin with a brief review of esports research that views sport and esport in terms of their continuities, rather than solely in terms of difference, so as to consider both in terms of how they are instrumented. Here, I mobilize the STS-driven notion of "media instruments" to explore how formalized sports (including esports) engage in different ways and to different degrees, in techniques of measurement, standardization, and increasingly, automated data recording and analysis. I then offer a brief description of LoL, currently the most popular esport in the world (Taylor 2018a), and I survey the current state of collegiate esports. This is a heterogeneous and dynamic terrain of intensifying professionalization, drastically diverse degrees and forms of institutionalization, and ad hoc techniques for recruitment, training, conditioning, and preparation that are often jealously guarded by individual teams.

Forming the core of this chapter is a description of the practices carried out by members of the competitive LoL team at NCSU. I examine the ways these players have learned to incorporate data provided by the game into their training and preparation regimes, over three years of being together in a relatively stable formation. This allows me to consider the ways data collection and analysis media form the "conditions of possibility" (Packer 2013) for their careers as elite competitive gamers—that is, the ways data constitute the epistemological grounds on which these players understand themselves and shape the kinds of work they carry out. I focus specifically on their use of statistical and video data, and the kinds of athlete-as-analyst subjectivity that the devices, platforms, and practices associated with this apparatus make possible. By way of conclusion, I gesture to the overlaps between this apparatus of esports datafication and the military's persistent push toward more powerful techniques for visualizing combat. This situates my concerns with the instrumentation of esports in a broader cultural politics, while acknowledging a further layer to the already rigorously interrogated connections between sports, the military, and digital play.

Theorizing Esports

Over the past decade, esports has attracted increasing attention from scholars, building on ethnographic research with various esports communities in the late 2000s (Harper 2014; Taylor 2009; Witkowski 2012). Concurrent with this scholarly attention, spectatorial competitive gaming has become more "normalized" (Partin 2017) and an integral component of an emerging media ecosystem of streaming platforms, such as Twitch.tv, supplanting traditional televisual content (Taylor 2018b). Running through much of the work on esports, and often drawing explicitly on STS research of games more generally (e.g. see Giddings 2007), is an attention to the agency of non-humans—code, screens, input devices, streaming platforms, recording technologies—in constituting spectatorial competitive gaming (Taylor 2015).

Another related and vital thread in esports research concerns its place in and relation to a globalized apparatus of spectator sport, which is itself undergoing rapid and often fundamental transformations. Countering the normative view that esports' relationship to conventional sports is primarily metaphorical and derivative—that esports merely appropriate the structural forms and discourses of sport in order to produce competitive gaming as a spectator sport—Emma Witkowski (2012) and Brett Hutchins (2008) articulate this relationship instead in terms of sociotechnical dis/similarities to, and dis/continuities with, other spectator sports. Hutchins acknowledges that other sports became "mediatized" throughout the twentieth century with the rise of mass media, the demise of amateurism, and formation of elite sport as a televisual commodity (pp. 857–858). He nonetheless insists that "physical sport remains steadfastly corporeal in character", whereas esport "is structured by computer code … put simply, a game of football remains possible with or without a media platform present" (p. 858). While insisting on this distinction, however, Hutchins concludes with a consideration of gene-doping and the problematization it poses to the notion that "physical" sport is ever purely, wholly thus. Echoing Latour (2005), Hutchins acknowledges that "it is no longer possible to think in terms of either humans *or* science *or* nature … the contemporary world demands that social and institutional demarcations be reflexively negotiated" (p. 865).

Witkowski (2012) takes a somewhat related approach to the relationship between esports and "physical" sport. She summarizes literature from sports sociologists and theorists on what makes an activity a sport, noting that "it is the *movement performance* of the human body which is placed as central to physicality in sports" (p. 356). Employing a phenomenological approach to ethnographic work with competitive *Counterstrike* players, Witkowski illustrates how "movement performance" is "central to the outcome of every match" (p. 359). As she articulates, elite *Counterstrike* play requires "maintaining a controlled body while quickly navigating the environment", executing precise movements on-screen "by means of the physicality executed in the muscles and tendons of hands and fingers and in the subtle control of breathing" (p. 359).

In her analysis, esports offers a lens to consider the ways in which *all* sports are technologized, involving mobile and ultimately porous boundaries between technologies and bodies. Like Hutchins, Witkowski concludes with the notion that while esports are *inherently* constructs of networked media technologies, "physical" sports are increasingly so.

This offers a useful point of engagement and extension for the account of collegiate esports I offer here. Given the intensified use of digital technologies to automatically record, quantify, consume, and analyze athletic performance, it is becoming increasingly unproductive to hang on to ontological distinctions between professional sports and esports; all are "mediasports" (Wenner 1998), actor-networks in which the actions of athletes are digitally selected, recorded, stored, and analyzed so as to produce further refinements in efficiency and effectiveness. My interest is in the ways these networks constitute relations between athletes and the instruments and sociotechnical practices associated with datafication, and with the relations of power that characterize collegiate esports in comparison to other adjacent domains including professional sports leagues like the National Basketball Association (NBA), Federation Internationale de Football Association (FIFA), and National Football League (NFL), professional esports associations, and elite amateur sports such as the National Collegiate Athletics Association (NCAA).[3] I argue that while it remains a deeply masculinized and gender-exclusive domain (Taylor et al. 2009), like other conventional mediasports (Witkowski 2013), the collegiate esports context I examine here engages in a politics of big data that is more accessible and transparent than its counterparts. The domain of collegiate esports is relatively unique in that it offers us the hybrid figure of the athlete-as-analyst. In contrast to adjacent mediasports, in which the quantification of "movement performance" is more often aligned with the economic interests of managers, owners, and league administrators, and in which players/athletes are treated primarily as *objects* of analysis, collegiate esports is a domain in which players "call the shots" when it comes to the uses of data. As I expand upon below, the more meaningful differences between collegiate esports and other domains of elite spectator sport, therefore, are not *whether* performance is translated into quantitative data, but rather *how* this happens.

Instrumenting Sports

Well before the systematic implementation of statistics-driven management introduced by "sabermetrics"[4] (Yarrow and Kranke 2016), measurement and record-keeping have been integral to the development of modern sport (Eichberg 1982; Finn 2016). The eighteenth-century stopwatch, for instance, not only subjected existing sports like horse racing to more accurate measurement and recording; it also brought about an instrumentation of time that helped convert recreational exercise such as running into quantified sport (Eichberg 1982, p. 22). Similarly, with leisure activities such as tennis, the imposition of "artificial spatial orders" legislated by a "bureaucratic administration"—both techniques of early manufacture capitalism—helped transform court-based games into standardized sports (p. 40). As Allen Guttmann (1978) argues, part of what makes modern sport recognizable as such is, precisely, the use of industrial-era media instruments to standardize the "playing field" and to record and quantify athletic performance. Such developments can be understood via

Jeremy Packer's articulation of media instruments (2013). Building on the STS work of Peter Galison (2003), Packer invites us to consider how technologies of measurement (clocks, for instance) do not simply measure phenomena, but constitute the epistemic grounds for what can be measured. Looking at media devices such as stopwatches, measuring sticks, and so on as instruments draws our attention to the transformations they affect "over the very possibilities for representing and processing the world into data" (Packer 2013, p. 14). This helps clarify the agential role of such tools in not simply representing phenomena, but constructing them in a way that makes sense for us, shaping what can be known about them, and how it can be known. Unlike approaches to the intersections of media and sport that focus on questions of what is broadcasted, and how, this approach to media instrumentation helps illuminate the role of data in constructing both conventional sports and esports such as LoL.

What Is *League of Legends*?

LoL is a multiplayer game viewed from a top-down, third-person camera perspective, in which two teams of player-controlled champions battle for territorial supremacy. In its most common format, two teams of five face each other in "Summoner's Rift", a terrain with team bases positioned at opposite corners, separated by a river and connected by three lanes (referred to as "top", "mid", and "bot", for bottom). Each lane is guarded by computer-controlled turrets and waves of minions. Teams must contend for territorial advantage, with the ultimate goal of destroying the enemy base, by efficiently "farming" experience points and gold (destroying enemy minions and turrets), in order to augment their champions with more effective abilities and items, winning encounters against player-controlled opponents, and securing temporary boosts by destroying special computer-controlled monsters appearing at key moments in the match. In tournament play, matches are usually determined by a best of three or best of five formats, with a single game averaging around 25–30 minutes.

The game is frenetic and, for newcomers and casual observers, opaque. Committed players must retain familiarity with the game's "meta", the set of constantly updating strategies and team compositions deemed optimal by the game's top players and expressed through a technical vocabulary describing the unique abilities and strategies afforded by each of the 139 selectable champions, along with the range of items players can equip on their champions, each with their own unique properties. It is a complex game with a demanding learning curve (Donaldson 2015) and a male-dominated player base notorious for its toxicity (Kou and Nardi 2014; Ratan et al. 2015), yet it has been the most popular esport since the early 2010s (Segal 2014). It is also the most popular game in the rapidly emerging and institutionalizing domain of collegiate esports.

Esports Gets Schooled

Colleges and universities in the United States and Canada have become sites of intensive experimentation and investment for the burgeoning esports industry. Since the early 2010s, there have been concerted efforts to organize the nebulous but vibrant culture of competitive gaming on college campuses into a more formalized network; organizations include the National Association of Collegiate Esports, which aims to be a governing body for collegiate esports; the Esports Association and Collegiate StarLeague, which provide infrastructural support for intercollegiate play; and the American Video Game League, which runs intercollegiate tournaments across a variety of games. Riot Games, publisher of LoL, runs its own league, College LoL, which offers the most lucrative awards and generally attracts the best collegiate talent. Accompanying this growing infrastructure is a proliferation of collegiate esports programs. Often either housed in athletics departments of smaller universities and technical colleges or run under the auspices of game design or computer science departments at larger universities, these programs offer scholarships to players, conduct recruiting efforts, retain coaching and training staff, and offer dedicated space and resources on campus for esports.

Teaming Up

The study reported on here is an ongoing ethnography, initiated in 2016, of the competitive collegiate LoL team at NCSU, carried out by myself and a shifting team of undergraduate and graduate students. Our work has involved periodic observations of weekly team meetings, particularly when the team runs tryouts in early autumn and when they train for the College LoL tournament in early winter. We also spectate and take notes on the team's matches, interview various team members one to two times per semester, and collect and review the documents they put together for tryouts, scouting, and so on. We devote a great deal of attention to the technologies that constitute the team's training and playing practices— from Discord (a VoIP platform popular among gamers) to Google documents, to Twitch, to their gaming machines and peripheral devices. In this, we are operating on the insight that none of the team's activities are unmediated, and almost all of it—including letting us research them— produces inscriptions, traces, and data.

The team was formed in late 2015—notably, one year after Robert Morris University established the first scholarship-granting collegiate esports program. The NCSU team is *not* part of a college esports program, and only obtained student organization status in 2018. Unlike their counterparts at universities with esports programs, none of the players were recruited from high school or are on scholarship to play university LoL. As I show below, this outsider status is key to their team identity. In their current configuration, they consist of five young men, pursuing degrees in either the hard sciences or computer engineering. Three of the original team members began in their first year, meaning that they have played together for three years—a duration that is remarkable given the four-year degree program, the time commitment required (upwards of 25 hours a week, including team meetings, practice sessions, and individual play), and the high turnover that characterizes elite LoL play. In winter 2016, the team began to use Circuit Studio, a media research studio that I co-direct, for their weekly meetings. Between then and spring 2019 (the time of this writing), they have earned over US$70,000 in scholarship prize money, including US$28,000 each year for two years that they placed in the top eight of the College LoL tournament (2016–2017 and 2018–2019). Over the same period of time, they have iterated upon and refined their tryout, training, and scouting practices, including forming a "junior varsity" team to compete in smaller tournaments. The 2018–2019 College LoL tournament was the last for the original three members that form the team's organizational backbone, meaning this ethnographic study neatly parallels a period of relative stability in the team's composition.

One player described the team as "one of the best non-program teams in the country"—meaning, they are better than many teams that are supported by an established varsity program and better than almost all teams that are self-organized. This characterization speaks to the shifting and heterogeneous conditions of collegiate esports, as teams with little to no institutional presence, constituted through ad hoc technical, spatial, and temporal arrangements, compete against teams that have dedicated administrative staff, support, and space. The University of California at Irvine (UC Irvine), for example, which bills itself as the "Duke Basketball" of collegiate esports (Partin 2017), offers ten scholarships a year to LoL players and boasts a 72-station esports arena.

As I detail below, a large part of the NCSU team's success in this unequal and shifting terrain is in their preparation, facilitated by their intensive use of video and statistical data.

Video Data: Now You See It, Now You Don't

In their inaugural 2015–2016 season of College LoL (which was then called uLoL), when the team first started using Circuit Studio, they made use of the space's large projection screens to watch video. Of particular use to them were videos on demand (VODs). These are replays of games recorded and stored on LoL's servers, rather than streamed for live broadcast by a particular esports tournament or organization. Compared to broadcasted games, in which the camera is operated by the broadcasters, VODs have the added benefit of offering viewers a "spectator" mode, meaning viewers can hone in on any part of the screen at any time. In their weekly meetings during the 2015–2016, which they called "VOD Meetings", the core activity involved watching VODs of upcoming opponents' previous matches, focusing on clips that illustrated particular strengths or weaknesses with individual players.

Much like in conventional competitive sports training, scrutinizing replays of opponents' past matches can reveal tendencies in the team's play styles that can be predicted and, thereby, exploited. As two players recounted in a group interview, this intensive VOD study proved highly effective in some instances, as in their match against the University of Ottawa:

Player 1:   When we played the University of Ottawa we watched enough of their games to realize every single time they're on red side they try to do this strat [strategy] where they walk into like the red buff on our side of the jungle and they try to make a play or get a ward down there. And we just—we played against them. They were on red side and we set up a counter attack and like they walked into us and we got three kills.

Player 2:   And then they said we were cheating.

Player 1:   And then they accused us of cheating. Yeah. It was really nice.

This kind of "lateral surveillance" (Andrejevic 2002) between competitors was enabled by a now-defunct third-party technology: during the 2015–2016 season, all LoL games could be automatically recorded and called up through replay.gg, a third-party service, giving teams free access to VODs of opponents' previous games. In early 2017, replay.gg was pushed out by Riot Games when they introduced their own much more restrictive VOD viewing system, integrated into the game client, tied to players' accounts, and facilitated through players' selecting which replays to publicly share. The collegiate LoL scene is already secretive and cautious; teams are often reluctant to scrimmage against their competitors for fear of giving away their preferred team strategies, and players often train on "smurf" accounts (secondary accounts not used in season play and therefore not linked to players' official College LoL profiles) to keep their training activity hidden. Within this framework, the more restrictive VOD sharing system means that college teams have effectively been cut off from the capacity to watch VODs of their opponents, the NCSU team's most valued source of data. They are left with broadcast games posted on video streaming sites, depriving them both of a wider selection of video data and of the ability to view it through "spectator" mode. The lack of VODs undermines their otherwise intensive preparation, which is, in turn, what they feel sets them apart from other college teams; as one member remarked, "if public VODs were available we'd be so much better than these other teams … it wouldn't even be close. I'm willing to just watch VODs all the time". With this lack of robust, up-to-date video data on opponents since early 2017, the NCSU team has come to rely more on statistical data.

Stats, Strats, and Comps

Similar to other popular esports titles such as *Counterstrike: GO*, *Dota 2*, and *Overwatch*, LoL engages in comprehensive data collection, storage, and analysis, made possible through the game's exhaustive and iterative instrumentation. Via its Application Program Interface (API), Riot makes much of this data available for free, enabling third-party programmers to construct websites and other services that aggregate and display LoL statistics. Two of the most popular are lolking.net, originally a fan-created site for hosting LoL data and player-authored strategy guides, and which is now part of the ZAM Network, a subsidiary of the Chinese gaming company Tencent; and op.gg, a South Korean-based site run by data scientists. Perhaps due to the traditions of freely available often player-produced strategy guides and walk-throughs that these sites are a part of (ZAM Network, for instance, grew out of Allakhazam, an online hub for information and knowledge-sharing among *EverQuest* players), these sites, and most others like them, provide their material to players for free and earn money primarily through advertising revenue. The information they gather and display includes years' worth of "Ranked" match histories played by individual users (searchable by their "Summoner", or account, name), displaying for each match the champion they chose and their kill/death/assist ratio for the match, which is often understood as a shorthand for player effectiveness. Most third-party sites also provide data on the "presence" of each of the 139 playable champions. Presence refers to the frequency with which a given champion is either selected or banned by players in a given match across all LoL matches played, and is expressed as a percentage. Presence data is a particular focus of the NCSU LoL team, whose members describe four ways in which they use statistics, honed over three years of playing together. In order of the relative importance the team reports to place on each, these are:

1. champion presence data from individual members of opposing teams they face in College LoL;
2. data from select professional players regarding the champions they select and the item build-outs they use;
3. their own champion presence data;
4. match data from select games, either their own recent team play or of their upcoming opponents.

This prevalence of champion presence data in the NCSU teams' use of statistics reflects both the way the game is designed as well as the team's understanding of their own strengths and needs. Selecting the most optimal champions against one's opponents is a key component of any match, but particularly in season and tournament play, where the relative stability of pre-formed teams means their tactics and team compositions (or "comps"—combinations of champions that either have synergistic capabilities and/or allow for particular tactics) can be researched ahead of time. The champion selection process begins once all players have entered the "lobby" (the pre-game interface). At the beginning and again halfway through the selection process, teams take turns "banning" a total of five champions each, removing them from the pool of selectable champions for either side, for that match. This means, in any given match, ten champions in total will be removed from the playable champion pool. A number of factors can go into deciding whether to ban a particular champion: its role in the current meta (i.e. whether the current state of the game renders that champion particularly powerful); its capacity to counter your own team's desired champions and team composition; and whether it is preferred by a specific opponent. Teams can, through careful planning, create a priori (and in some cases, insurmountable) advantages by selecting an optimal team comp while denying the same to their opponents.

Part of what makes the selection round such an integral part of LoL is simply the number of champions available to players. This creates a limited economy of proficiency—which is, ultimately, an economy of time, attention, and work. If a player develops expertise with a small handful of champions, they not only become one-dimensional in terms of their play style, but they risk being denied these champions through bans. If they instead develop moderate proficiency with a wide range of champions, they spread themselves too thin. For the NCSU team, champion selection plays a particularly key role in their preparation. The team has one team comp at which they excel; this is to have resilient, "tank" characters in the top and middle lanes (the three routes connecting the opponents' bases), a damage-dealing champion on the bottom lane accompanied by a support character, and a Jungler (the role that conventionally patrols the areas between lanes) capable of jumping into either the bottom or middle lanes at opportune moments. This comp is what they are most familiar and effective with; as a result, they spend a great deal of time in their meetings honing their approaches to selection and banning, so as to plot out as many paths to their preferred team comp as possible.

During the College LoL season, the team creates 10–20-page scouting documents in the days leading up to their weekly matches, with champion presence data (on themselves, their upcoming opponents, and professional players) culled from third-party sites, which team members review together in their Friday night meetings. The weekly scouting report begins with a bullet point profile for each member of the upcoming opposing team. Next are tables of which champions their opponents will likely ban and which they will try to pick. Underneath the table is commentary on the likelihood and/or rationale for specific champion selection and ban predictions. The last few pages of each document are given over to mock drafts; these are essentially decision trees, branching pathways of if/then nodes of champion selection and bans. Intended for group discussion, these mock drafts allow the team to predict and prepare for a number of likely team comp scenarios in their upcoming match.

This data-intensive approach requires very involved analytic and interpretive work by all members of the team, and in particular by the team member responsible for assembling the reports. This preparation is at the core of their self-identity as collegiate LoL players. As one of them said in a group interview, "we are way better" at data-driven preparation than other teams without an esports program (who often, though not consistently, have dedicated analysts), and this in turn is one of—if not the main—reason they describe themselves as one of the best non-program college teams. They have a team comp they excel at, and work vigorously with the game's readily available statistical data to support it. These practices—formed iteratively over the course of three years of playing together, and enacted without the support (and constraints) of a formal esports program at NCSU—stand in contrast to adjacent domains of instrumented athletic performance, especially men's professional sports leagues such as the NBA, Major League Basekball (MLB), and NFL.

"Moving Dots"

NBA basketball offers a particularly useful comparison to collegiate LoL in terms of the practices and politics of datafication. The NBA has been a site of well-documented experimentation in techniques of digital (and automated) data gathering, processing, and analysis, experiments which have recently generated broad transformations in the ways men's professional basketball teams are assembled. This is perhaps best represented by the recent successes of the Golden State Warriors and Houston Rockets (the former managed by Daryl Morey, co-founder of the MIT Sloan Sports Analytics Conference). In 2016, the NBA (together with its development league and the Women's National Basketball Association) negotiated a $250 million partnership with two sports technology firms—Second Spectrum and SportRadar—to replace the SportVU data gathering system.[5] Both SportVU and Second Spectrum make use of computer vision technology, which enables the automatic tagging and tracking of given objects in a video recording, to select and store granular data on each NBA players' motions in a given game. As Second Spectrum CEO, Rajiv Maheswaran exclaims in a TED talk on the topic, "We're instrumenting our stadiums, and our players, to track their movement every fraction of a second. So what we're doing is turning our athletes into, you probably guessed it, moving dots" (Maheswaran 2015). Here, the "movement performance" (Witkowski 2012) of NBA players is transformed via the logic of automated data collection and analysis into something more akin, (perhaps) ironically, to what we see on the user interface "minimap" of games like LoL: "moving dots" across a simplified depiction of the field of competition (whether an NBA arena or LoL's Summoner's Rift).

Attempts by sports technology firms to digitally record, store, and process athletes' movements are underway in other professional sports as well, including the NFL (Belson 2017) and National Hockey League (NHL) (though not without some resistance; see Wyshnynski 2018). Each of these innovations supplants, automates, and/or extends more conventional practices of manual data gathering, wherein workers would watch video replays of games and input data points as they went. As has been remarked on extensively (Furnas and Lezra 2012; Millington and Millington 2015), accompanying the instrumentalization of athletes, equipment, and playing fields, is the wide-scale introduction of data science (and scientists) into professional sports. Journalistic accounts abound with discourses of "nerds", "wizards", and "geeks", ambivalent new figures from elite engineering schools (and/or the military) whose technical prowess is often presented as a threat to conventional sports wisdom. While these changes have been addressed (and problematized) by sports professionals, fans, researchers, and journalists for decades (Guttmann 1978), they have greatly intensified in recent years with the deployment of the kinds of automated surveillance apparatuses described above.

The crux of this comparison I draw here between collegiate LoL and professional basketball (among other elite spectator sports) is not in *whether* or *why* data is being gathered and used, but in the ways this data is made available and operationalized. Whereas LoL data is offered in abundance through its API, and third-party developers package this data for players for free,[6] the instruments and techniques developed by firms like Second Spectrum are proprietary commodities, designed for (usually men's) professional leagues and franchises with deep pockets. They enter into (and often help reinforce) the heavily striated divisions of labor between managers, analysts, coaches, trainers, and athletes. Indeed, the expense associated with these analytics packages means that—at the college and amateur levels—the outcomes associated with their deployment will likely exacerbate existing divides between "haves" and "have not" sports and sports programs (Witz 2014). In what follows, I unravel some of the implications of these differential politics of datafication.

Athletes and/as Analysts

The bulk of critical work on sports and media outlines the political economies and practices involved in producing, marketing, and consuming the televisual spectacles of professional sports. Contemporary datafication is altering these conditions profoundly (Millington and Millington 2015); whether through fantasy leagues, video games, fan sites, and so on, we are growing accustomed to engaging professional sport through statistical media. To watch an NFL fantasy league enthusiast flipping through Sunday games in attempts to keep track of their team's performance, or to observe an expert *Madden NFL* or *Football Manager* player for whom the game is a matter of assessing and manipulating the numerical ratings of athletes and teams, is to confront some of the ways in which the audiovisual aspects of mediasport (with all their narrative trappings) are becoming subordinate to the consumption and configuration of sport statistics.

And yet, for leagues like the NFL and NBA, statistics must be generated after the fact; instruments must be grafted on, often with great expense, and the data then sold back to teams, colleges, franchises, broadcasters, and spectators. Digitized, automated surveillance instruments and the forms of analysis they make possible are relatively new (if not powerfully transformative) actors in contemporary professional sports; in contrast, esports is one among several applications of digital gaming in which the "big data" capacities of digital games are put to work. The point here is not to insist upon the divide between digital and corporeal domains and their attendant forms of sport—after all, digitality is also material (Hayles 1993)—rather it is to emphasize that while both esports and conventional sports are heavily invested in the datafication of human performance, esports is instrumented (literally) from the ground up. As such, it potentially (though by no means inherently) affords a politics of data collection in which it is possible for practitioners to have more agency in regards to how data about them is used to transform their own play. While both domains transform its players into "moving dots", in collegiate esports, the separation between athletes and analysts—between those who produce and those who collect, analyze, and operationalize the data—has not (yet) taken effect.

In a theorization passed on from Serres and Latour, Brian Massumi (2002) considers soccer athletes as "objects" of the ball, their actions coordinated and compelled by the ball's motion within the technologized event-space of the pitch. Viewed in light of the intensive media instrumentation of many professional sports, professional athletes might instead be seen as the objects of statistical data (and, by extension, its owners, operators, and analysts). In these media instrumented conditions, athletes are, increasingly, avatars—flesh and blood humans, certainly, but also "moving dots" who generate, and can be manipulated by, statistical analysis (Colás 2017). They are increasingly encountered through statistical media—whether by coaching, training, and management personnel, who attempt to account for, predict and control athletes' performances, or by fantasy league players and video gamers whose play consists of engaging with statistical expressions of athletic performance.

In contrast, the collegiate esports competitors whose practices I outline here embody a hybrid subjectivity. Operating in a less striated domain than professional sports (or, for that matter, college athletics and professional esports), and with access to abundant data, the NCSU LoL players I report on here are athletes-as-analysts. They are keenly aware that in a rapidly changing field of collegiate esports, in which attempts at the kind of institutionalization characteristic of other athletics programs (scholarships, coaching staff, practice areas) are already well underway, their success depends on their ability to effectively integrate data analysis into their preparation. They are figuring this out as they go along, developing a training regimen that makes robust use of the data available to them through experimentation and iteration. Along the way, they are articulating and enacting forms of sociotechnical practice that push past limiting conceptualizations of what constitutes "sport", at precisely the same moment that conventional sports are undergoing fundamental transformations in how we engage with and understand athletic performance. At a time when we are witnessing the datafication *of* sport, these players offer a glimpse of the kinds of sociotechnical activity involved in datafication *as* sport.

Who's Calling the Shots?

By way of conclusion, I want to gesture briefly toward two possible implications of this analysis. The first concerns how we make sense of esports in terms of the kinds of work it entails of participants, and the kinds of subjectivities it affords. While still acknowledging the rich and complex sets of connections between sports and esports (some of which I have addressed), it might be worth asking what other domains of sociotechnical activity esports draws from. I have sketched out the figure of the "athlete-as-analyst" here, as a way of describing the NCSU LoL team; but it may be that their work has less in common with athletics than it does with other domains involving statistical and audiovisual analysis, including military intelligence and scientific knowledge production. In this regard, it is telling that none of the players on the NCSU team will likely continue their involvement in esports after they graduate; but what will likely "stick" are the capacities for, and orientations toward, research and analysis that they have cultivated over three years.

This leads to a second implication, one that further problematizes the instruments and associated logics that transform "movement performance" into "moving dots". Perhaps more so than either digital games or sports, the military-industrial complex is heavily invested in technologies for automatically tracking—and thereby predicting and controlling—choreographies of kinetic bodies. It is well beyond the scope of this present work to chart the manifold connections and shared histories between the games industry and the military (see, for instance, Dyer-Witheford and de Peuter 2009; Stahl 2006) and between the military and sports (e.g. see King 2008; Schimmel 2017). Nonetheless, it is instructive that SportVU, the first technology to fully instrument professional basketball arenas, began as a missile-tracking system. This is no anomaly; related technologies like SitAware (https://www.systematicinc.com/), for instance, aim to provide military commanders and analysts with "god's eye" views of battlefields via a combination of networked location-based sensors and video surveillance (similar to what the NFL uses) that would give them the capacity to deliver orders from a safe location. It is no accident that the visualizations produced by these technologies look so much like those generated by SportVU or provided by LoL players via the interface's minimap: each transforms human action into "moving dots". That these instruments—what Donna Haraway, decades ago, called "god tricks" (1988, p. 583)—should be as readily deployed for warfare as for pleasure and play tells us much about the cultural values of contemporary mediasports.

Notes

1. In my understanding, and as of early 2019, only the United States and Canada yet have formalized infrastructures for college-based esports, with the highest concentration of activity in the United States. For these reasons, this analysis is primarily focused on the American collegiate esports scene.
2. This is an admittedly awkward construction, meant to include those team-based, competitive, and often (though not always) professional sports most often associated with leagues such as the NFL, NBA, MLB, and NHL and organizations such as FIFA and the NCAA.
3. While these are all rich sites of analysis, a comparison between collegiate esports and each of these adjacent domains is outside the scope of this chapter. My main contrast is therefore to professional North American sports associations, as these currently represent the most visible instances of automated data analysis in the sports world. For accounts of the practices and politics of data in professional esports and elite amateur sports, respectively, see Partin (2016) and Comeaux (2018).
4. As dramatized in the Hollywood film *Moneyball* (based on the book by the same name), "sabermetrics" refers to the statistical optimization of baseball management. Articulated before the widespread advent of digital datafication, sabermetrics made use of a long-standing collection of (and fascination with) statistics in professional baseball (Lewis 2004). This pre-digital datafication was made possible by the baseball scoreboard and fueled by the publication and trade of baseball cards, arguably a precursor to the consuming of statistical data via contemporary fantasy sports (Burton et al. 2013).
5. SportVU originated as a missile-tracking system for the Israeli military (Hickey 2012), a connection I return to in the conclusion.

6. The popular team-based shooter *Overwatch*, published by Activision-Blizzard, forms another interesting comparison to Riot's open-data policies. Activision-Blizzard has taken drastic steps in reducing the data available to third-party organizations. As Will Partin (2018) explains, this has less to do with their ostensible goal of preserving "competitive integrity" through regulation of its API, and more with ensuring that Blizzard maintains control over *Overwatch* data—likely, so they can monetize it.

References

Andrejevic, M. (2002). The work of watching one another: Lateral surveillance, risk, and governance. *Surveillance & Society, 2*(4), 479–497.

Belson, K. (2017, September 7). NFL expands use of chips in footballs, promising data troves. *New York Times*. Retrieved June 6, 2018, from https://www.nytimes.com/2017/09/07/sports/nfl-expands-use-of-chips-infootballs-promising-data-trove.html.

Burton, R., Hall, K., & Paul, R. (2013). The historical development and marketing of fantasy sports leagues. *The Journal of Sport, 2*(2), 185–215.

Colás, Y. (2017). The culture of moving dots: Toward a history of counting and what counts in basketball. *Journal of Sport History, 44*(2), 336–349.

Comeaux, E. (2018). Stereotypes, control, hyper-surveillance, and disposability of NCAA Division I Black male athletes. *New Directions for Student Services, 163*, 33–42.

van Dijck, J. (2014). Datafication, dataism and dataveillance: Big data between scientific paradigm and ideology. *Surveillance & Society, 12*(2), 197–208.

Donaldson, S. (2015). Mechanics and metagame: Exploring binary expertise in *League of Legends*. *Games and Culture, 12*(5), 426–444.

Dyer-Witheford, N., & de Peuter, G. (2009). *Games of empire: Global capitalism and video games*. Minneapolis, MN: University of Minnesota Press.

Eichberg, H. (1982). Stopwatch, horizontal bar, gymnasium: The technologizing of sports in the 18th and early 19th centuries. *Journal of the Philosophy of Sport, 9*(1), 43–59.

Finn, J. (2016). Timing and imaging evidence in sport: Objectivity, intervention, and the limits of technology. *Journal of Sport and Social Issues, 40*(6), 459–476.

Furnas, A., & Lezra, G. (2012, August 28). Make way for the soccer geeks. *The Atlantic*. Retrieved June 28, 2018, from http://www.theatlantic.com/technology/archive/2012/08/makeway-for-the-soccer-geeks/261634/.

Galison, P. (2003). *Einstein's clocks, Poincare's maps: Empires of time.* New York: W. W. Norton.

Giddings, S. (2007). Playing with non-humans: Digital games as techno-cultural form. In S. de Castell & J. Jenson (Eds.), *Worlds in play: International perspectives on digital games research* (pp. 115–128). New York: Peter Lang.

Guttmann, A. (1978). *From ritual to record: The nature of modern sports.* New York: Columbia University Press.

Haraway, D. (1988). Situated knowledges: The science question in feminism and the privilege of partial perspective. *Feminist Studies, 14*(3), 575–599.

Harper, T. (2014). *The culture of digital fighting games: Performance and practice.* New York: Routledge.

Hayles, N. K. (1993). The materiality of informatics. *Configurations, 1*(1), 147–170.

Hickey, W. (2012, June 22). Missile tracking technology is unlocking the game of basketball. *Business Insider.* Retrieved December 2018, from https://www.businessinsider.com/missile-tracking-technology-is-unlockingthe-game-of-basketball-2012-6.

Hutchins, B. (2008). Signs of meta-change in second modernity: The growth of e-sport and the World Cyber Games. *New Media and Society, 10*(6), 851–869.

King, S. (2008). Offensive lines: Sport-state synergy in an era of perpetual war. *Cultural Studies ↔ Critical Methodologies, 8*(4), 527–539.

Kou, Y., & Nardi, B. (2014). Governance in *League of Legends*: A hybrid system. In *Proceedings of the 9th international conference on the foundations of digital games.* Retrieved June 6, 2018, from http://www.fdg2014.org/proceedings.html.

Latour, B. (2005). *Reassembling the social: An introduction to actor-network theory.* Oxford: Oxford University Press.

Lewis, M. (2004). *Moneyball: The art of winning an unfair game.* New York: W. W. Norton & Company.

Maheswaran, R. (2015). The math behind basketball's wildest moves. Retrieved June 6, 2018, from https://www.ted.com/talks/rajiv_maheswaran_the_math_behind_basketball_s_wildest_moves.

Massumi, B. (2002). *Parables of the virtual.* Durham, NC: Duke University Press.

McMahan, I. (2017, March 8). Eight things we learned from the 2017 MIT Sloan Sports Analytics Conference. *Sports Illustrated.* Retrieved November 25, 2018, from https://www.si.com/edge/2017/03/08/mit-sloan-sportsanalytics-conference-nba-nfl-mlb-takeaways.

Millington, B., & Millington, R. (2015). 'The datafication of everything': Toward a sociology of sport and big data. *Sociology of Sport Journal, 32*(2), 140–160.

Packer, J. (2013). The conditions of media's possibility: A Foucauldian approach to media history. In J. Nerone (Ed.), *Media history and the foundations of media studies* (pp. 1–34). New York: Blackwell.

Partin, W. (2016, June 22). Dota 2 might be nearing its 'Moneyball' moment. *Killscreen*. Retrieved November 1, 2018, from https://killscreen.com/articles/dota-2-moneyball-moment/.

Partin, W. (2017, April 12). College esports programs are growing, but can they field a winning team? *Rolling Stone*. Retrieved June 6, 2018, from https://www.rollingstone.com/glixel/news/heroes-of-the-dorm-do-collegeesports-programs-matter-w476281.

Partin, W. (2018, September 18). Blizzard's ban on third-party *Overwatch* apps was never about competitive integrity. *Variety*. Retrieved December 1, 2018, from https://variety.com/2018/gaming/columns/blizzards-ban-on-thirdparty-overwatch-apps-was-never-about-competitive-integrity-1202961745/.

Puerzer, R. J. (2002). From scientific baseball to sabermetrics: Professional baseball as a reflection of engineering and management in society. *NINE: A Journal of Baseball History and Culture, 11*(1), 34–48.

Ratan, R. A., Taylor, N., Hogan, J., Kennedy, T., & Williams, D. (2015). Stand by your man: An examination of gender disparity in *League of Legends*. *Games and Culture, 10*(5), 438–462.

Schimmel, K. (2017). Not an 'extraordinary event': NFL games and militarized civic ritual. *Sociology of Sport Journal, 34*(1), 79–89.

Segal, D. (2014, October 10). Behind *League of Legends*, esports's main attraction. *New York Times*. Retrieved June 20, 2018, from https://www.nytimes.com/2014/10/12/technology/riot-games-league-of-legends-main-attractionesports.html.

Stahl, R. (2006). Have you played the war on terror? *Critical Studies in Media Communication, 23*(2), 112–130.

Taylor, N. (2009). *Power play: Digital gaming goes pro*. PhD Dissertation, York University, Toronto.

Taylor, T. L. (2012). *Raising the stakes: The professionalization of computer gaming*. Cambridge, MA: The MIT Press.

Taylor, N. (2015). Play to the camera: Video ethnography, spectatorship and e-sports. *Convergence, 22*(2), 115–130.

Taylor, H. (2018a, April 4). Research reveals most popular esports on Twitch. *Gamesindustry.biz*. Retrieved June 6, 2018, from https://www.gamesindustry.biz/articles/2018-04-04-research-reveals-most-popular-esports-ontwitch.

Taylor, T. L. (2018b). *Watch me play: Twitch and the rise of game live streaming*. Princeton, NJ: Princeton University Press.

Taylor, N., Jenson, J., & de Castell, S. (2009). Cheerleaders, booth babes, Halo hoes: Pro-gaming, gender, and jobs for the boys. *Digital Creativity, 20*(9), 239–252.

Wenner, L. A. (1998). Playing the MediaSport game. In L. A. Wenner (Ed.), *MediaSport* (pp. 3–13). London: Routledge.

Witkowski, E. (2012). On the digital playing field: How we 'do sport' with networked computer games. *Games and Culture, 7*(5), 349–374.

Witkowski, E. (2013). Eventful masculinities: Negotiations of hegemonic sporting masculinities at LANs. In M. Consalvo, K. Mitgutsch, & A. Stein (Eds.), *Sports videogames* (pp. 217–235). New York: Routledge.

Witz, B. (2014, March 24). College basketball data aplenty for those who can afford it. *New York Times*. Retrieved June 6, 2018, from https://www.nytimes.com/2014/03/25/sports/ncaabasketball/sportvu-offers-collegebasketball-data-for-those-who-can-afford-it.html.

Wyshnynski, G. (2018, February 28). Player tracking coming to the NHL? It's complicated. *ESPN*. Retrieved November 23, 2018, from http://www.espn.com/nhl/story/_/id/22604597/nhl-great-player-tracking-debate-ethicalquestions-fan-access.

Yarrow, D., & Kranke, M. (2016). The performativity of sports statistics: Towards a research agenda. *Journal of Cultural Economy, 9*(5), 445–457.

Part II

Bodies/Matter

Possibilities of Feminist Technoscience Studies of Sport: Beyond Cyborg Bodies

Kathryn Henne

Feminist studies of sport offer a rich literature on the gendered dimensions of physical activity and human movement. While critical examinations of women's participation in sport and physical activity are a cornerstone of this body of research, such work is not limited to generating knowledge about women's experiences or gender alone. Instead, projects also demonstrate how gendered, sexed, and intersectional differences inform practices and representations of human movement; the disruption of ideologies and tacit beliefs about embodied action; and how sport can contribute to naturalizing social hierarchies and injustices (e.g., Birrell 1988; Hargreaves 1994; Messner 2007).

Recent commentaries on feminist new materialism have emphasized the need for Sport Studies to attend to "how 'matter' is thought and constituted through entanglements between human and non-human bodies, affects, objects, and practices" (Fullagar 2017, p. 248). They point to an analytic privileging of discourse and human experience. In particular,

K. Henne (✉)
University of Waterloo, Waterloo, ON, Canada
e-mail: khenne@uwaterloo.ca

© The Author(s) 2020
J. J. Sterling, M. G. McDonald (eds.), *Sports, Society, and Technology*,
https://doi.org/10.1007/978-981-32-9127-0_7

they argue that language is not necessarily the primary mode of making meaning, nor are human subjects the main performers of agency (see Barad 2003; Fullagar 2017; Markula 2018). Reflecting on this "new materialist" shift, Katelyn Esmonde and Shannon Jette (2018) acknowledge the importance of these observations, but add a caveat: the emphasis on materiality as a novel contribution may unfairly suggest that other feminist approaches have negated it. Extending Sara Ahmed's (2008) criticisms, Esmonde and Jette (2018) point out that feminism has a long history of engaging material conditions, including (but not limited to) the biological, and that more recent materialist critiques disregard the important ways that poststructural theories aid in elucidating the constitutive relationships between the substantive and the discursive.[1] While Esmonde and Jette (2018) concede that the newness of new materialism may be overstated, they do highlight Science and Technology Studies (STS) as a field that offers many material-semiotic approaches that might be useful for studies of sport and physical culture (p. 44).

With these observations in mind, I explore the point further, considering what feminist technoscience might offer studies of sport. Feminist technoscience can be thought of as a specific (yet certainly not uniform) field of STS that has contributed significantly to analyses of materialism.[2] Through its examination of "the unpredictable liveliness of biology and matter" and how they "actively imprint the social," feminist technoscience can deepen analyses of "sociocultural inscriptions of power upon bodies and nature" (Foster 2016, pp. 128–129). Rather than draw distinctions between science, technology, and society, feminist technoscience illustrates their interconnectedness. Diverse in its range and scope, such analyses may be attentive to gender, but not exclusively so—a tendency that aligns with trends in women's and gender studies, which no longer emphasizes women or gender as its central concern. Instead, feminist technoscience, like women's and gender studies more broadly, offers many modalities through which to interrogate how different actors and relationships contribute to the fashioning—and refashioning—of power, politics, difference, and inequality.[3] However, the positioning of feminist technoscience, according to Cecilia Åsberg and Nina Lykke (2010), is a paradox—that is, the field is "simultaneously a marginalized area within feminist studies and a *locus* for famous innovators of feminist theorizing" (p. 301, emphasis in original).

Feminist analyses of the entanglements of science, technology, sport, and embodiment are increasing in number; however, the incorporation of feminist theories from STS is, for the most part, limited to a select few concepts. Notably, as discussed further in the next section, Donna Haraway's allegory of the cyborg has been influential in terms of making sense of how bodies, technologies, and sport are constitutive; however, they often retain a constrained focus on individual bodies. In doing so, such analyses miss opportunities for further engagement with other relevant concepts and ideas from feminist technoscience.

In what follows, this chapter offers a survey of existing and possible uses and adaptations of feminist technoscience to studies of sport, while attending to the aforementioned critiques of "feminist new materialism" and its advocates' assertion that it is a necessary intervention to correct for a seeming overemphasis on language (Barad 2003, p. 801). The next section considers how scholars have used the notion of the cyborg to study constitutive relations in sport. I then discuss feminist approaches employed to analyze technosocial relations, highlighting agential realism (Barad 2003, 2007) and assemblage (Puar 2012, 2017) as prominent, yet different analytical frameworks. I use them not only to show their utility but also to illustrate how adaptations of assemblage offer modes through which to address stated concerns around new materialist concepts. Throughout the discussion of both, I point to distinctions between them as well as their respective constraints. After reviewing how these ideas might support feminist analyses of the technosocial dimensions of sport, the chapter concludes with reflection on how existing feminist analyses of sport and physical activity also offer important insights for STS scholarship.

Cyborgs in Sport

While the cyborg is popularly understood as a being made of symbiotic human and cybernetic parts, its evocation in feminist analyses, STS, and Sport Studies flags a more complex set of relations. In "A cyborg manifesto: Science, technology, and socialist-feminism in the twenty-first century," Haraway (1991) argues that technosocial relations, cultural politics, and capitalist formations shape contemporary conditions in ways that are best understood as fragmented and transgressive. Reflecting critically on distinctions drawn between animal/human/machine, she argues that cyborgs transgress such dualisms, elaborating, "the difference between machine and organism is thoroughly blurred" (Haraway 1991, p. 165). Cyborgs are not fictions of the future; they characterize our present. Subscriptions to settled identities and notions of natural bodies are therefore romanticized notions—desires that, she contends, feminists must reconsider. Haraway refutes liberatory projects that make totalizing claims around appeals to a universal "women's experience" (as they evoke tacit beliefs about "woman" as an essential identity) and explains how their orientation does not capture the struggles of Women of Color (a category she frames as a productive fusion that reflects an enduring affinity among and with outsiders). These insights, taken together, support her point that our contemporary politics are cyborg politics, meaning that alliances can only be temporary. Thus, while the cyborg reflects the embodiment of technosocial relations, its analytical focus captures more than features of bodies.

This brief summary does not capture the nuances of Haraway's many claims about cyborg politics or the various interpretations and adaptations that have followed her initial publication (e.g., Prins 1995; Wilson 2009). Instead, it points to key features, not all of which have been taken up in sport scholarship. According to Tara Magdalinski (2008), cyborg bodies emerge from tensions that are emblematic of the "paradox" of modern elite sport (p. 1): that is, the quest for incredible human performances requires technological advancement and integration, generating various cyborg bodies that can challenge presumed distinctions between the organic (attributed to humans) and inorganic (attributed to technology). Elite sport, a domain known for pushing the boundaries of physical human achievement, therefore offers a site in which the notion of an innate "humanness" can be called into question. As such, many studies focus on how the cyborg problematizes the presumed binary division between human and machine, enabling further scrutiny of how "what is commonly assumed to be the 'natural' body is indeed a complex amalgamation of science, technology, and flesh" in the context of sport (Norman and Moola 2011, p. 1268). Specific applications range in topic, from issues related to athletes and disability (Howe 2011; Norman and Moola 2011), bodily enhancement (Miah 2003; Magdalinski 2008; Swartz and Watermeyer 2008), environment (Butryn and Masucci 2009), narratives of identity (Butryn and Masucci 2003; Rail and Lefebvre 2003), and sex/gender (Cole 1993). Although distinct, they collectively demonstrate the variety of ways in which athletes, as cyborgs, elicit pleasure—for example, their reverence and celebration in high-level competitions—and provoke anxiety—for example, the disdain for athletes who do not seem "natural," such as those who are suspected of doping (see Henne 2015; also Magdalinski 2008).

To explain how cyborg bodies prompt responses that exceed presumed binaries between pleasure and anxiety, consider Ted Butryn and Matthew Masucci's (2003) discussion of narratives around former Tour de France champion, Lance Armstrong (i.e., prior to findings of organized and premeditated doping). Rather than approach his story as evidence of a superior natural athlete, they trace shifts in his subjectivity—as an elite cyclist, cancer patient and survivor, and parent—as a "process of cyborgification" in which technologies become "infused in his self-narrative and the ways that Armstrong himself relates to his own physiological identity through technological means" (Butryn and Masucci 2003, p. 125). His narration exemplifies Haraway's proposition that the embodied self is not stable or whole. Butryn and Masucci also convey how Armstrong, as an embodied figure, is hybridized in ways that are etched and shaped by technosocial engagements. Thus, Armstrong—even before the findings of his doping-related violations—was "irreversibly 'polluted' through various degrees and methods of technologization" (Butryn and Masucci 2003, p. 126). In short, his identity was never singular, pure, or fully human, even though he was celebrated for his corporeal achievements.

Moss Norman and Fiona Moola's analysis of double-leg amputee sprinter Oscar Pistorius, a former Olympian and Paralympian, also illustrates how cyborg bodies can be both captivating and unnerving, particularly to onlookers who occupy a world built on the presumption of able-bodiness. Acknowledging debates regarding whether or not his prostheses unfairly enhanced his running ability, they contend that Pistorius, as a cyborg, transgressed the culturally construed "boundary between the included (i.e., ability, natural, and the normal) and the excluded (i.e., disability, the cyborg, and the abnormal)," revealing that the binary divide between them "is tenuous and unstable" (Norman and Moola 2011, p. 1273). While Olympic values uphold the ideal athletic body as natural and able-bodied, Pistorius and his quest to compete in the 2012 Olympic Games in London demonstrates how modern sport actually enables the contestation of these beliefs in practice, thereby pointing to the porous nature of the presumed boundary between those who are included and excluded.

These examples attest that the cyborg exceeds the traditional focus of many feminist analyses of sport, that is, women and/or gender. In fact, Haraway (1991, p. 150) wrote of the cyborg as "a creature in the post-gender world." Explicitly feminist readings of cyborgs in sport are often attentive to gender but do not limit their analysis to this concern. For instance, with regard to the policing of women athletes' biological traits under the guise of "fair play," Rayvon Fouché (2012) emphasizes that Haraway's cyborg allegory can help us find "a way out of the maze of dualisms in which we have explained our bodies and our tools to ourselves" (Haraway 1991, p. 181, as cited in Fouché 2012, p. 291). Specifically, he argues, the cyborg aids in thinking through the multiplicity of bodies, including their various physiological attributes and abilities, beyond the confines of sex/gender alone.

Adopting a different line of feminist inquiry, Sarah Rebolloso McCullough (2010) employs the cyborg to examine how technologies operate to shore up what we think of as "the natural" in sport. By asking how they do the work of *naturalization*, her analysis aligns with long-standing feminist efforts to understand and unveil how claims of natural or inherent difference have served to normalize inequality and justify differential treatment. Speedo's LZR Racer suit, which was worn by 38 of the 42 world record setters in swimming at the 2008 Olympic Games, serves as one such case. It, she argues, "creates an image of technological equity that ignores the unequal access to resources" (McCullough 2010, p. 18). Magdalinski (2008) extends this point in her reflection on the Fastskin technology used in other high-performance swimwear, explaining that this suit is perceived differently than other performance enhancers for two key reasons: (1) because it appears external to the body (whereas drugs are internal), and (2) because it is marketed as improving a specific function rather than wider bodily enhancement. The suit, as a technology, directs attention away from the myths sustained by the pursuit of continual improvements in performance—that is, that gains emerge from "progress and superior fitness of some bodies over others" and by "natural athletic bodies" (McCullough 2010, p. 19). The visibility of swimwear as an artificial enhancement operates almost paradoxically by both revealing and veiling the cyborg athlete. Moreover, by contributing to the sustenance of myths about athlete bodies, the suit is part of a wider network of relationships that undermine the scrutiny of broader inequalities that implicate sports and the bodies who participate and compete in them.

Sport-specific analyses retain core elements of Haraway's cyborg propositions in that they focus explicitly on the interconnections of organic and mechanical components, even though gender may seem to take a backseat to other concerns. One of their possible shortcomings, though, is the tendency to focus on athletes' bodies and their "body cultures," which reflects Susan Brownell's contention that "the horizons of an athlete's world can never stray far beyond her body" in part because their identity is intimately connected to corporeal action (1995, p. 10). Haraway, however, cautions against this narrow focus: she reminds us it is important to not simply acknowledge and describe cyborgs, but also to interrogate what they reveal about sociality and politics. For her, their existence illuminates the permeance of technosocialities as well as blurred boundaries that dislocate binary categories used to articulate difference about various bodies and actors. Cyborgs are evidence of wider ruptures and disruptions, enabling a rejection of claims based on inherent attributes. The metaphor is meant to advance a politics of affinity, not identity, and to aid in understanding and confronting conditions that have emerged as part of the influential and male-dominated nexus between militarism and capitalism (Haraway 1991). This observation suggests that it would be a mistake to think of the utility of the cyborg allegory—or other feminist technoscientific interventions—as simply destabilizing beliefs about bodies in movement. While analyses of cyborgs in sport are compelling in terms of their rethinking of embodied actors, there remains a notable gap in terms of making the broader connections that Haraway prescribes.

The next section considers two distinct analytics that feminists and other critical scholars have used to study technosocial relations that include, but are not limited to, sport: agential realism and assemblage. Recognizing that studies of cyborgs in sport retain a relatively narrow focus, it considers a wider array of STS-informed applications, with the aim of illustrating possibilities for studies of sport more generally and feminist studies of sport in particular.

From Bodies in Motion to Intra-Actions and Assemblages

Various approaches fall under the umbrella of feminist technoscience, many of which are not cyborg theories, including "cyberfeminisms, post-human feminisms, queerfeminisms, sexual difference feminisms, postcolonial, and anti-racist feminisms" (Åsberg and Lykke 2010, p. 300). Agential realism is perhaps among the most recognizable feminist materialist approaches in part because Karen Barad articulated it as a response to what she saw as a concern that "language and culture are granted their own agency and historicity while matter is figured as passive and immutable" (2003, p. 801). Specifically, she frames agential realism as rooted in *intra-action*, not interaction, an ontological position that renders "matter as an active agent in its ongoing materialization" (p. 822). As such, it reconsiders phenomena and things as co-constituted, not as the result of interactions between different agents. In contrast, adaptations of assemblage range widely in application and scope. The concept itself has roots in Gilles Deleuze and Félix Guattari's metaphor of the assemblage, which scholars have explained as a "multiplicity of heterogeneous objects, whose unity comes solely from the fact that these items function together, that they work together as a functional entity" (Patton 1994, p. 158). Both conceptual tools have been employed to analyze technosocial relations. While an in-depth reflection on their distinct foci is not possible in the space allocated here, this section considers how these frameworks aid feminist and critical projects that aim to unpack power and complexity, with a primary focus on sport and physical activity. Whereas agential realism emphasizes agency as an enactment that emerges from entangled relations (as opposed to coming from individual actors), assemblage provides a mode of interrogating multiple and sometimes seemingly disparate logics that can converge to inform specific events or situations (Ong and Collier 2005).

Agential Realism and Re(Con)Figurations as Intra-Action

A distinguishing feature of agential realism is that it does not posit individuals—human or otherwise—as pre-existing actors. According to Barad (2007, p. 33), "distinct agencies do not precede, but rather emerge through, their intra-action ... [T]hat is, agencies are only distinct in relation to their mutual entanglement; they don't exist as individual elements." Intra-action, she explains, "signifies the mutual constitution of entangled agencies" (p. 33). This ontological reorientation prompts a focus on how phenomena materialize, a distinctly different framing from more common examinations that look at interactions causing effects. Instead, agency involves "the ongoing reconfigurings of the world," not as a trait that actors possess (p. 141). This distinction has direct implications for how we think about human bodies. They are not autonomous agents who instigate changes independently, nor are they the outcomes of worldly processes. Instead, they are "part of the world in its open-ended becoming" (p. 150). Intra-action entails iterative practices, which, upon further scrutiny, reveal that matter and meaning are intertwined.

The embrace of materiality and its semiotic interconnections extends beyond agential realism (Alaimo and Hekman 2008). Barad's claims about intra-action, however, stand out in terms of their explicit and specific focus. She rejects the idea that technologies or other physical apparatuses simply measure objects; rather, they aid in the definition and creation. They are *entangled* in that the object does not exist without the apparatus, rendering them inseparable. Her reflection on one example, the fetus, serves as a case in point. Reproductive science has enabled advancements in surgical practice and biological understanding. Three-dimensional ultrasound technology presents the fetus as seemingly distinct from the womb of its mother (Barad 2007, p. 221). The fetus' existence as entity in the world reveals its constitutive relationships with technologies of visualization, which simultaneously can render the woman's body invisible. Her analysis of this example does not suggest that the meanings of the fetus result from these technologies or that they are fixed. Rather, for Barad (2007, p. 149), they are better understood as "an ongoing performance of the world in its differential dance," in which "part of the world becomes determinately bounded and propertied in its emergent intelligibility to another part of the world." Intra-action is not simply the generation of a thing or object through physical and discursive interconnections. Phenomena instead reflect productive and dynamic practices, which include perceptive, affective, and subjective elements. While the feminist sensibilities of agential realism may not at first appear clear, Barad (2007, p. 34) maintains that it has utility for "negotiating difficulties" around questions of materiality and materialization, particularly in relation to technology's "crucial role in public discourse as well as in feminist theories of the body."

Studies guided by agential realism vary in topic and scope. Employing intra-action to make sense of materialization, however, means being attentive to how non-human dimensions of entanglements. Daniel Nyberg's (2009) ethnography of a call center details how service calls reveal a kind of performativity that is materially grounded and transcends presumed boundaries between the telephone, the customer service operator, and computer systems (from screens, keyboards, and headphones to cables connecting parts, as well as one's physical connectivity to the mouse and cursor). Central to his analysis is the consideration of embodiment as it emerges through technosocial engagement. Rather than networked interactions between human and non-human actors, he explains their intra-action as an assembly of actors that materializes through a conjoined labor process (Nyberg 2009, p. 193). In a distinctly different vein, Rachel Colls (2007) examines the materialization of "fat" bodies, highlighting key aspects: first, that fat has its "own internal momentums" in which its texture, movement, and capacity to take up or react to different spaces enable it to be at times within and outside the body; and second, that fat can be a force that acts and is not simply acted upon by measurement devices or embodied practices (e.g., eating, cooking, exercising), doing so in ways that can render some actions unacceptable by normative standards (Colls 2007, p. 353). Taken together, they are the makings of "embodied topographies" (p. 363), which reorient fat so that it is not limited to an individual attribute. These topographies, Colls (2007) argues, offer an analytic alternative to the tendency to focus on discrimination against fat bodies and the condemnation of fatness—both of which minimize the role of agency.

These materialist insights into embodiment are arguably distinct from frameworks used in Sport Studies to conceptualize bodies, which often draw on Foucauldian approaches (e.g., Thorpe 2016; Fullagar 2017; Esmonde and Jette 2018). For instance, explorations of the "disciplined nature of bodily existence" have been central to cultural and sociological studies of sport. They have focused explicitly on the various ways and modalities through which power operates to encourage bodies to be both productive and docile (Andrews, 1993, p. 148). Feminist scholars of sport have also attributed Foucault's ideas as creating "an opening to question the modernist foundation of feminism's own categories of power, political action, resistance, and agency" (Markula 2003, p. 104). Thus, even though scholars reiterate the importance of asking "how matter comes to matter," developing the answers to shifting questions about bodies is arguably not easy (Barad 2003, p. 829).

According to Simone Fullagar (2017), materialist analyses require new kinds of qualitative research questions. She suggests moving away from "a hermeneutics of lived experience that has privileged the interpretive subject and towards the material-discursive relations that make the life of the body and its movement (im)possible" (p. 248). While some feminist scholars of sport, such as Holly Thorpe (2016), express enthusiasm for how these reconsiderations might enable new modes of interrogating the interplay between biology and culture, others highlight some notable complications. For example, Esmonde and Jette (2018) have incorporated feminist materialist insights to problematize claims that certain environments contribute to obesity and that human bodies can overcome them through more activity. They reframe the relationships between bodies and environments as entangled, not causal. While they acknowledge that both Barad and Haraway convincingly use feminist technoscience to unearth overlooked power asymmetries, they express concerns about whether "political and ethical claims" are "severely undercut if there is no posited difference between the agency of humans and non-humans" (Esmonde and Jette 2018, p. 44).

Despite somewhat cautious endorsements of feminist new materialism, analyses of intra-action do point to productive possibilities for studies of sport, especially in terms of reconsidering the anthropocentric tendencies of sport and studies of sport. According to Mary G. McDonald and Jennifer Sterling, these tendencies "promote binary thinking, falsely separating 'humans' as apart from—and in control of—'nature'" (forthcoming). Specifically, they incorporate Barad's insights on intra-action to draw attention to the range of actors and lives implicated in the controversies that emerged around the polluted waterways in and around Rio de Janeiro, Brazil, and gained international attention in the lead up to the 2016 Olympic and Paralympic Games. McDonald and Sterling acknowledge that media narratives tended to focus on the public health threats to athletes and tourists, as well as to the failures of technological solutions to prevent and remedy these risks. They point out that these foci "privilege a particular form of human need that creates deleterious effects and consequences" (p. 17). They argue for an ontological reorientation that attends to *trans-corporeality*, which recognizes how human corporeality cannot be disconnected from nature cultures—that is, the inseparability of nature and culture both ecologically and socially. Accordingly, McDonald and Sterling re-center the place of water, reaffirming both indigenous and feminist traditions that approach water as a central starting point for the study of human and non-human life and livelihoods (p. 18). Further, and aligned with Barad's (2007) call to reconfigure objects of inquiry, they reflect on how water intra-acts relationally with other organisms and actors in ways that disrupt assumptions that water can be understood as a thing distinct from or outside those relations. Their reading of the water pollution controversies, in turn, captures a wider range of actors, organisms, and inequalities that coalesce in the hosting of the Olympic and Paralympic Games and sheds light on overlooked forms of violence enabled by modern sport and its celebration of human-centered achievements. Importantly, they do so without losing sight of postcolonial legacies, capitalist practices, geographic distinctions, and social inequalities.

Others have employed intra-action to illuminate neglected dimensions of cross-species relationships. For example, Anita Maurstad, Dona Davis, and Sarah Cowles (2013, p. 322) examine human-horse partnerships in equestrian sports as embodied "anthropo-zoo-genetic practice, where species domesticate each other through being together." Their acknowledgment of nature cultures disrupts the oft-assumed dynamic of a (human) rider training a horse for a joint performance. Their analysis of these entanglements explains how horse and human become together through mutual engagement, verbal and "felt" co-communication, and recognition of the shifting boundaries between them. Their "co-being," to use Maurstad and colleagues' language, not only appreciates how non-human and non-organic actors engage and diverse expressions of agency that destabilize the oft-presumed authority of the (human) rider, but it also emphasizes their shared intra-action without losing sight of the importance of embodiment.

The distinct intra-active insights gleaned through the aforementioned analyses reveal multiple materializations of actors, bodies, and physicality. In doing so, they enable further scrutiny of how space and embodied activity emerge constitutively. While cyborg readings of athletes show how cybernetic connections are integral to modern sport, they, for the most part, remain preoccupied with relations revealed through bodies and body cultures. Inter-action, however, requires careful consideration of symbiotic relations that exceed presumed human/non-human divides, such as those inherent to nature cultures, which Sport Studies scholars have only recently begun to explore in depth (e.g., King and Weedon 2016; also in this collection; McDonald and Sterling forthcoming). However, it is worth noting that inter-action is also the subject of feminist critiques. Jasbir Puar (2017), for instance, points out that it may "privilege an essentialized truth produced through matter," missing an opportunity to interrogate the role of language because it is preoccupied with refuting the dominance of linguistic processes (Puar 2017, p. 172). The next section considers assemblage as a possible response to the limits of being preoccupied with materiality.

Tracing Multiplicity and (Re)Formations Through Assemblages

Scholars working in and across critical data, feminist, queer, and social scientific studies have drawn on the concept of assemblage to explore and query globalized and technosocial changes (see Ong and Collier 2005), exploring unpredictable and contingent features across various domains of activity, including science and its regulation (Prasad 2017), surveillance (Haggerty and Ericson 2000), and reproductive technologies (Lowry 2004). A key attribute of assemblages is their inherent multiplicity and contingency. They can materialize in the form of events, but they are not fixed. Instead, they fluctuate or dissipate along different temporal and spatial registers. In short, assemblages are not permanent or stable, nor are they straightforward or coherent. This approach to matter is distinct from agential realism in the sense that it attends to concerns of materialization, non-human agency, and the push to destabilize "humanist notions of the body" and "the politics of voice and visibility" without dismissing the contributions of language within dynamic processes (Puar 2017, p. 20). Given the seemingly amorphous nature of assemblages, grounded examples often provide more conceptual clarity than explanations of its theoretical tenets, three of which I highlight next.

Globalized Assemblages

The anthology, *Global assemblages: Technology, politics and ethics as anthropological problems*, features a number of anthropological examples to showcase how "global forms are articulated in specific situations" that reveal how assemblages "define new material, collective, and discursive relationships" and serve as "sites for formation and reformation" (Ong and Collier 2005, p. 4). Sport mega-events, such as the staging of the Olympic Games and the Commonwealth Games, are notable sites for interrogating global assemblages because they are international spectacles enabled by transnational networks of human and non-human actors, including participants, audiences, infrastructure, media and surveillance technologies, corporate sponsors, and governing sport bodies among others.

As global spectacles, sport mega-events require massive investment in infrastructure and security, which has meant the implementation of widespread and varied forms of surveillance. For Kevin Haggerty and Richard Ericson (2000), assemblage is an adept explanatory tool for making sense of these relations because it enables close scrutiny of the multiplicity of surveillance systems and the adjoining technosocial dynamics that accompany their expanding connections. As an assemblage can grow in multiple directions, they create additional modes of surveillance and extend into other locations with more subjects becoming visible under the gaze of overseeing authorities. This type of expansion carries notable implications for population governance, as surveillance generates and relies on multiple representations of human bodies (e.g., images, data inputs, and other signifiers) as grounds for understandings of human behavior and developing practices of social control. Analyses of mega-events follow suit: they reveal how both spectacle and surveillance are central to the production and governance of these events, thereby troubling Foucault's strong distinctions between spectacle and surveillance (Boyle and Haggerty 2009). Further, they demonstrate that legacies of security extend well beyond the actual sport mega-events themselves, operating across "structural, cultural, policy, technological, and relational" levels (Whelan 2014, p. 392). Within the assemblage, the staging of the mega-event remains important, even after its conclusion, because it facilitates the materialization of connections and enables the observation of what otherwise would appear as a diverse set of relations.

The surveillant assemblage has other applications as well. Consider Bryan Sluggett's (2011) use of assemblage to explain the globalized anti-doping regime in sport: it emphasizes the networks of widespread surveillance and decenters the disproportionate focus on the "doping problem" among athletes. Ophir Sefiha and Nancy Reichman (2016) offer a nuanced account of surveillance in cycling, looking beyond formal mechanisms adopted by authorities to discursive and pervasive aspects of the assemblage that reveal themselves in athletes' everyday lives. As such, they detail the extensive influence of required tracking, such as the bureaucratic requirements of whereabouts registration and random out-of-competition testing alongside athletes' self-surveillance of their food and supplement ingestion and peer-to-peer relations, including through social media. Their conclusion reveals the blurred lines between organizational and non-organizational, as well as external and internal, surveillance among athletes, all of which are enabled and sustained through an assemblage of sociotechnical relations (Sefiha and Reichman 2016, p. 213). Moreover, these practices often emerge in *anticipation* of formal regulatory requirements, not simply as a reaction to them, revealing a kind of preemptive governance that would otherwise be difficult to identify.

Digital Assemblages

The embeddedness of digital data in everyday life operates in ways that surpass social control through monitoring (Haggerty and Ericson's primary focus). Reflecting on encounters with digital data in everyday life, Deborah Lupton (2016, p. 1) elaborates on "digital data-human assemblages," offering a reminder that embodied practices actively contribute to the generation and employment of data. Specifically, she points out, assemblages are more than systems of extracting and using data about people; people also "learn from the assemblages of which they are a part" (Lupton 2016, p. 2). They engage and negotiate data, gleaning insights as they do so, which can lead to the use or manipulation of personal data collection as well as changes in behavior. Thus, according to Lupton (2016), it is important to remember "the inevitability of our relationship with our digital data assemblages and the importance of learning to live together and to learn from each other" (p. 2). In this way, data emerge more as companions in everyday life than as foes.

Extending these observations on the liveliness of data within assemblages, Sarah Pink et al. (2017) examine how data become a mundane part of physical experience and self-awareness. Drawing upon an ethnographic analysis of self-tracking cyclists, they document participants' micro-routines, everyday adaptations, and emotive shifts in relation to both the technologies of data collection and the data collected about them. They conclude that data are not the outcomes of embodied practices, but instead constitutive elements of embodied activity and subjectivity (Pink et al. 2017). Their observation that such assemblages can be central to notions of embodiment and self, however, is not necessarily new.

The advent of self-tracking wearable devices may bring about heightened awareness of our relationships with digital data, but our connections with biometric data can be traced to engagement with older technologies, such as the weight scale (Crawford et al. 2015). Although these historical predecessors did not harvest or share personal data digitally, Kate Crawford, Jessa Lingel, and Tero Karppi (2015) acknowledge that they nonetheless contributed to human subjectivity and behavior and operated in the service of regimes of social control, including weight management and health promotion agendas. What is distinct about digital self-tracking devices is their contributions to the growth of networks, not all of which can be anticipated, felt, or understood by the human bodies engaged with them. The connectivity enabled through technosocial connections can be multiple and unpredictable within assemblages—an observation that Roslyn Kerr (2016) has detailed in relation to sport science and medicine, the use of performance enhancement technologies, the incorporation of refereeing and judging technologies in different sports, and media broadcasting. Taken together, these analyses demonstrate how assemblage is a useful analytic for tracing cybernetic relations, such as those illustrated in the aforementioned cyborg theories. In contrast to most examinations of cyborgs in sport, though, assemblage requires reflecting on wider networked dynamics rather than the tendency to examine bodies or body cultures.

Queer Assemblages

Queer and feminist adaptations of assemblage shine additional light on issues of power that are often missed or under-interrogated in many studies of technosocial assemblages. As Puar is explicit in how assemblage can be employed to address the limitations of human-centric and identity-based frameworks and to avoid a kind of "ontological or material essentialism" that she associates with agential realism, her work figures centrally in this section (2017, p. 172).

Puar's (2007) engagement with assemblage responds directly to what she identifies as a consequence of surveillance studies scholars' preoccupation with data and digital representations of subjects. She criticizes their limited engagement with "the visual and its capacity to interpellate subjects" through "formations of race and sex that are under way in response to a new visual category, the 'terrorist look-alike'" (Puar 2007, p. 176). For Puar, the securitized conditions of the U.S. War on Terror have aided in refiguring these racialized subjects as perverse while also legally recognizing—and even applauding—certain kinds of "normative" gay and lesbian or homonormative citizens in the United States. Employing queer as an assemblage, she moves away from binary preoccupations (between, e.g., queer and non-queer subjects based on self-identification or the public and private sphere based on legalized norms) to examine articulations of U.S. nationalism. On the one hand, these discourses position secular values as more liberal and accepting of gay and lesbian subjects, and, on the other hand, they reiterate Orientalist ideas about Muslim sexuality as being repressive and backward through the visible condemnation (at least in the United States) of the abhorrent male terrorist body. This fantasy depicts "religious and racial communities are more homophobic than White mainstream communities are racist" (Puar 2007, p. 15). These refocusing techniques not only support what Puar refers to as "homonationalism," but they also divert the public's gaze from the ongoing violence of U.S. imperialism, both domestically and abroad. These maneuvers evidence a set of regulatory norms, which have life and death implications, particularly for queer subjects.

Puar (2007, 2017) rejects many individualized notions of race, gender, nation, and sexuality, suggesting that assemblages prompt a reconsideration of how bodies become implicated in and through interlocking inequalities and manifestations of violence. In her critique of common readings and applications of intersectional feminism, she elaborates how, as a heuristic device, intersectionality relies on the metaphor of a woman standing at the intersection of different axes of social difference in order to capture their impact on her (see also Liao and Markula 2016). Although Puar (2007) acknowledges intersectionality as an important intervention in feminist thought, she points to its risks, namely that its application can reify and stabilize identity categories. For example, the preoccupation with a human body standing within the intersection can lose sight of the dynamism of the forces at work and how they come to interact. In contrast, assemblages emphasize their importance, providing modes through which to interrogate the technologies and techniques of population governance as well as how they become enacted in ways that evoke and effect bodies differently. Instead of looking to the cyborg as a solution, which she suggests overemphasizes technological influences (see Puar 2012), she maintains that assemblages offer a productive mode through which to expose and interrogate shifting technosocial relations and interlocking formations of oppression and difference.

Rather than approach the body as an individuated subject, or even as necessarily human or organic, assemblages share agential realism's commitment to taking matter seriously and how it becomes in the world. Puar's articulation also reflects a clear concern for Foucauldian notions of power by retaining a focus on how "biopolitical apparatuses of control" contribute to larger practices of normalization and the exercise of disciplinary power (Puar 2017, p. 22). Identities, she argues, may emerge within and through these networks, but focusing on them or on individual bodies alone is not enough. In fact, she emphasizes that Foucault saw discipline as "a mode of individualization of multiplicities rather than something that constructs an edifice of multiple elements on the basis of individuals who are worked on as, first of all, individuals" (Foucault 1990, p. 146, as cited in Puar 2017, p. 23). Assemblage offers a compatible analytic for interrogating these dynamics.

Although feminist and queer scholars of sport have reflected on and extended Puar's concept of homonationalism (e.g., King 2009; Davidson 2013; Sykes 2016; Travers and Shearman 2017), analytic applications of assemblage have, as mentioned previously, tended to align with Haggerty and Ericson's (2000) notion of the surveillant assemblage. One exception is Judy Liao and Pirkko Markula's (2016) reading of media coverage about professional basketball player Diana Taurasi's 2010 drug charge as an assemblage. Through this approach, they illustrate that intersectional identity markers (e.g., race, ethnicity, and sexuality) were largely absent from narrations of her positive drug test and exoneration by the Court of Arbitration for Sport, even though the doping allegation itself is about Taurasi's body and drug taking. Instead, structural elements emerge as more prominent, namely "professionalism, legality, and U.S.-centerness" (Liao and Markula 2016, pp. 175–176). Their analysis, in turn, demonstrates how hybridized networks may yield important insights—in this case, about structures coalescing—that cannot be captured when privileging the individual body or identity.

When Feminist Technoscience Studies and Feminist Studies of Sport Meet

This chapter has mapped three theoretical frames—the cyborg, agential realism, and assemblage—to illustrate how scholars of sport have (and have not) incorporated them. This conclusion reflects on their possible utility for further incorporation and experimentation within studies of sport. First, though, I revisit some key contributions of feminist technoscience and expressed concerns about new materialism.

Although specific insights and contributions vary, feminist technoscience has advanced semiotic-material analysis. Its critical attention to materiality has revealed a distinct "more-than-human orientation"—an ontological repositioning that emphasizes embodied encounters as intertwined with the actions of objects, technologies, organisms (human and non-human) and other worldly conditions often discounted by human-centered studies (Fullagar 2017, p. 253). This shift in awareness has not meant a uniform, or even united, set of perspectives on the modes through which to interrogate materiality or incorporate feminist insights. I have discussed the adaptations of intra-action and assemblage as a case in point: whereas intra-action advocates for a notion of co-constitution that rejects agency as an individual (or humanistic) trait, assemblage has been employed in different ways, some of which retain a focus on biopolitics. Although distinct, both concepts facilitate engagement with dynamics that exceed traditional analyses of gender, reflecting the shift in feminism toward broader questions of power through the interrogation of "epistemological and ontological assumptions" (Foster 2016, p. 129). It is not surprising, then, that these concepts, as well as other ideas from feminist technoscience, such as the cyborg, have been incorporated to study questions that are explicitly feminist in nature.

Using feminist materialist approaches to make sense of biocultural dynamics has already, according to some scholars (e.g., Thorpe 2016), prompted reconsiderations of "both theoretical and empirical resources, and representational styles" (p. 10). In this chapter, I have noted some tradeoffs, including the possible political ramifications of giving comparable value to human and non-human agency (Esmonde and Jette 2018) and the potential for material essentialism (Puar 2017). According to Mieke Bal (2002), these kinds of questions and concerns are not unique to debates about new materialism: traveling concepts often confront obstacles. They have "solved major problems," but also have posed significant challenges, especially when they highlight disciplinary conflicts, discrepancies, or overlooked issues (Bal 2002, p. 4). This process of refutation and reassessment is arguably productive for feminist studies of sport in that it presents an opportunity to critically approach what traveling concepts offer as compared to ideas that (figuratively speaking) may have more road wear in the field. For the remainder of this conclusion, I consider these potential tensions and the uncertainties they provoke in a constructive light.

In fields dedicated to the sociocultural study of human movement, encounters with frameworks that reject foundational notions of human-centered agency, such as agential realism, or depart from the central focus on the body, such as assemblage, can be disruptive on multiple levels. Esmonde and Jette (2018, p. 44) acknowledge "expressed concerns about the ways that new materialisms create a falsely coherent and passé history of theory" in which "particular ways of knowing (often, subjugated ways of knowing) come to be dismissed as over so as to make way for the brave new theories." An uncritical embrace of materiality thus might not only reveal a disregard or neglect of other feminist approaches, but it also might contribute to the wider marginalization of those earlier ideas and their contributions.

Feminist scholars of sport are well equipped to engage the risks and possibilities of so-called "new" ideas around materiality in the context of sport. Feminist cultural studies of sport in particular have a "reflexive tradition" that pursues a "commitment both to exploring social difference and injustice and to contesting the relations of power that organize knowledge and disciplinary formations" (Adams et al. 2016, p. 76). Its insights align with recent reminders to value "the generative possibilities of an unbounded, eclectic scholarship that refuses to be over-disciplined or overdetermined by institutionally-privileged authorizing moves" and remains "cognizant of past contributions, while working toward a generative realm of 'productive conflict'" (p. 77).

In this spirit, we might, then, ask what are the generative offerings of materialist approaches? In the preceding pages, I have drawn attention to their contributions to the study of technosocial relationships in two ways: first, by addressing how agential realism productively reconsiders agency beyond human actors, and, second, by discussing assemblage as an alternative mode of interrogating material-semiotic relations between things and concepts without privileging matter, identities, or bodies. Taken together, they suggest that one answer to the question of generative offerings may not be about materialist approaches bringing about a heightened awareness of materialization. Instead, it may be rooted in reflexive reconsiderations of feminist sensibilities toward materiality, which can productively challenge, as well as reiterate, recognized traditions in studies of sport.

For Foster (2016, p. 129), feminist technoscience's appreciation of diverse materialities is fruitful precisely because it enables scrutiny of "affiliative kinship" among various objects and organisms across different domains. This affinity complements earlier articulations of feminist studies of sport. As C.L. Cole (1993, p. 93) argued over 25 years ago, such an agenda should prioritize "rethinking the categories of and relationships among sport, gender, sexuality, nature, the body, race, class, difference, science, power, representation, subjectivity, oppression" and "how the sport apparatus works in relation to and at the intersection of multiple technologies," doing so "in ways that always exceed institutional boundaries." Thus, while some scholars express apprehension about how the "material turn" may undermine past critical contributions, Cole's words point to another possibility: that the wider recognition and embrace of materialist sensibilities can reaffirm earlier commitments of feminist studies of sport. Of course, doing so requires first recognizing these traditions rather than erasing them.

At least two productive synergies become evident when considering connections and tensions across feminist studies of sport. On the one hand, feminist technoscience offers tools for thinking through the anthropocentric tendencies that accompany Sport Studies' focus on embodied human movement and their implications. On the other, feminist studies of sport provide myriad analyses that are attentive to discursive and embodied interrelationships etched and shaped by hierarchical relationships and social categories of difference. In doing so, they offer a reminder to STS scholars not to lose sight of interlocking inequalities—a criticism levied at both STS (e.g., Moser 2006) and feminist new materialism (see Puar 2017, pp. 20–21). As such, existing studies of sport offer examples to which STS scholars might look for guidance on how to retain valuable poststructural insights when interrogating material conditions.

While recognizing the value of cautious engagement, we would be remiss not to explore the possibilities of feminist technoscience studies of sport, especially given the acceptance of cyborg bodies and recognition of other technosocial bonds that coalesce through sport and physical activity. Forging a more explicit commitment to feminist technoscience studies of sport need not reject the past contributions of feminist studies of sport; instead, it has the potential to reinforce their generative commitments. Furthermore, it may aid in reviving feminist elements sometimes lost in the adaptation of feminist technoscience approaches when employed to study issues that lack overtly gendered contours.

Notes

1. Ahmed (2008) characterizes new materialism's "caricature of poststructuralism as matter-phobic" as both unfair (p. 34) and "motivated, as if the moment of 'rejection' is needed to authorize a new terrain" (p. 33). For more information about the debates around materialism, readers should consult a series of articles published in *European Journal of Women's Studies*, which span 2008 through the present.
2. Some important feminist technoscience theories—such as "situated knowledges" (Haraway 1991, p. 183), "strong objectivity" (Harding 1991, p. 138), and "agential realism" (Barad 2007, p. 132)—have wide

appeal within and beyond STS (Subramaniam 2009, p. 960). Situated knowledge, for example, reflects a recognition that robust knowledge cannot come from a bird's eye view of phenomena; rather, it emerges from "partial, locatable accounts of the world that are both accurate and explicitly embedded within the contexts of its own production" (Haraway 1988, pp. 575–599). Proponents of strong objectivity contend that persons and groups who occupy marginalized positions are more likely to be attentive to dimensions of social dynamics and systems often overlooked by more privileged observers; thus, in order to strengthen objectivity, their perspectives must feature centrally in knowledge production (Harding 1991).

3. While scholars of feminist technoscience acknowledge that this shift may pose challenges for political organizing and might endanger institutional gains made by earlier feminist efforts (see Subramaniam 2009; Foster 2016), Foster (2016) draws attention to the limited benefits secured through liberal feminist agendas as they failed to consider structural inequalities and the erasure of colonial legacies that disproportionately affect different groups of people.

References

Adams, M. L., Helstein, M. T., Kim, K., McDonald, M. G., Davidson, J., Jamieson, K. M., et al. (2016). Feminist cultural studies: Uncertainties and possibilities. *Sociology of Sport, 33*(1), 75–91.

Ahmed, S. (2008). Imaginary prohibitions: Some preliminary remarks on the founding gestures of the new materialism. *European Journal of Women's Studies, 15*(1), 23–39.

Alaimo, S., & Hekman, S. (Eds.). (2008). *Material feminisms*. Bloomington: Indiana University Press.

Andrews, D. L. (1993). Desperately seeking Michel: Foucault's genealogy, the body, and critical sport sociology. *Sociology of Sport Journal, 10*(2), 148–167.

Åsberg, C., & Lykke, N. (2010). Feminist technoscience studies. *European Journal of Women's Studies, 17*(4), 299–305.

Bal, M. (2002). *Traveling concepts in the humanities: A rough guide*. Toronto: University of Toronto Press.

Barad, K. (2003). Posthumanist performativity: Toward an understanding of how matter comes to matter. *Signs: Journal of Women in Culture and Society, 28*(3), 801–831.

Barad, K. (2007). *Meeting the universe half way: Quantum physics and the entanglement of matter and meaning*. Durham, NC: Duke University Press.

Birrell, S. (1988). Discourses on the gender/sport relationship: From women in sport to gender relations. *Exercise and Sport Reviews, 16*(1), 459–502.

Boyle, P., & Haggerty, K. D. (2009). Spectacular security: Mega-events and the security complex. *International Political Sociology, 3*(3), 257–274.

Brownell, S. (1995). *Training the body for China: Sports in the moral order of the people's republic*. Chicago: University of Chicago Press.

Butryn, T. M., & Masucci, M. A. (2003). It's not about the book: A cyborg counternarrative of Lance Armstrong. *Journal of Sport & Social Issues, 27*(2), 124–144.

Butryn, T. M., & Masucci, M. A. (2009). Traversing the matrix: Cyborg athletes, technology and the environment. *Journal of Sport & Social Issues, 33*(3), 258–307.

Cole, C. L. (1993). Resisting the canon: Feminist cultural studies, sport and technologies of the body. *Journal of Sport & Social Issues, 17*(2), 77–97.

Colls, R. (2007). Materializing bodily matter: Intra-action and the embodiment of 'fat'. *Geoforum, 38*(2), 353–365.

Crawford, K., Lingel, J., & Karppi, T. (2015). Our metrics, ourselves: A hundred years of self tracking from the weight scale to the wrist wearable device. *European Journal of Cultural Studies, 18*(4–5), 479–496.

Davidson, J. (2013). Sporting homonationalisms: Sexual exceptionalism, queer privilege and the 21st century international lesbian and gay sport movement. *Sociology of Sport Journal, 30*(1), 57–82.

Esmonde, K., & Jette, S. (2018). Fatness, fitness, and feminism in the built environment: Bringing together physical cultural studies and sociomaterialisms, to study the 'obesogenic environment'. *Sociology of Sport Journal, 35*(1), 39–48.

Foster, L. A. (2016). The making and unmaking of patent ownership: Technicalities, materialities and subjectivities. *PoLAR: Political and Legal Anthropology Review, 39*(1), 127–143.

Foucault, M. (1990). *History of sexuality, vol. 1, an introduction*. New York: Vintage.

Fouché, R. (2012). Aren't athletes cyborgs?: Technology, bodies and sporting competitions. *WSQ: Women's Studies Quarterly, 40*(1&2), 281–293.

Fullagar, S. (2017). Post-qualitative inquiry and the new materialist turn: Implications for sport, health and physical culture research. *Qualitative Research in Sport, Exercise and Health, 9*(2), 247–257.

Haggerty, K. D., & Ericson, R. V. (2000). The surveillant assemblage. *British Journal of Sociology, 51*(4), 605–622.

Haraway, D. (1988). Situated knowledges: The science question in feminism and the privilege of partial perspective. *Feminist Studies, 14*(3), 575–599.

Haraway, D. (1991). *Simians, cyborgs and women: The reinvention of nature.* New York: Routledge.

Harding, S. (1991). *Whose science? Whose knowledge? Thinking from women's lives.* Ithaca, NY: Cornell University Press.

Hargreaves, J. (1994). *Sporting females: Critical issues in the history and sociology of women's sport.* London: Routledge.

Henne, K. (2015). *Testing for athlete citizenship: Regulating doping and sex in sport.* New Brunswick, NJ: Rutgers University Press.

Howe, P. D. (2011). Cyborg and supercrip: The Paralympics technology and the (dis)empowerment of disabled athletes. *Sociology, 45*(5), 868–882.

Kerr, R. (2016). *Sport and technology: An actor-network theory perspective.* Manchester: Manchester University Press.

King, S. (2009). Virtually normal: Mark Bingham, the War on Terror, and the sexual politics of sport. *Journal of Sport & Social Issues, 33*(1), 5–24.

King, S., & Weedon, G. (2016, November 4). *Protein ecologies: Building surplus muscle, regenerating excess whey.* Presentation delivered at the annual meeting of the North American Society for the Sociology of Sport, Tampa, Florida.

Liao, J., & Markula, P. (2016). 'The only thing I am guilty of is taking too many jump shots': A Deleuzian media analysis of Diana Taurasi's drug charge in 2010. *Sociology of Sport Journal, 33*(2), 167–179.

Lowry, D. W. (2004). Understanding reproductive technologies as surveillant assemblage: Revisions of power and technoscience. *Sociological Perspectives, 47*(4), 357–370.

Lupton, D. (2016). Digital companion species and eating data: Implications for theorizing digital data–human assemblages. *Big Data & Society, 3*(1), 1–5.

Magdalinski, T. (2008). *Sport, technology, and the body: The nature of performance.* London: Routledge.

Markula, P. (2003). The technologies of the self: Sport, feminism, and Foucault. *Sociology of Sport Journal, 20*(2), 87–107.

Markula, P. (2018). What is new about new materialism for sport sociology? Reflections on body, movement, and culture. *Sociology of Sport Journal,* online first. https://doi.org/10.1123/ssj.2018-0064.

Maurstad, A., Davis, D., & Cowles, S. (2013). Co-being and intra-action in horse–human relationships: A multi-species ethnography of be(com)ing human and be(com)ing horse. *Social Anthropology, 21*(3), 322–335.

McCullough, S. R. (2010). Body like a rocket: Performing technologies of naturalization. *Thirdspace: A Journal of Feminist Thought and Culture, 9*(2). Retrieved from http://journals.sfu.ca/thirdspace/index.php/journal/article/viewArticle/mccullough.

McDonald, M. G., & Sterling, J. (forthcoming). Feminist new materalisms and the troubling waters of the 2016 Rio de Janeiro Olympic and Paralympic Games. In J. Newman, H. Thorpe, & D. Andrews (Eds.), *Sport, physical culture and the moving body: Materialisms, technologies, ecologies.* New Brunswick, NJ: Rutgers University.

Messner, M. A. (2007). *Out of play: Critical essays on gender and sport.* Albany: State University Press of New York.

Miah, A. (2003). Be afraid, very afraid: Cyborg athletes, transhuman ideals, and posthumanity. *Journal of Evolution & Technology, 13.* Retrieved from https://www.jetpress.org/volume13/miah.html.

Moser, I. (2006). Sociotechnical practices and difference: On the interferences between disability, gender, and class. *Science, Technology, & Human Values, 31*(5), 537–564.

Norman, M. E., & Moola, F. (2011). 'Bladerunner or boundary runner'?: Oscar Pistorius, cyborg transgressions and strategies of containment. *Sport in Society, 14*(9), 1265–1279.

Nyberg, D. (2009). Computers, customer service operatives and cyborgs: Intra-actions in call centers. *Organization Studies, 30*(11), 1181–1199.

Ong, A., & Collier, S. J. (Eds.). (2005). *Global assemblages: Technology, politics and ethics as anthropological problems.* Malden, MA: Blackwell.

Patton, P. (1994). Metamorpho-logic: Bodies and powers in *A Thousand Plateaus. Journal of the British Society of Phenomenology, 25*(2), 157–169.

Pink, S., Sumartorjo, S., Lupton, D., & La Bond, C. H. (2017). Mundane data: The routines, contingencies and accomplishments of digital living. *Big Data & Society, 4*(1), 1–12.

Prasad, A. (2017). Biopolitical excess: Techno-social assemblages of stem cell research in India. *Science, Technology and Society, 22*(1), 102–123.

Prins, B. (1995). The ethics of hybrid subjects: Feminist constructivism according to Donna Haraway. *Science, Technology, & Human Values, 20*(1), 352–367.

Puar, J. K. (2007). *Terrorist assemblages: Homonationalism in queer times.* Durham, NC: Duke University Press.

Puar, J. K. (2012). 'I would rather be a cyborg than a goddess': Becoming-intersectional in assemblage theory. *Philosophia, 2*(1), 49–66.

Puar, J. K. (2017). *The right to maim: Debility, capacity, disability*. Durham, NC: Duke University Press.

Rail, G., & Lefebvre, M. R. (2003). Sculling cyborg: Scientific discourses, media representations and the effacement of Silken Laumann's subversive potential. *Recherche sémiotique—Semiotic Inquiry, XXII*(1–2), 3–18.

Sefiha, O., & Reichman, N. (2016). When every test is a winner: Clean cycling, surveillance, and the new preemptive governance. *Journal of Sport & Social Issues, 40*(3), 197–217.

Sluggett, B. (2011). Sport's doping game: Surveillance in the biotech age. *Sociology of Sport Journal, 28*(4), 387–403.

Subramaniam, B. (2009). Moored metamorphoses: A retrospective essay on feminist science studies. *Signs, 34*(4), 951–980.

Swartz, L., & Watermeyer, B. (2008). Cyborg anxiety: Oscar Pistorius and the boundaries of what it means to be human. *Disability & Society, 23*(2), 187–190.

Sykes, H. (2016). Gay pride on stolen land: Homonationalism and settler colonialism at the Vancouver Winter Olympics. *Sociology of Sport Journal, 33*(1), 54–65.

Thorpe, H. (2016). Athletic women's experiences of amenorrhea: Biomedical technologies, somatic ethics and embodied subjectivities. *Sociology of Sport Journal, 33*(1), 1–13.

Travers, A., & Shearman, N. (2017). The Sochi Olympics, celebration capitalism and homonationalist pride. *Journal of Sport & Social Issues, 41*(1), 42–69.

Whelan, C. (2014). Surveillance, security and sporting mega-events: Toward a research agenda on the organization of security networks. *Surveillance & Society, 11*(4), 392–404.

Wilson, M. W. (2009). Cyborg geographies: Towards hybrid epistemologies. *Gender, Place and Culture, 16*(5), 499–516.

Enacting Bodies: The Multiplicity of Whey Protein and the Making of Corporealities

Samantha King and Gavin Weedon

This chapter is about how bodies are enacted—how they are literally brought into being and sustained—and about why Sport Studies scholars should take ontological politics seriously. If bodies are made (and unmade) through practices, not static or given in nature, then their making is a matter of concern, as opposed to an immutable matter of fact (Latour 2004).

Opening up the question of how bodies are enacted means thinking expansively about what constitutes a body. In kinesiology and Sport Studies, bodies in motion are a shared empirical focus. This body is usually understood as a singular, physically-bounded entity whose biological, social, psychological, and phenomenological forma-

S. King (✉)
Queen's University, Kingston, ON, Canada
e-mail: kingsj@queensu.ca

G. Weedon
Nottingham Trent University, Nottingham, UK
e-mail: gavin.weedon@ntu.ac.uk

J. J. Sterling, M. G. McDonald (eds.), *Sports, Society, and Technology*,
https://doi.org/10.1007/978-981-32-9127-0_8

tion, capacities, and behaviours constitute the major objects of study. With few exceptions, these fields have also tended to understand the body as distinctly and distinctively human. Indeed, "humanist" has long been a label that positively distinguishes those scholars with an interest in holistic personhood from those deemed to take a rational, technocratic, and all together colder approach to human kinetics (Ingham 1997). Notwithstanding the merited critiques of technoscientific rationality and instrumental conceptions of the body advanced in Sport Studies (Pronger 2002), we are proposing, instead, a conceptualization of bodies as "indeterminate" (Waterton and Yusoff 2017) organisms that are multiple, variegated, porous, dispersed, and not delimited in advance within the category "human." These bodies are situated in multispecies, organismic, and technoscientific assemblages, co-constituted and co-shaped by the other bodies (bacterial, viral, fungal, animal, vegetable, digital, etc.) with which they intra-act (Barad 2007). This relational emphasis is important, lest we be read as (re)instantiating a naturalistic and pre-discursive body, albeit in plural form. Our interest, on the contrary, lies in exploring the particular contexts and practices out of which bodies materialize (King and Weedon accepted).

In our work we are engaging with feminist philosophers, Science and Technology Studies (STS) scholars, and political ecologists, whose shared concern lies with the process of how objects (such as bodies) materialize. Deleuze and Guattari (1987) call the extension of the body beyond its discreetly organic composition *agencement* or assemblage; Donna Haraway (2008) writes about bodies "becoming-with" the full gamut of life in the biosphere amid technoscientific practices, and Karen Barad (2007) argues for the performativity of matter (including biological matter) to materialize without the prerequisite of discursive arrangements to animate its capacities or propel it into motion. Once bodies are opened up in the various ways that these authors invite, what counts as and constitutes "a body" shifts accordingly.

Each of these authors and their fields of study make distinct contributions to apprehending what Rosi Braidotti (2016, p. 13) has called the "posthuman predicament": the multispecies, ecological, technoscientific embeddedness of human embodiment at a time of converging economic, social, and environmental crises. Unable to fully survey these crises and attempts to comprehend them (see Braidotti 2018), we delimit our focus in this chapter to how one particular author's approach can help sport and exercise scholars study and capture the ontologically multiple and situated characters of embodiment.

Annemarie Mol is a STS scholar and philosopher whose ethno-graphic research spans illness, care, and food, among other subjects (Berg and Mol 1998; Law and Mol 2002; Mol 2002, 2008; Mol et al. 2010). Like other scholars associated with the STS tradition, Mol's fundamental premise is that reality is performed and materialized through a variety of practices. "The radical consequence" of this insight, according to Mol (1999), is that "reality itself is multiple" (p. 74). In Mol's oeuvre, "the body" (her preferred term) is frequently the reality under investigation, with her work revealing its multiplicity. This is not "only" an epistemological claim, in terms of the disciplinary views we might hold about the body, but a material one, insofar as bodies are distributed across space and time. Mol is at pains to point out that the practices through which the body is "done" are socially, culturally, and economically located and thus malleable. That configurations of practices can shift, and that particular arrangements may be better than others for living and dying well, reveals what is at stake, politically, in her analysis.

Mol's work offers a range of generative biomedical, sociocultural, and philosophical insights about bodies and embodiment, yet outside of this volume her ideas have not been taken up within the study of sport, exercise, or physical culture. Persuaded by the utility of her approach, and of STS more broadly, our aim in what follows is to introduce Mol's concepts for understanding how bodies are made and sustained, and to show how those same concepts help inform and explain our ongoing study of whey protein powder, a nutritional supplement best known for enacting fit and healthy bodies. Let us set the scene for this study.

Over the past three decades, protein has been heralded as a transcendent nutrient—the "old reliable" of fickle dietary regimes. Protein deficiency in the industrialized west is extremely rare, manifesting primarily among a small number of elderly adults, but its association with lean limbs, boundless energy, and physical and intellectual performance has been packaged and sold to consumers with astounding success. The resulting demand for protein-rich and protein-enriched foods sees manufacturers inject amino acids into substances ranging from bread to chocolate bars. Key to their ability to do this, and to protein's ascendance, is whey protein powder, a desiccated byproduct of cheese production that has been hailed by the dairy industry as an eco-friendly manifestation of a substance—liquid whey—that otherwise manifests as troublesome toxic waste. At once a ubiquitous "hidden" ingredient in contemporary processed foods *and* the most popular type of nutritional supplement among the many on sale in this $7 billion market, whey powder has, in the last decade, moved from the niche realm of serious bodybuilding to the cultural mainstream (Millot 2016; Schmidt 2014).

Initially curious about the cultural status of protein powder, we have since expanded our interest to include the physical, material, and ontological status of whey protein and the political-economic, technoscientific, and biocultural practices involved in its reiterative "transcorporeal" journeys (Alaimo 2010). As we explain later in the chapter, we feel it significant to note that whey itself demanded such attention from us, as our research gradually revealed that this was no stable object passing through different contexts—economic, environmental, cultural—but an "indeterminate organism" that contingently and unpredictably co-constitutes the substances, bodies, processes, and technologies with which it comes into contact (Waterton and Yusoff 2017). For Claire Waterton and Kathryn Yusoff (2017), an "indeterminate organism," is "that which is not (and perhaps will never quite be) a thing, a body" (p. 4). We find it useful to understand whey—a mutable, multispecies bodily substance that is irreducible to a classifiable, individual entity (Waterton and Yusoff 2017, p. 9)—in these terms.

Our subsequent focus has been with what whey protein *is* and *does* as it travels and mutates in this manner. In foregrounding ontological politics, we are not discounting questions of capital, empire, and identity that have driven much sociological scholarship on sport, exercise, and physical culture hitherto. On the contrary, and as we hope to show, ontological politics, as elaborated by Mol, help us understand bodies as at once economic and ecological, cultural and biological, social and natural. As whey protein refuses to stay loyal to any singular reality, we have submitted to following it on its travels—and its stops—through and in the indeterminate bodies with which it intra-acts, documenting and deliberating over the versions of embodiment that are enacted along the way.

To open the chapter, we elaborate upon Mol's interrelated concepts of multiplicity and situatedness to demonstrate how bodies are enacted through practice. Here, we set about mapping the horizons of purely perspectival approaches and the stakes of ontological politics. Next, we elaborate how whey protein powder emerges as multiplicity, exceeding and troubling a focus on the supplement's nutritional elements or the individual human embodiment it is designed to mould. Our purpose here is to draw out the implications of a focus on practice and multiplicity for kinesiological research on the body. Finally, we discuss how persistently "following" whey protein led us to broader considerations about body-environment relations, thereby extending the scope of much of Mol's work and demonstrating the ecological embeddedness of the moving body in sport and physical culture.

Annemarie Mol: Multiplicity, Situatedness, and the Body

A Dutch ethnographer and philosopher, Annemarie Mol has been at the forefront of the social studies of science, technology, and medicine over the past two decades. Most well known for her work on the enactment of materially different realities through scientific and corporeal practices in the realm of embodiment, Mol's intellectual project is driven by an interest in how to investigate, and how best to convey, the multiplicity and situatedness of bodies. Her contributions—richly textured accounts of events that range from clinical encounters between doctors and patients, to the everyday experience of eating an apple—are at once theoretical, methodological, and empirical.

In *The Body Multiple: Ontology in Medical Practice*, Mol (2002) draws upon ethnographic work conducted in an atherosclerosis clinic to investigate how medicine "attunes to, interacts with, and shapes its objects" through its "various and varied practices" (p. vii). While a definition of atherosclerosis would usually be well-placed here, Mol's project is to open up the question of what exactly this disease "is," and the role of different medical practices in enacting it. That it is a disease known to inhibit blood circulation, one that predominantly affects elderly people, is only the beginning of what needs to be investigated. Over four years of field-work at a clinic observing patients and doctors and immersing herself in this institutional and intellectual domain, Mol finds that different ver-sions of atherosclerosis are materialized by different kinds of medical practice. Rather than a given, stable object to be analysed, atherosclerosis is shown to be "brought into being, sustained, or allowed to wither away in common, day-to-day, sociomaterial practices" (p. 6).

By focusing on how objects are "enacted," Mol (2002) seeks to shift the terrain of critical studies of bodies and disease away from a perspec-tival approach, in which objects are articulated as singular, passive things about which people hold different views, and towards an approach that centres objects as they come into being—or fall apart—through prac-tices. Implicit in this manoeuvre is a critique of the limits of social con-structivism, insofar as this usually equates to an "addition to existing medical knowledge" (p. 7) by social scientists who cannot comment on, less still complicate, the objectivity of the body itself. Hence, the multi-plicity of atherosclerosis is not "just" an epistemological acknowledge-ment but an empirical observation, supporting the bolder claim that "[n]o object, no body, no disease, is singular" (p. 6).

Importantly, Mol is interested in how "versions" of the body are coor-dinated in particular scenes or locations. By "versions" she means mani-festations of disparate kinds of bodies, at once physical and social, that emerge as "events in *time*" in "different circumstances" (2012, p. 513). Her project is to understand how such versions are held together, without allowing them to "recede" behind interpretation (2002, p. 12) in ways that reinscribe perspectival approaches. She writes: "[A]s long as the prac-ticalities of enacting a disease are kept unbracketed, out in the open, the varieties of 'atherosclerosis' multiply" (p. 51). In her fieldwork, different versions of atherosclerosis (the anatomical version, the physiological ver-sion, the daily life version) are shown to accompany different versions of the body (a spatial body served by arteries narrowed through the accumu-lation of plaque; a processual body that is transformed by the buildup of plaque over time; a lived with body that experiences pain upon walking). Such distinctions not only are interesting but hold "practical consequences": regular walking can help solve a patient's pain but it doesn't increase the width of their veins (Mol 2018, p. 3). These different versions of the body are neither entirely distinct nor reducible to one another, for even as the body is multiple, "it still hangs together" (2002, p. 55). If we take this approach, we begin to see, with Mol, that bodies are "more than one and less than many" (2002, p. 55).

This interest in coordination stems from one of Mol's foremost influences, actor-network theory (ANT). Developed through laboratory ethnographies that sought to observe science in action (i.e., science as it is practised; see Latour and Woolgar 1979), ANT outlines a series of methodological premises discernable in Mol's work, notably the importance of tracing how one's object of inquiry is made—quite literally—through its connectivity with other "actors" (Latour 2005). Actors are understood not (necessarily) as human subjects but as things, substances, and forces that perform certain functions in holding an object (such as atherosclerosis) together. Thus, atherosclerosis emerges through its association with actors (or "actants" when they are in the process of modifying other actors) such as stethoscopes, patients and patient disclosures, doctors and doctors prescriptions, blood vessels, clots, and tests, hospitals, treatments, and medical knowledges. And, in the pathbreaking contribution of Mol's work, it manifests in different forms depending on its tethering to particular actors. Mol's contention is that the atherosclerosis clinic is not so much a site for contestation between competing accounts or "versions" of the disease, but instead incubates the multiplicity of these versions as they multiply in a situated clinical context. Continuity and coordination are the key interactions in her analysis, but if situated in a different clinic, scene, or context, things could be otherwise.

Mol extends the work of *The Body Multiple* in a provocatively titled essay, "Layers or Versions: Human Bodies and the Love of Bitterness" (2012), by posing a question that preoccupies many a theorist of embodiment and technology: How can social science researchers best capture the fleshiness and physicality of the human body in their work? Traditionally, Mol notes, researchers have conceptualized the body in layers, with the singular, natural, physical entity assumed to lie underneath the learned and constructed social skin. Building on the critique of the "addition of the social" put forth in *The Body Multiple*, she writes: "In a layered reality the body is just a single thing. It may have many abilities that can each be observed from a variety of perspectives, but when it comes to it 'the body' *is* a unity, a whole" (2012, p. 11). This conceptualization, Mol argues, works in tandem with a disciplinary divide that tasks biologists with studying the body's physicality and social scientists with studying how the body is shaped by culture, politics, the economy, and so on.

The same issue also animates Mol's recent collaborative research on omega-3 supplementation (Abrahamsson et al. 2015), in which the enactment of reality through practices is again the central claim. Here, though, the objective is as much to complicate the claims of the en vogue "new" materialisms as it is to open up the multiplicity of commodified fish oil. The accusation levelled here at "new" materialists—and Jane Bennett's (2010) vitalist brand of materialism in particular—is that, in taking up the lesson that matter and things be recognized as active, even vital, in social science and humanities research, they have veered too close to a detached realism in which things act autonomously. Abrahamsson et al.'s counterclaim, borne of an STS-inspired study of scientific methods addressed to omega-3's health benefits, is that "omega-3 is not matter *itself* all by itself, but rather matter *in context*. It is engaged in many relations" (Abrahamsson et al. 2015, p. 5, original emphasis). Thus, the authors advocate for a relational materialism, in which ontology (reality) can never be untethered from epistemology (knowledge-making and representation). The ancient philosophical debate about reality and its mediation cannot be rehearsed here, though it is of continuing relevance to those scholars interested in the making of the athletic body and its relation to technoscience. That said, the following passage on the alteration of bodies through the practice of ingestion is akin to what we have observed in the movements of whey protein, and thus warrants quotation in full:

> [O]mega-3, absorbed and transformed into a part of a human body, is a very peculiar example of nonhuman agency. For, as a mode of doing, *eating* crucially includes transforming: food into eater and eater into a well-fed rather than an undernourished creature. But, as it is through eating and feeding that diverse beings or substances fuse, in the end you never quite

know *who or what has done it.* Has omega-3 acted, or, since you absorbed it, have you? Eating interferes with 'doing' in a fascinating way not just by relating the creatures and substances that 'do', but also, crucially, irreversibly, by transforming them—and their agential abilities. (Abrahamsson et al. 2015, p. 15)

Note that adjudicating who has done what to whom (or what) gives way to observing and carefully documenting the "transformations" that occur in situated encounters between bodies of all kinds.

By way of summary, Mol's contention is that objects of inquiry are not only affected by perception (epistemology) but enacted through practice (ontology). That is to say, the substance of the world and its bringing-into-being through contextually contingent knowledge-making practices and technological devices are entwined. It would not be controversial to state that there exist different perspectives on bodies, diseases, and so on. Indeed, kinesiology departments are comprised of precisely this multidisciplinary model, where biomechanists, sociologists, psychologists, physiologists, historians, and others bring their disparate disciplinary expertise to bear on a common object of study: the moving body. As Mol points out, though, such "perspectivalism" implies a stable object to which different lenses can be applied (and, accordingly, a stable concept of objectivity at its centre). Mol's contention is more radical and more consequential. To say that objects are situated is to say that they emerge differently depending on the knowledge-making apparatus to which they are tethered.

Versions of Whey Protein

It would be possible to study whey protein powder from a variety of perspectives (biochemical, nutritional, political-economic, feminist, Foucauldian) and to produce a provocative analysis, critical or otherwise, of its numerous biological and social functions (adequate nutrition, muscle replenishment, biopolitical governance) to which various cultural meanings (strength, energy, longevity, masculinity, whiteness, responsibility, freedom) are ascribed. Indeed, this is the multidisciplinary format that predominates in kinesiology and sport and exercise science. But to what would we be referring when we spoke of "whey protein powder" in such an analysis? A sequence of amino acids? A dehydrated milk product? A bovine bodily substance? A solution to dairy industry waste? A scoop of nutritional powder? A component of the recommended daily allowance? A hegemonic "health" food? Foregrounding this question might lay us open to the accusation that we remain stuck in the register of representation. Yet probing what whey protein is, identifying the profusion of signifieds to which it alludes, can begin to nudge us away from a focus on "gathering knowledge—whether objective or subjective" about a stable object and towards a focus on multiplicity and the variety of contexts in which whey protein is done (Mol and Law 2004, p. 45).

To illustrate whey protein's multiplicity, we might begin by considering whey at the scene where it materializes at the dairy processing plant. Here, whey is made—and makes itself known—as the liquid that remains from milk and cheese production. Whey has always been part of the cheese-making process, but the industrialization of agriculture through the twentieth century led to unprecedented dairy production capacities and, in turn, an unprecedented surplus of whey waste. About 90.5 billion pounds of whey effluent are generated by the U.S. cheese-making industry alone each year (United States Department of Agriculture 2014). This protein- and acid-rich substance manifests as an environmentally devastating toxin if leached into groundwater or discarded in waterways, which was its fate in many North American contexts through the last century (Lougheed 2013). While intentional dumping has declined in the face of greater regulation, whey spills, which result in aquatic algae blooms and oxygen depletion, continue to occur (Bergquist 2008; Environmental Protection Agency 2011; James 2015). Thus, this version of whey, a toxic byproduct of dairy production, is enacted in ways that pose problems to the plants and fish that become starved of the oxygen they need to survive, and subsequently to the dairy researchers, manufacturers, and engineers tasked with mitigating toxicity at its point of co-production.

Like all versions, though, this iteration of whey is situated. In this instance, it is the commodification of whey protein in North American dairy farms that warrants our scrutiny. Geoffrey Smithers, who declares funding from dairy industry sources, has extolled the 50 years of innovation in whey protein manufacture. In a celebratory storying of whey protein's commodification, he notes that "increases in the value of [whey] products in an increasingly sophisticated marketplace have resulted in enhanced wealth to dairy manufacturers and the communities that rely on them" (2008, p. 702). Notwithstanding an ominously undefined notion of dependent "communities," Smithers is correct. Working with the version of whey protein that is co-produced in industrialized dairy farms, the commodification of whey "from gutter to good" and "good to gold" (Smithers 2008, p. 695) is a triumph for industry: a harmonious joining of technoscientific innovation and economic imperatives that convert a toxic waste byproduct into a healthy, popular consumer product that is fed to both human and nonhuman animals. The enactment of this reality is premised on a series of technoscientific practices—concentration, separation, and drying of whey to make it more versatile and palatable for consumption—that bring into being the desiccated powder that presently lines store shelves and is infused into all manner of products.

Our analysis might end here, or we might thicken the story by elaborating on legislation designed to deter Big Dairy from whey dumping, or the plight of incarcerated cows whose lives are organized in the service of producing milk, or the implications for the more-than-human communities still exposed to the pungent toxicity of whey waste because of lack of oversight or accidental spills, but the version in question and the scene of enactment would stay essentially the same.

Many readers will know that this version of whey protein, focused as it is on the moments and consequences of its materialization as a toxin, is by no means the most prevalent in kinesiological, nutritional, or sport and exercise circles. If we centre these circles instead, whey is enacted through its purchase in ready-to-eat items like protein bars or as a supplement to be incorporated, by the consumer, into smoothies, baked goods, or other snacks and meals. The quantity and timing of its ingestion is the subject of both countless physiological studies and inexhaustible "protein talk" among buyers seeking to extract optimal value from this nutritional resource valued for its untold health promises and fitness-enhancing capacities. Its processing and repurposing for consumer use—that is, its enactment first as poison and then as panacea—are not part of this version of whey protein. For the dairy industry, in other words, whey protein has become an economic solution to the environmental hazards and species threats presented by the dumping of untreated waste, its status as a versatile and popular commodity helping to offset the costs associated with its technoscientific transformation. But for kinesiologists and their ilk, whey protein is a solution for a very different set of problems, most often those related to building and sustaining musculature, but also, and increasingly, to a broader variety of issues ranging from sluggish cognition to problem pregnancies.

The complexity and specificity of this picture are further heightened when we consider how the bodies implied by the different versions of whey protein vary. In the agricultural and food engineering version of whey, when protein is enacted as a waste stream that must be disposed of, or an edible repurposed from a toxin, the bodies of the humans and agricultural animals to whom it is fed manifest as consumer-processors whose finicky tastes and digestive systems must be accommodated through innovations in processing that make whey transportable, preservable, and safe and palatable to eat. An exercise physiology version of protein, in contrast, brings into being a body made of components and dimensions that shift in accordance with variables such as diet and exercise. Protein intake can affect this body's size, shape, and mass and the job of the exercise physiologist is to determine optimal protein intake. A daily life version of whey protein, where whey is enacted as muscle (through the efficacious constellation of exercise, sleep, broader nutrition, lactose tolerance, and more), materializes the body as an ongoing project, a valuable investment that requires constant maintenance.

Critically minded readers might imagine that the multiplicity of whey protein and its corporealities exist in a paradoxical state that can be revealed to the initiated and enlightened eye. For example, and as we have already suggested, there is an apparent contradiction in the contemporary uptick in protein consumption in regions where protein deficiency is extremely rare. Why produce and consume unprecedented amounts of something our bodies are not lacking? We might also envisage that the versions of protein enacted through particular practices—production, consumption, ingestion, filtration—are at odds with each other, at least in the eyes of scientists trained to help bring particular, disciplinary, versions into view. Where the exercise physiologist sees muscle mass increases and subsequent health benefits, the sociologist might see the cultural pressures to build and sustain muscle, control weight, or mitigate ageing. The ecologist, on the other hand, might find greenhouse gas emissions and contaminated air, soil and water stemming from the ongoing overproduction of milk, to which whey protein powder offers only a band-aid solution.

Just as Mol's approach dissuades us from asking whether one of these versions is true, and from presuming that social context is "layered" on top of the natural matter of the body, it also guards against the a priori suspicion that different realities will necessarily conflict with one another. To give one example, the dairy industry version of whey powder does not necessarily undermine or run counter to the exercise physiology version of whey powder. Indeed, the industry has been a major sponsor of physiological research on protein supplementation, such that these versions are, at certain moments—though not infinitely or predictably—coordinated. Whereas the clash of dialectical forces or competing ideologies often implies a single, contested reality over which different parties struggle, the premise here is that reality itself is multiple, and crucially, *no less real for being enacted*. This means taking seriously the versions of reality which one might be tempted to discard as false, partial, or limited, and to understand them as coterminous, coordinated, and only possibly contested. As Mol (2002, p. 5) puts it, "[t]he driving question no longer is 'how to find the truth?' but 'how are objects handled in practice?'"

Of course, guarding against suppositions of conflicting realities does not mean that such engagements will be tension free, or that the bodies or versions of protein that emerge from such an approach will harmonize in a kind of multidisciplinary nirvana free of politics or power. As Mol herself writes, "[R]ather than a whole, the body *is* a list. The entries on the list are not necessarily coherent. They may have linkages between them, but also tensions. They do not fit within a single set of coordinates" (Mol 2012, p. 539). But moving away from a model in which physical scientists explain the substance and activities of whey protein up to a certain level (their truth), at which point the social scientists take over (our truth), allows different question to emerge. To paraphrase Mol's list of such questions: How do different versions of protein happen to relate in practice? What kind of frictions are there between them? And where and how do they depend on one another? What is linked up with different versions of protein and how might specific configurations be valued? In this approach, "explanation is no longer the horizon of our inquiries. Articulation is" (p. 11). "Rather than a quest for mechanisms," Mol continues, "research comes to resemble a cartographic exploration. A different model of intervention ensues" (p. 11). For Mol, this model entails not the adjustment of physical or social variables to produce a different outcome, but reflection on the version of the body, or protein, we wish to value or fortify, "where, when and how" (p. 11).

More-Than-Human Multiplicities and the Moving Body in Sport Studies

In keeping with Mol's emphasis on the specificity and situatedness of knowledge production, it is important to note that her approach is not a template to be applied to any and all contexts. Nor, for that matter, has it been our only guide for understanding the complex, circuitous journey of whey protein through bodies multiple. By way of conclusion, we continue our pursuit of whey out of the bodies that consume it as a way to consider the horizons of Mol's insights. We focus on two key points: ontological politics beyond the limits of social constructivism and the place of the environment in analyses of the moving body.

That the body is multiple is at once a radical constructivist claim and perhaps an understatement. While Mol demonstrates how socio-material practices enact different versions of bodies within specific contexts, her approach stops short of fully expressing the physical, material mutations that occur as bodies are enacted, or the agentic capacities of bodies to frustrate or exceed the demands of the practices and instruments designed to regulate them. In our efforts to "follow" whey on its circuitous travels, we have been struck by the shape-shifting character of this slippery substance, not least its shift from toxic byproduct of dairy production to ostensibly healthy and valuable commodity. With Mol, it is worth emphasizing here the significance of the economic, environmental, technoscientific, and sociocultural practices implicated in these multiplicitous enactments. For example, whey's desiccation into powder is made possible by innovations in filtration, concentration, and drying techniques, innovations that followed from environmental concerns about whey dumping in public waterways, though these innovations have been driven as much by economic imperatives to produce more milk as by environmental activism and policy aimed at addressing pollution. Agency here is not so much an attribute of whey as it is a relational outcome of its co-constitutions and effects. That said, there is also a sense in which whey compelled its own methodological pursuit; for whey's proclivity to alter and eclipse the bodies it encounters demanded a persistence on our part, and led us to move beyond familiar economic and cultural analytical terrain—and beyond Mol to a certain extent. Just as "sociomaterial practices" (Mol 2002, p. 6) bring about the enactment of multiplicitous phenomena, so those phenomena partake in and *make a difference to* those practices. Here we are navigating with care debates about agency, particularly the agency of nonhuman matter, in which Mol has herself been engaged, as both exemplar and critic (Abrahamsson et al. 2015).

The crucial point for us is that whey protein does not disappear—its effects do not halt—at the point of production, where a political-economic analysis, critical or otherwise, might cease; nor does it disappear following consumption, where a biomedical or constructionist analysis might cease; nor does it disappear as it is embodied and felt, where a phenomenological, sociological, or psychological analysis might cease. While Mol's approach encourages us to explore how whey is done in each of these disciplinary contexts, what it does not necessarily invite is an exploration of whey protein's movement *across* space and time, or of the ways in which it changes shape, form, and purpose along the way, reflecting but also confounding knowledge regimes and practices. Thus, if our analysis were to stop—if we did not remain alert and sensitive to the dynamic materiality of protein—we might not think to ask what happens to these assemblages of amino acids following their ingestion and metabolism by the humans and animals incorporated into their recycling. That is, we might not question what happens to the excess of this rich nitrogenous nutrient content—the very biochemical properties that give whey its appeal as a dietary supplement—as it is excreted. And we might not come to understand that whey's ecological entanglements endure as the protein-rich urine of humans and animals manifests as nitrogen pollution—"one of the most pressing environmental issues that we face" (Erisman et al. 2013, p. 3).

Thus, whey's proclivity is not "only" an intellectual curiosity, just as it not attributable to some alchemic property or singular capacity. Attentiveness to the liveliness of its movements through social relations eventually led us, quite literally, to consider the role of nitrogen-dense protein in the problem of nitrogen pollution, and to understand this not as an extraneous "environmental issue" but as one that is intimately entangled with corporeality, with economic imperatives, and with the cultural status of protein. The precise dynamics of whey protein's relation with nitrogen pollution remain an open question for us, one that is complicated by the complex role of synthetic nitrogen fertilizer, which is cast as both hero and villain in relation to global population growth. Human and animal excretion is just one of a multitude of sources of anthropogenic nitrogen pollution, with synthetic nitrogen fertilizer, which acidifies soils and leaches into drinking water, rivers, and seas, representing the major source of reactive nitrogen in the environment. While the world's population cannot presently be fed without the use of industrially produced fertilizer (Page 2016), the demand for protein-rich foods has exacerbated nitrogen pollution. Even before humans consume a protein shake, then, substantial volumes of nitrogen are lost to the environment through the cultivation of feed for the cattle who produce the milk, and yet more are lost in the cows' manure.

Thus, if we recognize and take seriously the multiplicity of whey, approach it as *matter in context* while also attending to how it actively reshapes those contexts, we come to see that there is neither a simple solution to the problems it poses nor a simple problem to which it emerges as a solution. Whether in its materialization as toxic byproduct of the cheese-making process, or as nitrogen pollution in wastewater systems, whey inevitably confounds attempts to purify its properties and harness its value. And the problems to which whey responds ultimately precede its enactment as an excess of milk production. Indeed, "it" is no longer it in this extension of Mol's framework. Whey has become something else, and that something else in turn mutates as other versions are enacted within a multiplicity of contexts—large scale industrial agriculture, environmental remediation, climate change, shifts in the global diet—that appear to hang together (there is no world shortage of protein yet!), even as relations among them are uncertain, complex, and contested.

Finally, whey's persistent ecological entanglements have encouraged us to think anew about body-environment relations in kinesiology and Sport Studies. Mol's focus seldom broadens to consider environmental issues, and though her approach is not antithetical to doing so, there are several fields of inquiry concerned with how ecological issues intra-act with health and embodiment that seem relevant here (Guthman and Mansfield 2012; Senanayake and King 2017). Sport Studies and kinesiology are curiously not among these fields, despite the well-established "turn to the body" in recent decades and despite a growing literature on sport and the environment (Bunds and Casper 2018; Millington and Wilson 2016). Whey protein is an "unruly" object insofar as it will not be contained to either of these categories, bodily or environmental, and as such it invites explorations of how athletic bodies are quite literally entangled in ecologies, shifting shape and meaning in rhythm with social relations. The body enacted in these scenes might not present itself as a body at all, at least not in the received terms of an athletic body: whole, bounded, and human. Whey remains elusive in this sense, an "indeterminate" organism that gives cause to follow its enactments across bodily borders.

References

Abrahamsson, S., Bertoni, F., Mol, A., & Martin, R. I. (2015). Living with omega-3: New materialism and enduring concerns. *Environment and Planning D: Society and Space, 33*, 4–19.

Alaimo, S. (2010). *Bodily natures: Science, environment and the material self.* Bloomington: University of Indiana Press.

Barad, K. (2007). *Meeting the universe halfway: Quantum physics and the entanglement of matter and meaning.* London: Duke University Press.

Bennett, J. (2010). *Vibrant matter: A political ecology of things.* Durham, NC: Duke University Press.

Berg, M., & Mol, A. (1998). *Differences in medicine: Unraveling practices, techniques and bodies.* Durham, NC: Duke University Press.

Bergquist, L. (2008, October 31). Dairy plant to pay fine in river whey spill that killed fish. *Journal Sentinel.* Retrieved from http://archive.jsonline.com/news/wisconsin/33670594.html/.

Braidotti, R. (2016). Posthuman critical theory. In D. Banerji & M. R. Paranjape (Eds.), *Critical posthumanism and planetary futures* (pp. 13–32). Springer, India.

Braidotti, R. (2018). A theoretical framework for the critical posthumanities. *Theory, Culture and Society*, Online First.

Bunds, K., & Casper, J. (2018). Sport, physical culture, and the environment: An introduction. *Sociology of Sport Journal, 35*, 1–7.

Deleuze, G., & Guattari, F. (1987). *A thousand plateaus: Capitalism and schizophrenia*. Minneapolis, MN: University of Minnesota Press.

Environmental Protection Agency. (2011). Summary of criminal prosecutions. Retrieved from https://cfpub.epa.gov/compliance/criminal_prosecution/index.cfm?action=3&prosecution_sumary_id=2138.

Erisman, J., Galloway, J., Dise, N., Sutton, M., Bleeker, A., Grizzetti, B., et al. (2013). *Nitrogen: Too much of a vital resource*. World Wildlife Fund Netherlands. Retrieved from http://www.nprint.org/WWFReport.

Guthman, J., & Mansfield, B. (2012). The implications of environmental epigenetics: A new direction for geographic inquiry on health, space, and nature-society relations. *Progress in Human Geography, 37*(4), 486–504.

Haraway, D. (2008). *When species meet*. Minneapolis, MN: University of Minnesota Press.

Ingham, A. G. (1997). Toward a department of physical cultural studies and an end to tribal warfare. In J. M. Fernandez-Balboa (Ed.), *Critical postmodernism in human movement, physical education, and sport* (pp. 157–182). Albany: State University of New York Press.

James, M. (2015). Cheese whey spill: $80,000 fine. Retrieved from https://www.siskinds.com/envirolaw/cheese-whey-spill-80000-fine/.

King, S., & Weedon, G. (Accepted). Embodiment is ecological: The metabolic lives of whey protein powder. *Body & Society*.

Latour, B. (2004). Why has critique run out of steam? From matters of fact to matters of concern. *Critical Inquiry, 30*, 225–248.

Latour, B. (2005). *Reassembling the social: An introduction to actor-network theory*. Oxford: Oxford University Press.

Latour, B., & Woolgar, S. (1979). *Laboratory life: The construction of scientific facts*. Beverly Hills: Sage.

Law, J., & Mol, A. (2002). *Complexities: Social studies of knowledge practices*. Durham, NC: Duke University Press.

Lougheed, S. (2013). *An actor-network theory examination of cheese and whey production in Ontario* (Unpublished master's thesis). Queen's University, Kingston, Ontario.

Millington, B., & Wilson, B. (2016). *The greening of golf: Sport, globalization and the environment.* Oxford: Oxford University Press.

Millot, J. (2016, December 22). Do you even lift bro? Weighing protein powder performance online. *1010Data.* Retrieved from https://www.1010data.com/company/blog/do-you-even-lift-broweighing-protein-powder-performance-online/.

Mol, A. (1999). Ontological politics: A word and some questions. *The Sociological Review, 47*(1), 74–89.

Mol, A. (2002). *The body multiple: Ontology in medical practice.* Durham, NC: Duke University Press.

Mol, A. (2008). *The logic of care: Health and the problem of patient choice.* London: Routledge.

Mol, A. (2012). Layers or versions? Human bodies and the love of bitterness. In B. Turner (Ed.), *The Routledge handbook of the body* (pp. 119–129). New York: Routledge.

Mol, A. (2018). Multiple bodies, political ontologies, and the logic of care: An interview with Annemarie Mol. D. Martin, M. J. Spink & P. P. G. Pereira. *Interface: Comunicação Saúde Educação, 22*(6), 5–8.

Mol, A., & Law, J. (2004). Embodied action, enacted bodies: The example of hypoglycaemia. *Body & Society, 10*(2–3), 43–62.

Mol, A., Mosser, I., & Pols, J. (Eds.). (2010). *Care in practice: On tinkering in clinics, homes and farms.* New York: Columbia University Press.

Page, A. (2016). 'The greatest victory which the chemist has won in the fight (…) against Nature': Nitrogenous fertilizers in Great Britain and the British Empire, 1910s–1950s. *History of Science, 54*(4), 383–398.

Pronger, B. (2002). *Body fascism: Salvation in the technology of physical fitness.* Toronto: University of Toronto Press.

Schmidt, C. (2014, April 8–9). The rise of protein in the global health and wellness and supplement arenas. *Global Food Forums.* Retrieved from https://www.globalfoodforums.com/wpcontent/uploads/2014/04/Chris-Schmidt-Euromonitor-2014-Protein-Trends-Technologies.pdf.

Senanayake, N., & King, B. (2017). Health-environment futures: Complexity, uncertainty, and bodies. *Progress in Human Geography*, Online First.

Smithers, G. (2008). Whey and whey proteins: From 'gutter-to-gold'. *International Dairy Journal, 18*(7), 695–704.

United States Department of Agriculture. (2014). *Whey to ethanol: A biofuel role for dairy cooperatives?* Research Report 214. Retrieved from http://www.rd. usda.gov/files/RR214.pdf1.01.

Waterton, C., & Yusoff, K. (2017). Indeterminate bodies: Introduction. *Body & Society, 23*(3), 3–22.

The (In)Active Body Multiple: An Examination of How Prenatal Exercise 'Matters'

Shannon Jette and Katelyn Esmonde

Dominant medical advice around exercise during pregnancy has changed significantly in the United States over the past three decades. When the American College of Obstetricians and Gynecologists (ACOG) released its first guidelines in 1985, they cautioned against overexerting the pregnant body, a position informed largely by a legacy of gendered ideologies about the inherent fragility of female bodies (Jette 2011; see also Verbrugge 2012 and Vertinsky 1994). For instance, it was stated that "[a]lthough the risk of fetal injury is probably small, there are insufficient scientific data to support this belief. Therefore, exercise recommendations should err on the conservative side" (ACOG 1985, p. 316). One of the concerns about prenatal exercise was its potential to limit fetal growth and cause 'small for gestational age' (SGA) infants (Hopkins and Cutfield 2011; see also Jette 2011).

S. Jette (✉)
University of Maryland, College Park, MD, USA
e-mail: jette@umd.edu

K. Esmonde
Johns Hopkins University, Baltimore, MD, USA
e-mail: kesmond1@jhu.edu

© The Author(s) 2020
J. J. Sterling, M. G. McDonald (eds.), *Sports, Society, and Technology*,
https://doi.org/10.1007/978-981-32-9127-0_9

In contrast, the most recent 2015 ACOG Committee Opinion on the topic urges obstetric care providers to encourage their patients "to continue or to commence exercise as an important component of optimal health" (ACOG 2015, p. 2). Perhaps even more significant is the emphasis on the risk of *not* exercising: "physical inactivity and excessive weight gain have been recognized as independent risk factors for maternal obesity and related pregnancy complications, including gestational diabetes mellitus" (p. 2). A 'complication' not mentioned in the above quote, but which is central to the growing emphasis on the risk of physical inactivity, is a concern that excessive weight gain during pregnancy—which is purportedly on the rise—contributes to 'large for gestational age' (LGA) babies and ultimately, the epidemic of childhood obesity (Hopkins and Cutfield 2011; see also Jette and Rail 2013). Thus, earlier cautions that physical activity might negatively impact the fetus, in part by limiting fetal size, have shifted to optimism that prenatal exercise can help reduce the incidence of excessive 'gestational weight gain' (GWG) and LGA infants, even though scientific evidence about the impact of exercise on fetal growth is conflicting (Hopkins and Cutfield 2011).

The optimism that prenatal exercise can allegedly help prevent childhood obesity is informed by the rapidly growing field of Developmental Origins of Health and Disease (DOHaD) and the related field of environmental epigenetics which seek to demonstrate how 'exposures' in the womb or early postnatal life can influence developmental pathways, in effect 'programming' the fetus for future chronic disease or preventing it (Waterland and Michels 2007). Exposures of interest are often environmental, meaning that they focus on material factors such as air pollution or pesticide exposure and psychosocial factors such as emotional stress (Müller et al. 2017). The focus on environmental stimuli also extends to lifestyle practices, with physical inactivity during pregnancy posited as a behavior that influences the maternal environment and, by extension, maternal obesity (Blaize et al. 2015; see also Jette et al. 2017). It is against this backdrop that the risk of physical inactivity has taken on new significance and become the target of intervention by health researchers and practitioners.

In this chapter, we explore how this particular caution about prenatal exercise—the risk of physical inactivity—has come to 'matter' in the contemporary moment. Our use of matter has a double meaning (Barad 2008; Butler 1993). We use it as a verb to denote our interest in examining the significance of prenatal exercise in the present moment, and we use it as a noun to refer to 'matter' as a physical or material entity. With the latter, we build upon scholarship from the field of Science and Technology Studies (STS) which has been influential in bringing awareness to the role of material entities such as laboratory equipment—and related material-discursive practices such as lab work—in shaping social life (Latour and Woolgar 1986; Mol 2002). Feminist STS scholars have been important contributors to this focus on the entanglement of the material and social (Barad 2008; Haraway 1985, 2003). More specific to our focus in this chapter, feminist STS scholars (Balsamo 1996; Casper 1998; Mamo 2007) have explored the merging of human and non-human as well as the merger of subject and object in the technoscientific practices of reproduction.

The emergent fields of DOHaD and epigenetics are of particular interest when bringing materiality to social inquiry, including as it relates to the (in)active pregnant body. STS scholars (Kenney and Müller 2017; Landecker 2011; Meloni 2016; Müller et al. 2017), as well as researchers in the neighboring fields of feminist materialisms (Frost 2011, 2016; Warin 2015) and geography (Guthman 2012; Guthman and Mansfield 2013), note the potential of DOHaD and/or epigenetics to open space for theorizing the human body as indistinct from the social. They also suggest that these frameworks potentially support a social justice agenda as emergent research in the fields of DOHaD and epigenetics demonstrate how social and material inequities literally get 'under the skin' and are manifested in population health disparities. Scholars exploring DOHaD and epigenetics as they relate to obesity note these frameworks' potential to disrupt the overly simplistic and oft-stigmatizing narratives dominant in mainstream obesity science (Guthman 2012; Guthman and Mansfield 2013; Warin 2015; Yoshizawa 2012). Guthman (2012, 2014), for instance, points to research suggesting that pathways to obesity have less to do with access to food or genetics, and can instead be traced to environmental exposures such as chronic stress, endocrine disrupting chemicals (EDCs), and undernourishment in utero, all of which alter developmental pathways via epigenetic mechanisms—regardless of calories consumed. Such findings, she suggests, bring attention to structural inequities that produce higher rates of pollution, chronic stress, and under-nutrition in disenfranchised communities, especially in communities of color.

However, critical scholars' optimism that DOHaD and epigenetics might offer fresh theoretical possibilities and inform a social justice agenda is tempered by the recognition that the life sciences have historically been—and continue to be—bound up with political projects that "exacerbate and perpetuate inequality and injustice" (Frost 2016, p. 14; see also Müller et al. 2017). A common concern across the work of these scholars (Müller et al. 2017; Richardson et al. 2014), including those focused on maternal obesity (Mansfield and Guthman 2015; McNaughton 2011; Warin et al. 2011), is that despite the potential to challenge genetic and behavioral determinism by focusing on how the environment shapes health outcomes, scientific research on DOHaD and epigenetics often is not mobilized in such a fashion. Collectively, these scholars have demonstrated how DOHaD and epigenetic theories are enacted in ways that promote a narrow view of the environment, often reducing it to the uterine environment and thus rendering pregnant women as responsible for managing their behaviors. Simultaneously, the myriad factors that shape maternal health and childhood development over the life course and across generations are often ignored.

Our chapter contributes to this body of STS and related scholarship by attending to DOHaD as applied to the physically (in)active pregnant body, a topic not yet engaged using the tools and techniques of STS scholarship which we describe in more detail below. In doing so, we also build upon the scholarship of those who have developed Foucault's (2003) concept of governmentality to examine how 'risk' has functioned as a technique of governance, one of the "heterogeneous governmental strategies of … power by which populations and individuals are monitored and managed so as to best meet the goals of democratic humanism" (Lupton 1999, p. 4; see also Rose 2007). Feminist Foucauldian scholars, in particular, have illustrated how 'risk' has become a central construct around which pregnancy is framed in both the popular and medical realm such that women are pressed to manage an ever-increasing number of risk factors in order to be considered a responsible mother (see Lupton

1999; Weir 2006). Following this line of feminist Foucauldian scholarship, Jette (2017, 2018) has argued that across varying historical contexts, and as enacted through differing exercise prescriptions, prenatal exercise 'risk' functions as a technique of governance intended to discipline individual pregnant bodies while regulating population health. The result is that women are pressured to be 'fit for two', whether it be by cautioning against the risk of doing 'too much' and/or advising against the risk of not doing 'enough'.

In this chapter, we extend previous feminist Foucauldian analyses by tracing the networks of material relations that make the risk of not doing enough 'matter' in the contemporary moment. In doing so, we move beyond the Foucauldian tendency to treat risk as a social construct without sufficiently attending to its materiality. Rather, we make visible the devices, tools, practices, and techniques mobilized to enact risk pertaining to prenatal exercise. Within STS scholarship, we look in particular to Mol's (2002) concept of the body multiple which demonstrates that there is not just one version or 'truth' of the body, but multiple versions that are performed by differing health professionals depending upon where they are enacting and with what assemblage of equipment and/or methods (Mol 1998, 2002). Thus, we attend to the material practices mobilized to enact a particular version of prenatal exercise—despite the fact that multiple versions exist, including both the risk of activity during pregnancy and the risk of inactivity during pregnancy as they relate to fetal size. As such, we also bring to our analysis a feminist STS concern with the gendered politics of knowledge production (see Haraway 1988, 1997).

Our empirical site of investigation is the growing number of physical activity interventions that are intended to help women manage their weight gain during pregnancy. We view these interventions as exemplifying the current trend toward cautioning women against being inactive during pregnancy with the aim of improving the health of two generations (mother and child). Our analysis looks at 'practices'; that is to say, although we examine interventions discursively via the text of medical journals, we also seek to make visible the network of relations mobilized in interventions—both human and non-human—to enact a particular version of prenatal exercise. This chapter begins with an overview of relevant theoretical and methodological insights that shape our investigation of the activity-related interventions, followed by a discussion of two key findings that demonstrate how prenatal exercise is made to 'matter' in the contemporary moment. This information, particularly a fuller account of the insights provided by Mol, offers a grounding necessary for illuminating contemporary prenatal interventions.

Situating the (In)Active Body Multiple

Central to STS scholarship has been the decentering of human actors, often through what has been termed actor-network theory (ANT) or a material-semiotic approach, the latter of which is our preferred terminology as it captures the multiplicity and fluidity of networks (see Latour 1999; Law 2009). A material-semiotic approach takes the semiotic insight that words give each other meaning, and extends it to all material entities with the effect that entities in a network of relations bring each other into being or 'enact' each other. With this commitment to relationality, the distinction between human and non-human loses its analytic relevance, as do other dualisms (e.g., macro and micro, nature and culture). Moreover, agency is disentangled from its 'human' association with intentionality; instead, an entity counts as an actor by making a perceptible difference within the relationally linked network (Knappett and Malafouris 2008). Thus, the focus of a material-semiotic approach is to understand how it is that entities get performed, and perform themselves, into relations or articulations that did not previously exist. Although these relations can become relatively stable, this stability can be difficult to achieve as these relations are dynamic and could connect otherwise (Latour 1999; Law 2009; Mol 2002; Slack and Wise 2015).

Particularly influential in our examination of prenatal exercise interventions are Mol's case studies of how different objects of inquiry (e.g., atherosclerosis, hypoglycemia, anemia) are performed via a range of scientific and technical practices (Mol 1998, 2002, 2013; Mol and Berg 1994). In her detailed ethnography of how atherosclerosis is enacted in a hospital in the Netherlands, she demonstrates that there is not just one version or 'truth' of atherosclerosis but multiple versions, or multiple ontologies, that are performed by the differing health professionals, depending upon location of enactment (e.g., the pathology lab, the radiology lab, the clinical examination room) and with what assemblage of equipment and/or methods (Mol 1998, 2002). Used here the term assemblage refers to the network of actors needed to enact a particular ontology of atherosclerosis, with differing versions existing throughout the hospital. Pointing to the material and performative nature of atherosclerosis, Mol (2002) explains that disease ontologies are "brought into being, sustained, or allowed to wither away in common day-to-day sociomaterial practices" (p. 6). With this description, she locates knowledge in activities, events, instruments, and procedures, as well as individuals (i.e., experts, patients, technicians).

A key insight of Mol is that while multiple versions of an object are enacted, be it a particular disease or advice about exercise during pregnancy, we are often presented with a singular version which requires 'work' by health professionals to coordinate multiple, and possibly contrasting, versions into a singular object or reality (Mol 1998, 2002; Mol and Berg 1994). This 'work' might consist of interpreting inconsistencies in disease diagnosis as limitations in practice; viewing one version of disease diagnosis, with its accompanying technologies and practices, as the gold standard while other versions are ignored; or using the rhetoric of principles-and-practice whereby principles of 'pure' science are understood as becoming muddied once mobilized in the messy social world of practice (Law 2004; Mol 2002; Mol and Berg 1994). According to Mol (2002), these strategies support the maintenance of the modernist, Euro-American version of reality, namely that a single 'real' version of the disease exists prior to, and independent of, medical intervention, and that the singular disease might simply be interpreted differently by various practitioners or experts. The goal of Mol's work is to illustrate that we are not dealing with different and possibly flawed perspectives on the same object; instead, we are dealing with different objects produced in different networks.

We bring to our own analysis an interest in exploring how a particular version of prenatal physical activity is being performed in the interventions we reviewed. More specifically, we are interested in how multiple versions of prenatal exercise are made into a (seeming) singularity whereby it 'matters' in a particular way. Such an investigation, while not drawing on explanatory frameworks such as 'power' or 'context', is not apolitical (Haraway 1988, 1997). As Mol (2013) contends, if "realities are adaptive and multiple, if they take different shapes as they engage, and are engaged, in different relations, then questions of ontological politics become important" (p. 381). In other words, the questions of *which* reality gets to take shape and *how* are political ones (Mol, 2013). Acknowledging the insights of Foucault, Mol (1999, 2013) uses the concept of political ontology to suggest that assumptions about the nature of objects and being neither escapes nor precedes power relations. With this attention to political ontology come questions such as the following: What does this version of reality mean for those who have to live with(in) it? How are bodies being valued? What are the norms embedded in practices and how might we interfere in them through our analysis? These are the questions that guided our examination of the pregnancy exercise interventions in our research sample.

To be included in our sample, an article had to report on a peer-reviewed, English language physical activity-related intervention or program for pregnant women, focus on reducing obesity, and make reference to DOHaD or epigenetics as part of the rationale for the physical activity intervention. We did not limit our search to studies that utilized randomized control trials (RCTs) though they were the dominant form of research; rather non-RCTs, programs without a control group, and qualitative studies were eligible for inclusion as we sought a diverse sample of approaches to prenatal exercise promotion. Publications were selected from a search of PubMed and CINAHL (Cumulative Index to Nursing and Allied Health Literature) databases, using the date range of database inception until January 2017, and search terms were organized into the categories of pregnancy, physical activity, body weight, and interventions.

The initial search yielded 503 possible articles and, after applying the inclusion and exclusion criteria described above, we identified 30 relevant articles. The most common reasons for exclusion were a lack of focus on an intervention or program and/or pregnant women not being the target population. Once we identified the articles for our sample, we read the publications and extracted the following information: country in which study was conducted; number of participants; participant demographics; rationale for study, including citations to support the rationale; study design; study outcome(s) of interest; intervention or program description; study findings. We then reviewed the information extracted for patterns pertaining to how physical activity during pregnancy was being discussed and/or practiced in the interventions or programs.

Making Physical Activity During Pregnancy 'Matter': Enacting Singularity

Through our review of the prenatal intervention literature, it became apparent that a particular version of physical activity during pregnancy is enacted: the 'environment' is equated with women's behaviors during pregnancy, and physical activity comes to 'matter' by its ability to control GWG and prevent LGA infants that risk becoming obese children. Thus, although DOHaD and epigenetics have the potential to account for how the broader environment, or the 'social', shapes the biological, that potential is not realized in the interventions that we examined, a finding that echoes the scholarship discussed above (Mansfield and Guthman 2015; McNaughton 2011; Warin et al. 2011). In what follows, we explore two combined practices—mobilizing the over-nutrition hypothesis from the DOHaD literature and privileging a linear model of causality—that work to create this singular version of prenatal exercise. However, and as explored below, this is not the only version that is possible.

Mobilizing the Over-Nutrition Hypothesis as Rationale

In the interventions reviewed, physical activity is made to 'matter' through the mobilization of scientific literature citing the various risks of maternal obesity such as postpartum weight retention, complications in delivery, and future offspring obesity. DOHaD literature is cited to support concerns that obese mothers are more likely to produce obese children, and that prenatal exercise is therefore a preventative measure.[1] However, a particular aspect of the DOHaD literature is put to work in this regard.

DOHaD has its roots in the work of David Barker, a British epidemiologist who, in the 1980s, drew attention to data demonstrating how under-nutrition during pregnancy, often a consequence of poverty and social trauma, is associated with SGA infants who have increased risk for developing cardiovascular disease, type 2 diabetes, metabolic syndrome, and hypertension in adulthood (Wadhwa et al. 2009). As such, under-nutrition has been suggested as an underlying cause of metabolic conditions that are associated with obesity, a move that has captured the interest of feminist scholars seeking to bring materiality to their gendered analyses of DOHaD and obesity. Warin (2015) and Yoshizawa (2012), for instance, argue that Barker's work shows that fatness is not necessarily a moral failing but rather a marker of poverty and nutritional deprivation across generations, a condition which is often gendered in nature. In this view, argues Yoshizawa (2012), obesity—and how to intervene in order to challenge any negative health effects—is not only a scientific and/or medical issue, but also a social and economic one.

However, within the field of DOHaD, and in the vast majority of the literature cited in our sample of articles, an over-nutrition hypothesis has gained prominence. The over-nutrition hypothesis has been popularized by Oken and colleagues (Oken and Gillman 2003; Oken 2009) through their epidemiological research showing an association between LGA babies and future obesity and type 2 diabetes in childhood. Oken (2009) views the intergenerational transfer of obesity from mothers to daughters as especially threatening, explaining: "[i]ncreasing trends of maternal weight and gestational weight gain may be propagating an intergenerational 'vicious cycle' of obesity, as heavier mothers give birth to heavier daughters, who are then even more likely to be obese and diabetic entering their own pregnancies" (p. 361). McNaughton (2011) and Warin et al. (2011) argue that a focus on maternal overweight—and LGA babies—has eclipsed the previous public health focus on under-nutrition and SGA babies originally initiated by Barker. McNaughton (2011) further suggests that while all women are held responsible for the future, fat-free health of their offspring within this now dominant thesis, marginalized women are singled out as posing the greatest risk to their offspring and positioned as in need of greater degrees of intervention and surveillance.

In our own analysis, we found that the 30 studies mostly focused on the epidemiological research documenting the association between over-nutrition and obesity/type 2 diabetes. This literature was mobilized to provide the rationale for the prenatal exercise interventions that sought to limit maternal weight gain and prevent LGA infants. For instance, in the rationale for their intervention entitled 'The Maternal Obesity Management (MOM) Trial Protocol: A Lifestyle Intervention During Pregnancy to Minimize Downstream Obesity', Adamo et al. (2013) explain that:

> Obesity and excessive gestational weight gain (GWG) alter the intrauterine environment and contribute to increased risk of obesity in children. Both are independently and positively associated with infant birth weight and frequently used as a surrogate marker of the intrauterine environment. In fact, a recent meta-analysis confirmed the association between high birth weight (>4000 g) and increased risk of downstream obesity ... It is important to note that maternal overweight or obesity more than doubles the risk of obesity in offspring at 24 months of age and ... [s]imilarly, epidemiological evidence has illustrated the independent effect of GWG on downstream offspring BMI, with women who exceed GWG recommendations being over 4 times more likely to have a child who is overweight by their preschool years. (p. 88)

Koivusalo et al. (2016) similarly assert: "GDM [gestational diabetes mellitus] and obesity are both independently associated with adverse maternal and neonatal outcomes. Maternal overweight and GDM may also increase the offspring's predisposition to obesity, impaired glucose regulation, and GDM, creating a vicious cycle leading to an accumulating risk in the next generation" (p. 25). In the various rationale sections, the authors then hypothesize that physical activity during pregnancy can help to intervene in this cycle of obesity, justifying the intervention. Thus, prenatal exercise is made to 'matter' by its purported ability to limit maternal weight gain, thus preventing LGA infants and, in turn, future obesity.

Notably, the optimism that physical activity during pregnancy might limit infant size is a significant departure from how prenatal exercise was imagined when the exercise science community first turned its attention to the topic in the mid-1980s (Jette 2011). At that time, researchers hypothesized that since exercise brings about physiologic alterations similar to those during pregnancy (i.e., changes to heart rate, ventilation rates, and substrate utilization), it was possible that when pregnancy and exercise were combined, the physiological impact would be doubled, with the fetus suffering the consequences in terms of fetal hypoxia and distress, fetal growth restriction, as well as premature labor and/or lower birth weight. Thus, the potential for physical activity during pregnancy to lead to SGA infants was the primary area of concern and research focus. However, while the effects of exercise in pregnancy have been studied extensively since that time, authors of a review of the literature on how prenatal exercise impacts fetal growth note that "a dearth of well controlled randomized studies has led to conflicting evidence as to the impact of exercise on fetal growth"[2] (Hopkins and Cutfield 2011, p. 120). Amidst this scientific uncertainty, the concern that exercise in pregnancy might lead to SGA infants still remains prevalent within the scientific community.

Given this information, it appears, then, that two versions exist as to how physical activity in pregnancy matters: it might lead to SGA babies which brings with it potential risks (i.e., preterm birth, future metabolic disorders); or it might help prevent LGA babies and obesity across two generations by preventing GWG and reducing infant birth size (i.e., the hypothesis tested in the interventions). Despite remaining concerns and conflicting evidence about exercise and SGA, within the contemporary scientific literature there is very little sign of controversy, and certainly none in the prenatal exercise interventions that we reviewed. Instead, the epidemiological research concerning the fetal over-nutrition hypothesis is put into action within many articles' rationale sections and in detailing the prenatal exercise interventions. For example, the article by Adamo et al. (2013) discussed above cites research (see Oken et al. 2007) that found that women who exceed GWG recommendations are 4.35 times more likely to have a child who is overweight by age 3 as compared to women with inadequate GWG.

This use of epidemiological research and related facts about the association between maternal GWG and offspring adiposity can be understood as what Mol (1998) has called a 'transportable link'. Mol uses this term to capture the manner in which associations that are difficult to make in routine medical practice may be practiced in a specific setting with careful monitoring. For example, in her discussion of atherosclerosis, she explains that even if a doctor is not certain that smoking cessation by an individual patient will decrease their risk of atherosclerosis:

> it is possible to evaluate the histories of large populations of people and see if there is a correlation between smoking habits and the onset, severity, and course of atherosclerosis. If such links are monitored and noted, they may be published. In that way, mobile connections are created that can later be quoted somewhere else. (Mol, 1998, p. 157)

These mobile connections or transportable links, she explains, can then be used (i.e., cited elsewhere) to influence treatment policies or practices "even in the absence of any sensible story about the way in which, inside the body, [hormones] act upon vessel walls" (p. 159). Thus, as a form of legitimation, these associations or links are transported and put into practice by suggesting something to do or to avoid doing. In the articles we studied, there is a similar lack of clarity as in the case of atherosclerosis regarding the biological mechanisms at work (Blaize et al. 2015; Ruchat and Mottola 2012). Indeed, most authors suggest that 'something to do' is to use physical activity during pregnancy to intervene and prevent two generations of obesity, making physical activity 'matter' as epidemiological facts—or transportable links—are put into practice within the rationale section of the intervention articles.

It should not go without notice, however, that these transportable links are the end product of prospective cohort studies whereby a cohort of pregnant women is assessed on a number of health measures including GWG and infant birth weight, and infant weight gain monitored at intervals over the ensuing years. Thus, the transportable links are the relational effect of multiple practices in a network—weigh scales, charts to record demographic information, skinfold calipers to measure infant or child skinfolds, phone calls to schedule appointments to make measurements, statistical tests run on data, human interpretation of that data—that allow the materiality of bodies to be represented as a number such as a 4.35 odds ratio of overweight by age 3. These practices and relations (both human and non-human, social and material) are folded into the final statistic of 4.35 and made invisible as the link is transported to the rationale section of the intervention paper, becoming part of a new network of relations: the prenatal exercise interventions for which they provide the rationale.

The mobilization of these transportable links is a strategic, even political, decision made by researchers conducting the interventions at the same time that it is an established, even required, practice in their profession. By drawing on these citations or 'allies' as Latour (1987) has called them, researchers make the rationale for their projects and (hopefully) translate the interests of differing parties to align with their own. It helps them to obtain funding to conduct the study and generate public interest in the topic as a relevant public health issue. Moreover, it may well be in line with their views about overweight and obese bodies as in need of intervention while simultaneously constituting these bodies in exactly this way by enacting a recommendation of physical activity during pregnancy. Questions about the potential of prenatal exercise to lead to SGA infants are not raised in the intervention articles that we reviewed, possibly because it is thought that there is no risk of an overweight or obese woman having a baby that is too small.[3] Rather a singular version of prenatal exercise is presented for this population, namely the risk of not being physically active and having an LGA infant that will become an overweight or obese child.

Privileging a Linear Model of Causality

With this in mind, we turn to the practice of the articles' physical activity interventions. Notably, intervening to prevent obesity via prenatal exercise is not an American-only project, although the United States does appear to be leading this type of research in terms of quantity. Rather, the prenatal exercise interventions that we reviewed were conducted in 16 different countries, with the United States and Finland being the most frequently represented at six and three studies respectively, followed by a number of countries with two studies (Canada, New Zealand, Australia, Sweden, Germany, Denmark, and England) and several with one (Spain, Chile, China, Belgium, Brazil, Wales, and Norway).

However, despite this global representation, albeit an over-representation of Western nations, the interventions shared several commonalities. The majority (23 of the 30) are randomized control trials (RCTs), which are considered to be the 'gold standard' in the life sciences. RCTs are put into practice by randomly assigning participants (or hospitals, as is the case in some of the interventions) into one of two groups: the intervention group, which receives the exposure (i.e., physical activity) or the control group, which does not receive the exposure. The researchers then measure various factors of interest at differing intervals over the course of the intervention, with the goal of comparing how the two groups differ at specified points in time. The logic underpinning the RCT is that any observable changes are caused by the intervention; it is a linear model of cause-effect. The goal is to minimize the chance of bias—on the part of participants and researchers—and increase the validity of the intervention results by preventing disparate 'social' factors from interfering with the intervention and the presumed biological facts or reality it is intended to reveal. Thus, RCTs attempt to preserve a separation between the 'inside' and 'outside' of science, although STS scholars have turned the purported separation of inside and outside on its head, demonstrating how the social infuses laboratory life (Haraway, 1997; Latour and Woolgar 1986).

In all the interventions analyzed, physical activity is an exposure of interest although sometimes it was paired with diet as part of an overall lifestyle intervention. While multiple outcomes were assessed in many of the studies, participant GWG was an outcome common to all of the research interventions in our sample. In addition to GWG, just over half of the interventions (18 of 30) also assessed the impact of the intervention on infant birth weight which is a commonly used marker of fetal growth and assumed to be influenced by maternal weight gain. To make physical activity 'matter' in this linear model of causality, another causal model—this time of the body—is put into action: the energy balance model (Gard and Wright 2005; Guthman 2012). This approach, which is dominant in obesity science, treats the human body mechanistically, presuming that body weight—and obesity—is a result of excess calorie intake relative to energy expenditure or calories out. As Guthman (2012) notes, "[r]esearchers who take this approach also tend to assume that the problem of obesity in relation to poor health is clear-cut and noncontroversial" (p. 952).

Guthman suggests that the energy balance model has allowed for the body to be 'black boxed', drawing on the term used by Latour (1987) to describe the situation whereby an object's internal nature is taken to be objectively established, thus erasing the network of actors—human and non-human, social and natural—required to construct a scientific 'fact'. The black boxed model of obesity focuses on inputs (calories from food) and outputs (expenditures via physical activity) with little to no attention paid to the biophysical workings of the human body which is in turn treated as a machine that processes calories in a predictable manner. In response to this construction, Guthman (2012) points to emergent epigenetic research that suggests that chronic stress and chemical pollutants shape gene expression and influence adiposity. She argues that this research disrupts the simple equation of the energy balance paradigm while illustrating the necessity of opening the body's 'black box' to explore not only its biophysical workings, but also how it is inseparable from its ecological, geographical, and historical contexts.

A similar ontology is also at work in our reviewed articles whereby physical activity constitutes the energy expenditure portion of the energy balance equation, helping women to reduce their GWG with the goal of reducing infant birth weight and ultimately, childhood obesity. For example, Guelinckx et al. (2010) explain that "[t]he total amount of GWG is determined by many factors, of which maternal dietary intake and physical activity (PA) may be the most modifiable factors" (p. 373) and Adamo et al. (2013) similarly note that "[a]ppropriate nutrition and regular PA are critical mediators of weight gain and weight maintenance at all ages and have been specifically identified as predictors of excessive GWG" (p. 88). Thus, physical activity comes to matter by its purported ability to tip the body's energy balance into a deficit that will limit GWG within the range researchers deem healthy for pregnant women and their offspring thus rendering the intervention a success. Notably, what is considered healthy in terms of GWG is defined in relation to pre-pregnancy body mass index (BMI) and this concept has been subject to revision in recent years in light of concern about excessive maternal weight gain (Jette and Rail 2013). More specifically, many of the research interventions use Institute of Medicine (IOM) GWG guidelines which were revised in 2009, with weight gain recommendations for obese pregnant women being lowered from a range of 15–25 lbs. to 11–20 lbs., and the BMI cut-off points altered so that more pregnant women are now classified as overweight and thus in need of intervention.

The dominance of the energy balance model in our sample of research articles supports an ontological view of the body as a closed, linear system whereby the 'environment' continues to be equated with women's behaviors during pregnancy, and physical activity comes to 'matter' by its ability to control GWG and prevent the birth of large babies that risk becoming obese children. Left unfulfilled is the potential of DOHaD to provide a different and more complex version of obesity that places the body within its larger ecological, political, and historical context and implicates structural inequities in the materialization of health disparities (Guthman 2012, 2014).

Conclusion

In this chapter, we have argued that the combined practices of mobilizing transportable links that support the over-nutrition hypothesis as well as the logic of a linear model of causality enact a version of prenatal exercise that forecloses the possibility of illustrating the complex interplay of biology and society that is promised by DOHaD and which could, in turn, underpin a social justice agenda. Instead, the 'exposure' of interest shaping the intrauterine environment is too often limited to the behavior of physical activity and in some cases diet, with little to no acknowledgment of the forces that shape this environment—including such factors as environmental toxins, and mothers' stressors due to poverty and/or discrimination. Our intent is not to suggest that the prenatal interventions we reviewed do not 'matter', or in other words, that prenatal physical activity does not have the potential to positively impact the health of women and their offspring. However, we are wary of the over-simplified version of physical activity and women's bodies that we found in our analysis.

While this investigation did not explicitly draw upon explanatory frameworks such as 'power' or 'context', we have attempted to get at what Mol (1999) has termed the political ontology surrounding prenatal exercise by using STS approaches to trace the networks of practice that allow a particular version to be enacted. That is to say, we suggest that *which* version of the body gets to take shape out of the multiple ontologies possible is reflective of political processes. And indeed, there are norms at work in the version of prenatal exercise that is being enacted in the interventions we examined. As mentioned above, many of the interventions use the IOM guidelines pertaining to GWG to evaluate intervention success. The IOM guidelines prescribe GWG amounts based on women's pre-pregnancy BMI, or in other words, based on whether they are considered underweight, 'normal' weight, overweight, or obese according to this classification system (IOM & NRC 2009). Critical obesity scholars (Evans and Colls 2009; Gard and Wright 2005; Jette and Rail 2013; Nicholls 2013) have questioned the utility of the BMI on several accounts, including its capacity to measure what it is intended to measure, its ability to predict future health outcomes, the application of population-level data to individual bodies in the clinical context, and the arbitrary nature of BMI category cut-offs.

While these are certainly relevant concerns, we are most interested in the normative assumptions embedded in the BMI classification system itself, which marks some bodies as 'good' (i.e., normal weight, and even perhaps underweight) and others as 'bad' (i.e., overweight and obese) (Nicholls 2013). Here, physical activity comes to 'matter' as it promises to act on the bodies of overweight and obese pregnant women, expending energy to help them succeed in achieving a healthy amount of weight for themselves and their offspring—and aiding researchers in achieving intervention success. In doing so, particular bodies are being valued over others, just as inequalities are glossed over, all of which has implications for how non-normative fetal and adult bodies are judged by the medical profession and the women themselves.

Notes

1. Only one of the articles cited epigenetic literature in the rationale (see Aparicio et al. 2016), with the others citing DOHaD literature. One possible reason is that the molecular mechanisms involved in translating fetal exposure to excessive GWG into offspring obesity are largely unknown, and this emphasis on mechanisms would be the focus of epigenetic research.

2. Regardless of their recognition of the conflicting evidence around the impact of exercise on fetal growth, the authors are optimistic about the potential of using prenatal exercise to prevent obesity across two generations.

3. In a few articles (see Guelinckx et al. 2010; Koivusalo et al. 2016), the authors cite DOHaD scholarship that demonstrates the impact of fetal under-nutrition on the development of future disease, even though the focus of their project rationale is the danger of over-nutrition in pregnancy. The DOHaD under-nutrition citation—also a transportable link—was thus used to emphasize the plasticity of early development and the importance of maternal lifestyle in shaping offspring health. However, the authors then focused exclusively on the dangers of overweight and how an intervention into diet and exercise can assist with excess GWG.

References

Adamo, K. B., Ferraro, Z. M., Goldfield, G., Keely, E., Stacey, D., Hadjiyannakis, S., et al. (2013). The maternal obesity management (MOM) trial protocol: A lifestyle intervention during pregnancy to minimize downstream obesity. *Contemporary Clinical Trials, 35*(1), 87–96.

American College of Obstetricians and Gynecologists (ACOG). (1985). Technical bulletin number 87: ACOG guidelines: Exercise during pregnancy and the postnatal period. In R. Artal Mittelmark, R. Wiswell, & B. Drinkwater (Eds.), *Exercise in pregnancy* (2nd ed., pp. 313–319). Baltimore and London: Williams & Wilkins.

American College of Obstetricians and Gynecologists (ACOG). (2015). Physical activity and exercise during pregnancy and the postpartum period. Committee opinion no. 650. *Obstetrics and Gynecology, 126*(6), e135–e142.

Aparicio, V. A., Ocón, O., Padilla-Vinuesa, C., Soriano-Maldonado, A., Romero Gallardo, L., Borges-Cósic, M., et al. (2016). Effects of supervised aerobic and strength training in overweight and grade I obese pregnant women on maternal and foetal health markers: The GESTAFIT randomized controlled trial. *BMC Pregnancy and Childbirth, 16*(1), 290.

Balsamo, A. (1996). *Technologies of the gendered body.* Durham, NC: Duke University Press.

Barad, K. (2008). Posthumanist performativity: Toward an understanding of how matter comes to matter. In S. Alaimo & S. Hekman (Eds.), *Material feminisms* (pp. 120–154). Bloomington, IN: Indiana University Press.

Blaize, A. N., Pearson, K. J., & Newcomer, S. (2015). Impact of maternal exercise during pregnancy on offspring chronic disease susceptibility. *Exercise and Sport Sciences Reviews, 43*(4), 198–203.

Butler, J. (1993). *Bodies that matter: On the discursive limits of 'sex'*. New York, NY: Routledge.

Casper, M. J. (1998). Working on and around human fetuses: The contested domain of fetal surgery. In M. Berg & A. Mol (Eds.), *Differences in medicine: Unraveling practices, techniques, and bodies* (pp. 28–52). Durham and London: Duke University Press.

Evans, B., & Colls, R. (2009). Measuring fatness, governing bodies: The spatialities of the body mass index (BMI) in anti-obesity politics. *Antipode, 41*(5), 1051–1083.

Foucault, M. (2003). Governmentality. In P. Rabinow & N. Rose (Eds.), *The essential Foucault: Selections from essential works of Foucault, 1954–1984* (pp. 229–245). New York and London: The New Press.

Frost, S. (2011). The implications of the new materialisms for feminist epistemology. In H. Grasswick (Ed.), *Feminist epistemology and philosophy of science: Power in knowledge* (pp. 69–83). Springer Netherlands.

Frost, S. (2016). *Biocultural creatures: Towards a new theory of the human.* Durham, NC: Duke University Press.

Gard, M., & Wright, J. (2005). *The obesity epidemic: Science, morality and ideology.* New York, NY: Routledge.

Guelinckx, I., Devlieger, R., Mullie, P., & Vansant, G. (2010). Effect of lifestyle intervention on dietary habits, physical activity, and gestational weight gain in obese pregnant women: A randomized controlled trial. *The American Journal of Clinical Nutrition, 91*(2), 373–380.

Guthman, J. (2012). Opening up the black box of the body in geographical obesity research: Toward a critical political ecology of fat. *Annals of the Association of American Geographers, 102*(5), 951–957.

Guthman, J. (2014). Doing justice to bodies? Reflections on food justice, race, and biology. *Antipode, 46*(5), 1153–1171.

Guthman, J., & Mansfield, B. (2013). The implications of environmental epigenetics: A new direction for geographic inquiry on health, space, and nature-society relations. *Progress in Human Geography, 37*(4), 486–504.

Haraway, D. (1985). Manifesto for cyborgs: Science, technology, and socialist feminism in the 1980s. *Socialist Review, 80*, 65–108.

Haraway, D. (1988). Situated knowledges: The science question in feminism as a site of discourse on the privilege of partial perspective. *Feminist Studies, 14*, 575–599.

Haraway, D. J. (1997). *Modest_Witness@Second_Millenniun. FemaleMan©_ Meets_OncoMouse™: Feminism and technoscience*. New York, NY; London: Routledge.

Haraway, D. (2003). *The companion species manifesto: Dogs, people, and significant otherness*. Chicago, IL: Prickly Paradigm Press.

Hopkins, S. A., & Cutfield, W. S. (2011). Exercise in pregnancy: Weighing up the long term impact on the next generation. *Exercise and Sport Sciences Reviews, 39*(3), 120–127.

IOM (Institute of Medicine) and NRC (National Research Council). (2009). *Weight gain during pregnancy: Reexamining the guidelines*. Washington, DC: The National Academies Press.

Jette, S. (2006). "Fit for two?": A critical discourse analysis of *Oxygen* fitness magazine. *Sociology of Sport Journal, 23*(4), 331–351.

Jette, S. (2011). Exercising caution: The production of medical knowledge about physical exertion during pregnancy. *Canadian Bulletin of Medical History/Bulletin canadien d'histoire de la medicine, 28*(2), 383–401.

Jette, S. (2017). Pregnant bodies. In D. Andrews, M. Silk, & H. Thorpe (Eds.), *Routledge handbook of physical cultural studies* (pp. 313–320). New York: Routledge.

Jette, S. (2018). Sport for all, or fit for two? Governing the (in)active pregnancy. In R. Dionigi & M. Gard (Eds.), *Critical perspectives on sport and physical activity across the lifespan* (pp. 211–226). London: Palgrave Macmillan.

Jette, S., & Rail, G. (2013). Ills from the womb? A critical examination of clinical guidelines for obesity in pregnancy. *Health, 17*(4), 407–421.

Jette, S., Maier, J., Esmonde, K., & Davis, C. (2017). Promoting prenatal exercise from a sociocultural and life-course perspective: An "embodied" conceptual framework. *Research Quarterly for Exercise and Sport, 88*(3), 269–281.

Kenney, M., & Müller, R. (2017). Of rats and women: Narratives of motherhood in environmental epigenetics. *Biosocieties, 12*(1), 23–46.

Knappett, C., & Malafouris, L. (2008). Material and non-human agency: An introduction. In C. Knappett & L. Malafouris (Eds.), *Material agency: Towards a non-anthropocentric approach* (pp. ix–xix). Springer Science & Business Media.

Koivusalo, S. B., Rönö, K., Klemetti, M. M., Roine, R. P., Lindström, J., Erkkola, M., et al. (2016). Gestational diabetes mellitus can be prevented by lifestyle intervention: The Finnish gestational diabetes prevention study (RADIEL). *Diabetes Care, 39*(1), 24–30.

Landecker, H. (2011). Food as exposure: Nutritional epigenetics and the new metabolism. *BioSocieties, 6*(2), 167–194.

Latour, B. (1987). *Science in action: How to follow scientists and engineers through society*. Cambridge, MA: Harvard University Press.

Latour, B. (1999). On recalling ANT. In J. Law & J. Hassard (Eds.), *Actor network theory and after* (pp. 15–25). Oxford: Blackwell Publishers.

Latour, B., & Woolgar, S. (1986). *Laboratory life: The construction of scientific knowledge*. Princeton, NJ: Princeton University Press.

Law, J. (2004). *After method: Mess in social science research*. New York, NY: Routledge.

Law, J. (2009). Actor network theory and material semiotics. In B. Turner (Ed.), *The new Blackwell companion to social theory* (pp. 141–158). Malden, MA: Wiley-Blackwell.

Lupton, D. (1999). Risk and the ontology of pregnant embodiment. In D. Lupton (Ed.), *Risk and sociocultural theory: New directions and perspectives* (pp. 59–85). Cambridge: Cambridge University Press.

Mamo, L. (2007). Negotiating conception: Lesbians' hybrid-technological practices. *Science, Technology, & Human Values, 32*(3), 369–393.

Mansfield, B., & Guthman, J. (2015). Epigenetic life: Biological plasticity, abnormality, and new configurations of race and reproduction. *Cultural Geographies, 22*(1), 3–20.

McNaughton, D. (2011). From the womb to the tomb: Obesity and maternal responsibility. *Critical Public Health, 21*(2), 179–190.

Meloni, M. (2016). *Political biology: Science and social values in human heredity from eugenics to epigenetics*. New York, NY: Palgrave Macmillan.

Mol, A. (1998). Missing links, making links. In M. Berg & A. Mol (Eds.), *Differences in medicine: Unraveling practices, techniques, and bodies* (pp. 144–165). Durham and London: Duke University Press.

Mol, A. (1999). Ontological politics. A word and some questions. *The Sociological Review, 47*(1 suppl), 74–89.

Mol, A. (2002). *The body multiple: Ontology in medical practice*. Durham and London: Duke University Press.

Mol, A. (2013). Mind your plate! The ontonorms of Dutch dieting. *Social Studies of Science, 43*(3), 379–396.

Mol, A., & Berg, M. (1994). *Principles and practices of medicine. Culture, Medicine and Psychiatry, 18*(2), 247–265.

Müller, R., Hanson, C., Hanson, M., Penkler, M., Samaras, G., Chiapperino, L., et al. (2017). The biosocial genome? Interdisciplinary perspectives on environmental epigenetics, health and society. *EMBO Reports, 18*(10), 1677–1682.

Nicholls, S. G. (2013). Standards and classification: A perspective on the 'obesity epidemic'. *Social Science & Medicine, 87,* 9–15.

Oken, E. (2009). Maternal and child obesity: The causal link. *Obstetrics and Gynecology Clinics of North America, 36*(2), 361–377.

Oken, E., & Gillman, M. W. (2003). Fetal origins of obesity. *Obesity, 11*(4), 496–506.

Oken, E., Taveras, E. M., Kleinman, K. P., Rich-Edwards, J. W., & Gillman, M. W. (2007). Gestational weight gain and child adiposity at age 3 years. *American Journal of Obstetrics and Gynecology, 196*(4), 322.e1–322.e8.

Richardson, S. S., Daniels, C. R., Gillman, M. W., Golden, J., Kukla, R., Kuzawa, C., & Rich-Edwards, J. (2014). Don't blame the mothers. *Nature, 512,* 131–132.

Rose, N. (2007). *The politics of life itself: Biomedicine, power, and subjectivity in the twenty-first century.* Princeton, NJ: Princeton University Press.

Ruchat, S. M., & Mottola, M. F. (2012). Preventing long-term risk of obesity for two generations: Prenatal physical activity is part of the puzzle. *Journal of Pregnancy, 33.*

Slack, J. D., & Wise, J. M. (2015). *Culture and technology: A primer* (2nd ed.). New York, NY: Peter Lang Publishing.

Verbrugge, M. (2012). *Active bodies: A history of women's physical education in twentieth-century America.* New York, NY: Oxford University Press.

Vertinsky, P. (1994). *The eternally wounded woman: Women, doctors, and exercise in the late nineteenth century.* Champaign, IL: University of Illinois Press.

Wadhwa, P. D., Buss, C., Entringer, S., & Swanson, J. M. (2009). Developmental origins of health and disease: Brief history of the approach and current focus on epigenetic mechanisms. *Seminars in Reproductive Medicine, 27*(5), 358–368.

Warin, M. (2015). Material feminism, obesity science and the limits of discursive critique. *Body & Society, 21*(4), 48–76.

Warin, M., Moore, V., Zivkovic, T., & Davies, M. (2011). Telescoping the origins of obesity to women's bodies: How gender inequalities are being squeezed out of Barker's hypothesis. *Annals of Human Biology, 38*(4), 453–460.

Waterland, R. A., & Michels, K. B. (2007). Epigenetic epidemiology of the developmental origins hypothesis. *Annual Review of Nutrition, 27,* 363–388.

Weir, L. (2006). *Pregnancy, risk and biopolitics: On the threshold of the living subject.* London & New York: Routledge.

Yoshizawa, R. S. (2012). The Barker hypothesis and obesity: Connections for transdisciplinarity and social justice. *Social Theory & Health, 10*(4), 348–367.

Ignorance and the Gender Binary: Resisting Complex Epistemologies of Sex and Testosterone

Madeleine Pape

In recent decades, Science and Technology Studies (STS) scholars have increasingly taken up the study of ignorance and non-knowledge as part of a broader effort to reveal the political and institutional processes that underpin scientific knowledge-making. Also known as agnotology, this area of scholarship brings attention to absent or unrecognized knowledge, showing that these are not simply the passive corollary to that which *is* known but rather are actively produced (Gross 2007; Tacke 2001). Sites of unknown and unrecognized knowledge are also sites of contestation, since the exclusion of certain topics from dominant ways of knowing can be highly advantageous for the interests and agendas of powerful stakeholders (Frickel and Vincent 2007; McGoey 2007; Proctor and Schiebinger 2008). In other words, the non-production and marginalization of alternative knowledge forms is as political as the knowledge that *is* produced and granted recognition, with both reflecting epistemic investments that stakeholders and the institutions they reside in may seek to protect (Hess 2007; Frickel et al. 2010).

M. Pape (✉)
Northwestern University, Evanston, IL, USA
e-mail: mpape@wisc.edu

© The Author(s) 2020
J. J. Sterling, M. G. McDonald (eds.), *Sports, Society, and Technology*,
https://doi.org/10.1007/978-981-32-9127-0_10

The politics of marginalized knowledge can be charted to reveal the institutional dynamics that explain how and why some knowledges are resisted relative to others (Proctor and Schiebinger 2008, p. 6). Yet social scientists in general, and STS scholars and feminist STS scholars in particular, have typically privileged only the study of those knowledges that *do* achieve institutional viability and visibility. As a result, less is known about the production (or non-production) of ignored knowledge forms and the gendered political and social practices that may underpin their marginalization (McGoey 2012).

The scientific study of sex difference constitutes one area where certain ways of knowing are dominant while others have not received the same degree of institutional recognition and support. For several decades, feminist STS scholars have generated an artillery of empirical research contesting dominant scientific understandings of sex difference and particularly the notion that sex is binary and purely biological (Fausto-Sterling 2000; Fujimura 2006; Lorber 1993; Martin 1991; Tuana 1988). This scholarship suggests that researchers in the biological sciences produce knowledge about sexed bodies in ways consistent with socially conditioned expectations and paradigmatic assumptions about the nature of sex difference: as binary, distinct from gender, and discoverable through science. Despite these efforts, the dominant scientific narrative about human sexual variation as divisible into two distinct and opposite biological categories has largely remained in place in Western cultures (Westbrook 2016; Sanz 2017). This is also despite recent developments in feminist biology, a field where researchers combine feminist STS insights with their training in the biological sciences to empirically examine gender and sex as dynamic, non-binary, and entangled (Fausto-Sterling 2012; Ritz 2018; van Anders 2012). This development further prompts the question: what has prevented the broader recognition of these alternative feminist accounts of sexed bodies?

Olympic sport, and international track-and-field in particular, offers a highly visible setting where answers to this question can be pursued. Feminist scholars have long critiqued the application of allegedly objective scientific claims about sex difference to regulate the participation of women athletes (Birrell and Cole 1990; Henne 2014; Kane 1995; Pape 2017). Since the late 1950s, the International Olympic Committee

(IOC) and International Association of Athletics Federations (IAAF) have worked in tandem to establish gender eligibility rules for women's competition (Henne 2014). After decades of using other technologies such as chromosomal testing, which was ultimately recognized as a scientifically inaccurate measure of sex differences in athletic ability, the IOC and IAAF have most recently ushered in a new "era of hyperandrogenism," in which regulations posit a simplistic understanding of naturally occurring testosterone levels in women (but not men) as a marker of athletic ability. Specifically, those women whose bodies naturally produce higher levels of testosterone than is deemed "normal" are thought by the IOC and IAAF to be benefiting from an unfair athletic advantage over their competitors (IAAF 2011; IOC 2012).[1]

However, the assumption of a straightforward relationship between testosterone and athletic ability in men or women—and the subsequent legitimacy of using such an approach to determine women's eligibility—has been contested on both scientific and ethical grounds (Karkazis et al. 2012). For instance, some male athletes competing at an elite international level in track-and-field are known to have testosterone levels in the so-called women's range (CAS 2015). Ethical concerns have also been raised about the implementation of such regulations, given numerous breaches of confidentiality surrounding those who have been tested for hyperandrogenism as well as an apparent targeting of women of color from the Global South (Henne and Pape 2018; Karkazis and Jordan-Young 2018). For the most part, however, recent appeals of these regulatory efforts have largely focused on scientific questions. The 2011 Hyperandrogenism Regulations of the IAAF were suspended for a two-year period by the Court of Arbitration for Sport (CAS) in 2015, with the adjudicating panel citing a lack of scientific evidence to support the claim that naturally occurring testosterone levels serve as a reliable measure of athletic ability (CAS 2015). When the IAAF's revised Eligibility Regulations for Female Classification were challenged in 2019 by Caster Semenya, a Black South African athlete and double Olympic champion, the CAS ruled in this instance that these discriminatory regulations should stand (CAS 2019). Nevertheless, the extent of international debate over the legitimacy of the 2019 ruling reveals a divided scientific landscape (see WMA 2019).

This chapter considers how sports governing bodies are able to use scientific accounts of binary sex and endogenous (naturally occurring) testosterone to determine eligibility for women athletes, in spite of significant concerns surrounding such policies.[2] More specifically, I explore how certain ways of knowing embodied sex circulate within the elite international track-and-field community, which in turn helps to legitimate the rule-making efforts of sports governing bodies. To do so, I analyze data from interviews conducted following the 2016 Rio Olympic Games. In this chapter, I ask: did this decision prompt the elite track-and-field community to revisit their understandings of sex difference, testosterone, and athletic ability? If not, how did these stakeholders avoid reconfiguring their existing epistemic commitments? More specifically, how were track-and-field stakeholders able to *ignore* unsettling scientific and ethical claims about the regulation of women with high testosterone, thereby protecting their investment in the notion that male and female bodies are characterized by distinctly different—and scientifically measurable—ranges of testosterone and athletic ability?

More broadly, this chapter attends to a puzzle that has not received sufficient attention from feminist STS scholars, nor from STS scholars concerned generally with the politics of knowledge production, namely: that binary and biological accounts of sex difference appear to prevail *in spite* of scientific evidence (and political efforts) to the contrary. Turning to the concept of ignorance, I develop a conceptualization in which ignorance is understood not only as an outcome, as has primarily been suggested in the literature to date, but also as a *process*: as an act of turning away in a given moment *when it was possible to know differently.* This approach to ignorance is consistent with the concept of "undone science" advanced by Frickel et al. (2010), where an alternative research agenda exists—and has been recognized by some stakeholders as worthy of pursuit—but has been systematically undermined by a lack of institutional investment and recognition (see also McGoey 2007). I suggest further that ignorance can be understood as an *institutional* process in that it is reproduced and compelled through the formal rules and informal cultural and normative practices that organize a given institutional sphere and reproduce its gender relations (Acker 1990; Lopez and Scott 2000). Ignorance as a form of institutional resistance may unfold in particular ways when long-standing investments in binary understandings of sexed and gendered bodies are at stake. In the case of sport, and track-and-field in particular, it can serve as a "strategic" means by which stakeholders protect institutional practices, norms, and structures from the destabilizing effects of recognizing the complexities of sex and testosterone's role in the body (McGoey 2012).

I begin by situating recent events in the longer history of gender eligibility regulations for women, focusing in particular on the post-2009 efforts of sports governing bodies to bolster the scientific case for testosterone-based regulations. After describing my methodological approach, I then present data from my interviews that reveal three different forms of ignorance unfolding simultaneously as track-and-field stakeholders seek to protect their existing epistemic investments. First, I present an overview of common misunderstandings and misrepresentations that arose during interviewees' accounts, which I term ignorance-as-misinformation. I then explore how track-and-field stakeholders justify their commitment to a particular policy agenda *despite* the absence of supporting scientific evidence, or what I call ignorance-as-ideology. Finally, I reveal the various means by which track-and-field stakeholders actively resist becoming more informed on the topic of regulating women with high testosterone, or ignorance-as-avoidance. While I largely focus on the perspectives of athletes, coaches, managers, and the media, I also show that the actions taken by governing bodies set the terms for how particular notions of gendered bodies can be known and others *not* known.

Background: Defining the Female Athlete in the Era of Hyperandrogenism

During earlier eras of gender verification, sex testing was a mandatory and hence highly visible part of the elite female athlete experience. Formal testing practices began with genital examinations in the late 1950s before moving to a chromosome-based testing regime that lasted over three decades, during which chromosomally "certified" female competitors were required to present "certificates of femininity" or "femininity cards" in order to compete (Wackwitz 2003). This arrangement changed in the late 1990s when, following decades of critique from geneticists and endocrinologists, both the IOC and IAAF quietly moved to measures of endogenous testosterone as an allegedly more accurate way to identify "hypermuscular" women with a natural but "unfair" athletic advantage (Pieper 2016). Rather than subject all women to testing, only those athletes deemed "suspicious" by designated medical staff would be subjected to examination. As a result, the hyperandrogenism regime unfolded with little accountability and broader awareness (Henne and Pape 2018).

This changed following the 2009 World Championships in track-and-field, where a controversy erupted around the victory of the then 18-year-old Caster Semenya in the women's 800-meter competition. On the eve of the final, the IAAF announced that they were conducting tests to determine whether Semenya was "100 percent" a woman (Longman 2016). In this extraordinary move, the IAAF broke with its own protocol by disregarding Semenya's right to confidentiality amongst such an accusation, leading to unprecedented public scrutiny of Semenya's body and right to compete. The IAAF's reckless actions drew considerable critique, particularly in South Africa, where they were framed as racially motivated (Cooky et al. 2013). Following the Championships, the IAAF revisited their procedure for investigating women athletes believed to have high testosterone, culminating in 2011 with the public release of the Hyperandrogenism Regulations (IAAF 2011). Reflecting their long-standing collaboration with the IAAF on this issue, the IOC quickly followed suit and introduced parallel regulations applying to all women's Olympic sports (Henne 2014; IOC 2012).

The IAAF's 2011 Regulations specified a limit of 10 nmol/L for endogenous testosterone in women athletes.[3] The criteria for identifying athletes "suspected" of having hyperandrogenism were left vague and open-ended, with potential sources described as including *any* information received by IAAF medical officials (IAAF 2011, p. 3, emphasis added). "Suspect" athletes were subjected to initial blood testing and, if their testosterone was found to be above the specified limit, a clinical examination followed to assess the extent of "virilization" (visible signs of high testosterone exposure in the breasts, pubic hair, skin, etc.). This clinical examination was presumed to be a proxy for measuring the extent of an athlete's "unfair" performance advantage. Athletes believed to be benefiting from higher than "normal" testosterone were required to medically lower their levels before returning to competition. Scholars and activists note that this approach has largely targeted gender nonconforming athletes and especially women of color from the Global South, reflecting the entanglement of race and nation with normative constructions of femininity (Bohuon 2015; Henne and Pape 2018; Karkazis and Jordan-Young 2018; Magubane 2014).

In 2014, an 18-year-old Indian sprinter, Dutee Chand, was barred from international track-and-field competition for ostensibly having "violated" the Regulations. Instead of agreeing to medical interventions, Chand contested this regulatory regime before the CAS in Switzerland in 2015. During the appeal, expert witnesses for Chand and the IAAF debated the relationship between testosterone, sex difference, and athletic ability, including whether endogenous and exogenous (artificially administered) testosterone had similar or different effects on the body.[4] Ultimately, the CAS adjudicating panel ruled that the Regulations were *not yet* sufficiently supported by scientific evidence, suspending them for two years but encouraging the pursuit of new research to support their reinstatement. In other words, the CAS supported a policy aimed at excluding women athletes with high testosterone and endorsed the post hoc pursuit of scientific evidence, rather than awaiting the outcome of a broader research agenda.

Following the decision to suspend the Regulations, Caster Semenya returned to career-best form, culminating in her victory at the 2016 Olympic Games in Rio de Janeiro where an additional two 800 m competitors, both women of color from Sub-Saharan African nations—Francine Niyonsaba and Margaret Wambui—were also publicly accused by media commentators and track-and-field stakeholders of having elevated testosterone. In 2018, the IAAF announced a revised set of regulations, this time with a limit of 5 nmol/L and applying only to those women's events where IAAF-affiliated researchers claimed to have established a correlation between testosterone levels and performance (IAAF 2018).[5] Though initially suspended as Semenya and Athletics South Africa pursued an appeal process, in May 2019, the CAS contradicted concerns within the broader scientific community by deciding that the revised regulations, though discriminatory, provided "a necessary, reasonable and proportionate means of achieving the IAAF's aim of preserving the integrity of female athletics" (CAS 2019, p. 2; Tannenbaum and Bekker 2019; WMA 2019).

In sum, the scientific and ethical controversies that have plagued the hyperandrogenism era—and indeed, all previous eras of gender eligibility regulation (Henne 2014)—have not dissuaded governing bodies and the IAAF in particular from seeking seemingly more sophisticated "scientific" ways to define the boundaries of the female body and "fairness" amongst women athletes. This state of affairs reveals a deep institutional investment in particular constructions of sex difference and testosterone that is driven by motivations other than science. Since governing bodies do not operate in a vacuum, the legitimacy of their regulatory efforts depends upon the support of diverse stakeholders (Parker and Braithwaite 2003). As I will show below, decision-makers and stakeholders in the sport of track-and-field frequently work in concert to "turn away" from and ignore that which could otherwise be known about the female athlete body. Before addressing these issues, I first discuss my data collection methods.

Data and Methods: Perspectives on a Controversy

In the wake of the renewed scrutiny of women alleged to have high testosterone during the 2016 Rio Olympic Games, I conducted semi-structured interviews with diverse individuals associated with elite track-and-field with the aim of understanding how their convictions, knowledge, and non-knowledge reflected their particular social and institutional environment. In all, I collected 62 semi-structured in-depth interviews with athletes, coaches, team staff, managers, officials including governing body representatives, media personnel, academics, and activists. All of these interviewees either were involved in track-and-field at the elite international level between 2009 and 2016 or had engaged in some way with decision-making processes related to the regulation of women with high testosterone. The sample encompassed ten countries, the majority of which were English-speaking and located in the Global North. Few of the interviewees were scientists, reflecting my interest in understanding how ideas about biological sex and testosterone circulate within the broader sport of track-and-field and legitimate associated regulatory regimes (Parker and Braithwaite 2003).

I asked interviewees to describe various aspects of their experiences related to the regulation of women with high testosterone, including the following: what they knew about the CAS appeal in 2015; how they felt about the claim that testosterone's effects on performance were not yet well established; the kinds of conversations about the topic they had engaged in; their reaction to the women's 800 m during the Rio Olympic Games; and their overall position on the regulation of women with high testosterone. The majority of the interviews were completed before the 2018 announcement of the IAAF's revised regulations, meaning this study offers insights into the views of key stakeholders at a moment when the future of regulating women with high testosterone was especially uncertain. Some interviewees had been involved in the sport for many years and were able to reflect on the 2009 World Championships or even earlier events, thereby offering some important historical context to contemporary debates.

I imported the transcribed interviews into NVivo, a qualitative data analysis software, to aid in the coding process. I iteratively read and coded the data, working with small excerpts at a time and applying existing theories to the data in order to identify opportunities for novel theoretical insights (Timmermans and Tavory 2012). I found three emergent themes: adherence to *misinformation* and harmful misrepresentations; *ideologically* motivated rather than scientifically informed policy priorities; and *avoidance* of becoming informed.

Findings: Three Modes of Ignorance

Ignorance as Misinformation

Charting the flows and non-flows of knowledge within the elite track-and-field community begins with an exploration of how they feel about the regulation of women with high testosterone and the extent to which these views are well informed. As I show below, various forms of misinformation and misrepresentation abounded. First, and contrary to the IAAF's claim during the 2015 appeal to the CAS that "the 'community of athletes' supports the Hyperandrogenism Regulations" (CAS 2015, p. 27), a few athletes as well as coaches, officials, team staff, and media personnel were ambivalent about or even opposed to the regulation of women with high testosterone. Even two female 800 m runners I interviewed, who had competed against Caster Semenya, stated that they supported her right to compete. According to one, "my feelings have changed as more information has come out" and "I'd love [Semenya] to break the world record … I'm supportive of Caster now." Overall, however, women and especially athletes in my sample were more likely to call for the reinstatement of the Hyperandrogenism Regulations, particularly if they competed in the 800 m.

Yet many interviewees also confessed they knew little about the content of the Hyperandrogenism Regulations or the scientific issues raised during the CAS appeal in 2015. Those that did have some knowledge often had a background in sports science and had either encountered critiques of the policies as part of their education or were sufficiently curious to seek out further information. As recalled by one coach, "the only reason why I had an idea of [the CAS decision] was because I'm interested in physiology, so I had read further [and] knew a little bit more than some of the athletes." Amongst other interviewees, it was common to (erroneously) believe that the CAS had suspended the Hyperandrogenism Regulations purely for ethical reasons. For example, one middle-distance coach believed the Regulations were suspended "because of human rights … that's what I seem to recall, but all the details I don't know anything about." One journalist and coach described a conversation with the lead track-and-field journalist for a major French newspaper, who "had this misconception about the whole story regarding the Dutee Chand case" and believed "it's unethical to not let her compete, and that's why CAS suspended the rule." The interviewee had explained, "no, if you read the conclusion of the case, it's not about being unfair or unethical ... the IAAF didn't have the science to back up the rule." The mis-casting of the issue as purely ethical enables stakeholders to ignore the existence of scientific debate, the presence of which threatens their ability to claim an indisputable relationship between testosterone, sex difference, and athletic ability.

Many interviewees were also not aware of the history of gender verification practices in the sport of track-and-field, especially current athletes without a sports science background who had not experienced the compulsory testing regime of earlier decades. For example, one athlete advocated for testing based on chromosomes, without realizing that such an approach had previously been implemented and ultimately discarded for lack of scientific rigor and relevance:

> [My teammate] had a really good and a fair way of looking at it, where instead of looking at testosterone levels he's actually like "well, let's just look at chromosomes" ... Maybe there needs to be a reclassification of individuals with XX chromosomes and then individuals with XY chromosomes and then we separate categories like that.

In other words, the lessons of the 1980s—when the IAAF and IOC were eventually forced to acknowledge that sex chromosomes are neither binary nor correspond with athletic ability—had not become part of the general knowledge base within the sport. Nor had critical awareness of the scientific challenges associated with such practices.

The interview data also reveals a significant amount of uninformed, derogatory, and harmful language in relation to women with high testosterone. Many interviewees were uncertain about what constituted respectful terminology. For instance, when describing the scrutiny of certain women during the Rio Olympic Games, one athlete said "excuse any improper terminology, but [women] who happened to be a hermaphrodite or hyperandrogenous ... I don't even know what the terms are."

Indeed, it was not uncommon for athletes and coaches to use the problematic term, "hermaphrodite." One journalist recalled an article in a major Italian newspaper using the "outdated" term "hermaphrodite," the author of which was also the President of the International Sports Press Association.

It was also not uncommon for interviewees to have heard of women with high testosterone being referred to as "men." One athlete described the following scene during the Rio Olympic Games:

> It's coming from these people high up the chain. You know, the talk coming out onto the track or sitting in the stands, there are things from the [team] leaders … they're saying things like, "Oh it's a race for 4th" or "the men are on the track again."

As another Rio Olympian reflected, "in any other situation you'd say it quietly, if it was going to be a negative comment or an assumption or anything like that, but it seems with Semenya it's just fair game [to comment openly] … it's pretty bad."

Additional forms of pathologizing language also surfaced. As stated by one media commentator, who was part of the television coverage of the Olympic Games in his home country, his "superficial understanding is that we've got a different species here. You've got males, you've got females, and you've got intersex … it's a different sort of person." A middle-distance coach interviewee referred to one athlete with high testosterone as "a disabled person because she has an illness or a disease that gives her a very, very high testosterone level." Overall, all interviewees had either encountered or used harmful and derogatory language toward women with high testosterone. There was some evidence of change, with numerous interviewees suggesting that they and the broader track-and-field community had become much more informed and sensitive in recent years. However, disrespectful and harmful descriptions of women with high testosterone remained normalized. Combined with misinformation, these discursive misrepresentations protect the dominant scientific epistemology of the binary sexed body by objectifying—and even dehumanizing—the women affected by Regulations, thereby enabling stakeholders to turn away from thoughtful reflection on the complexities of athletic performance and the real-life impacts of such regulations.

Ignorance as Ideology

In order to develop and legitimate their rule-making efforts, governing bodies may draw selectively on expert scientific advisors, in the process establishing privileged and private spaces for scientific knowledge production that enable the pursuit of certain research agendas to the exclusion of others (Frickel et al. 2010; Jasanoff 1990). When the politics underpinning the designation of certain scientific research agendas and claims as policy-relevant are not broadly recognized, it becomes possible to ignore the existence of alternative approaches (Hess 2007; Frickel et al. 2010). In circumstances where existing epistemic and ideological commitments are strong, policy priorities are likely to *precede* the pursuit of scientific knowledge, rather than policy agendas following from independently conducted (and potentially disruptive) research (Kleinman and Suryanarayanan 2012; Richardson 2013). The regulation of women with high testosterone shows how the a priori and ideologically driven determination of policy is a form of ignorance, one based on the active disinvestment in and exclusion of claims that in this case might prompt the track-and-field community to consider alternative policy agendas. According to gender scholar, Judith Lorber (1993), "believing is seeing": biological scientists "discover" binary sex in their data because they are socially conditioned to expect two discrete sex categories (p. 569). The same phenomenon applies outside of the research laboratory.

The strong commitment of interviewees to the belief that testosterone is the basis of performance differences between men and women was unaffected by scientific debates concerning the actual magnitude of testosterone's effects on athletic ability. When asked about the 2015 CAS decision to suspend the Hyperandrogenism Regulations because the IAAF lacked the scientific evidence to justify the exclusion of women based on testosterone levels, many interviewees expressed incredulity. This was particularly the case for those without a background in sports science, for whom the question of whether there was a relationship between testosterone and athletic performance was presumed long settled. Any suggestion to the contrary contradicted what the majority of interviewees had accepted as the conventional wisdom of the sport: testosterone underpins both athletic ability and sex difference, and therefore also explains average differences between male and female athletes. The presence of scientific disagreement about this relationship was incomprehensible.

Within this ideological context, interviewees widely accepted the unsubstantiated rumor that the three women who medaled in the 800 m at the Rio Olympic Games benefited significantly from having elevated testosterone levels. According to one competitor, "well of course they're running these times, of course they're beating all of us if they have more testosterone." One coach from the Rio Olympic Games stated it was "very predictable how [a female athlete] with high testosterone levels runs, because we can just see, particularly in those middle-distance races, the amount of power and the finishing speed and the ability to hold that pace." Another coach similarly stated that "naturally occurring testosterone is the key, in terms of maintaining muscle mass, increased metabolism, production of energy," alleging further that the three Rio medalists who "*obviously* had elevated testosterone levels" were "more manly, larger than all of the other girls, [they] run like a man" (emphasis added). These kinds of anecdotal observations were frequently presented as evidence to justify existing beliefs and dismiss scientific claims about the disparate ways that bodies process testosterone during athletic performance. As stated by one Olympic coach, "we *know* testosterone is critical to performance, so for the CAS to ask for more evidence is nonsensical" (emphasis added).

As stated above, a core issue during the CAS appeal was whether endogenous and exogenous testosterone equally affected athletic performance. When I informed interviewees that the CAS panel had determined this question could not be answered given the limited amount of available evidence, many interviewees opted to embrace a simplified narrative of testosterone. Most commonly, they collapsed the distinction between endogenous and exogenous forms of testosterone in order to claim the performance-enhancing effects of the latter as evidence for their convictions:

> I think that most people do believe that there is an unfair biological advantage [associated with testosterone] and that we'd be hard-pressed to believe otherwise ... If there was no advantage ... there would be no distinctions between women who choose to take testosterone ... If there was no advantage, then why would women dope? (Rio Olympian, woman)

In response to such accounts, I often suggested that expert witnesses for Chand had questioned whether endogenous and exogenous testosterone acted similarly in the body. When I did so, many interviewees again turned to doping as evidence of testosterone's performance-enhancing effects. As one athlete stated, "the thing is, if [testosterone] didn't affect [performance], then it would be legal ... [but] it's been put on the prohibited list." This epistemic investment in testosterone as *always* a decisive performance enhancer preceded the available evidence and relied on a simplified narrative that erased the possibility of an endogenous/exogenous divide, instead representing testosterone's effects as universal regardless of its origins.

When reflecting on the IAAF's rule-making responsibilities, interviewees implied that scientific evidence could be pursued post hoc. For instance, a former 800 m runner turned television commentator suggested that the IAAF—and the broader track-and-field community—were committed to the Hyperandrogenism Regulations regardless of the scientific evidence:

> If you were the IAAF, what would you do? Because we wanted to exclude [women with high testosterone], but we don't have the science to do it ... We wish we could have come up with a better argument to exclude them, but we couldn't ... [Now] we're just waiting for our language and *our science to catch up with the reality that we can see.*

Interviews also revealed that even the experts involved in drafting both the IOC and IAAF Hyperandrogenism Regulations were committed to their policy stance despite recognizing the lack of supporting evidence. For example, an activist and researcher described a conversation with one such expert, where she "ran everything by him ... most especially that I didn't think the evidence was there, and he agreed with everything I said."

However, he publicly disagreed with her arguments once they were published.

A similar story was recounted by a researcher and intersex rights advocate who had been invited to participate in a working group convened in 2013 to review the IOC Hyperandrogenism Regulations. Several members of the IAAF Medical Commission were also present, reflecting the long history of the two organizations working together to establish their gender eligibility rules (Henne 2014). The interviewee described repeatedly pointing out anomalies in the IOC and IAAF's logic, such as the observation that women with complete androgen insensitivity syndrome—meaning their bodies derive no benefit from the testosterone in their bodies—are able to compete at the international level, suggesting that testosterone cannot be as decisive as IOC and IAAF decision-makers claim. Although they acknowledged such anomalies, other working group members "really couldn't understand the difference between data and policy" and were "quite determined to put this hyperandrogenism policy through." She reflected:

> The science to me was sort of the window dressing, the reasoning behind the decision that was already made. There is the famous quote … that a judge knows what he'll decide before the case is over and then he'll come up with the reasons afterward. And that's the way humans are.

Thus, despite claiming there exists "broad medical and scientific consensus … that the high levels of endogenous testosterone circulating in athletes with certain DSDs [Differences of Sexual Development] can significantly enhance their sporting performance" (IAAF 2018), the IAAF's rule-making agenda—like the attitudes of other stakeholders in the sport—precedes and exists in spite of current scientific debate, particularly in relation to the precise relationship between testosterone levels and male and female athletic ability. Maintaining an ideological commitment to testosterone as the basis of athletic ability and binary sex categories emerged as a more urgent priority than supporting the pursuit of a more balanced and open scientific process. This constituted a "turning away" from inconvenient scientific evidence and debate, which might otherwise call current policy commitments into question and destabilize a regulatory agenda aimed at maintaining a strict binary definition of who may "legitimately" be recognized as a female athlete.

Ignorance as Avoidance

The presence of expert advisors—alleged to be the purveyors of objective facts—offer decision-makers a means of deferring responsibility for key decisions and justifying their lack of engagement with alternative knowledge claims that might undermine their existing policy commitments (Jasanoff 1990; McGoey 2007). This kind of avoidance emerged during my recruitment efforts. For example, when I approached individuals associated with the women's committees of the IAAF and IOC to request an interview, they indicated that the regulation of women with high testosterone was not their area of expertise and instructed me to approach the relevant medical committee instead. One of my interviewees, who had previously served on the IOC Women's Commission, had experienced similar avoidance. In his words, "most of those people were very reluctant to accept advocacy on this [issue] … for the most part they said 'we will defer to the Medical Commission and the physicians,' and basically that's where things end." Similarly, an IAAF official I interviewed stated that he "had not tried to second guess" the organization's medical committee and "perhaps therefore [hadn't] understood … their research justification" for excluding women with high testosterone.

But there was also evidence of more concerted efforts by the IAAF to avoid open and informed discussion amongst key stakeholders on the topic of regulating women with high testosterone. In one account of practices during the early 2000s, at a time when the IAAF had moved to a less visible testing regime for women athletes, an international official described trying to obtain more information about the new rules at successive World Athletic Congresses.[6] In 2003, he was "brushed off by the chairman of the IAAF Medical Commission," who assured him that "they most certainly knew what they were doing concerning gender testing." Unconvinced, in 2005, the official again requested to discuss the regulations:

> I submitted a proposal along with substantial background materials ... I came much more prepared ... I had sent a lot of materials to the IAAF, but they were never given on to the other countries, to the [other] delegates ... When I criticized that and tried to reveal what was going on, the [IAAF] President took away my right of speaking.

Historical actions of the IOC Medical Commission similarly suggest an institutionally sanctioned culture of avoidance. Archival materials reveal that its leadership avoided engaging with critiques of their chromosome-based testing regime that were repeatedly lodged by endocrinologists and various professional scientific associations throughout the 1970s and 1980s.[7] The chairperson at the time resisted raising such concerns at Commission meetings and defended their policy stance as "practical and economical" even if not scientifically sound.[8]

Avoidance of a different kind was visible at the level of national federations, with one national coach and administrator describing his federation as preferring "to leave the decision to the IAAF ... [and] not to worry too much about it unless the Regulations actually end up affecting one of our athletes." The notion that certain countries were less likely to have athletes affected by the Regulations emerged in several interviews and was linked to the unsubstantiated belief that women with high testosterone are over-represented in Sub-Saharan Africa relative to countries in the Global North (see Henne and Pape 2018; Karkazis and Jordan-Young 2018). For instance, when I asked one physical therapist from a Global North country whether the Regulations could impact athletes on his national team, he responded that "the general wisdom is that in Africa, the prevalence of certain gender presentations is a lot higher." This logic was offered by numerous interviewees as justification for why their home national federations could afford to be uniformed about the regulations. It also reproduces the racialized and imperialist notion that women of color from the Global South are somehow biologically different and hence the legitimate targets of such regulatory efforts, enabling decision-makers from other nations to avoid responsibility for such actions.

Another factor prompting national federations to avoid engagement was a fear of backlash. One athlete perceived that her national federation was "too scared to get involved in the argument ... just putting their hands up and going 'I'm not getting involved' … They don't want to open themselves up to the response they might get." A board member from a national federation that was considering protesting the Regulations described a colleague who "feels that this is maybe not the fight we should be fighting against the IAAF. People that think we should just stick our head in the sand and let other people take this," since not only were their athletes perceived as not being targeted under the rules, but also "we are not a powerhouse … They just don't feel this is the [issue] we should be sticking our necks out for." However, as acknowledged by this interviewee, avoidance also serves another purpose: "if anything, we have athletes who would benefit from the rules staying in" if other competitors were disqualified.

Athletes also engaged in various forms of avoidance. Some reported being preoccupied with their own training and racing. One female long-distance runner reflected on her lack of awareness during the Rio Olympic Games, stating she didn't "recall being too savvy … I think I was just so caught up in my training and preparation." Some women athletes who were ambivalent toward or supportive of women with high testosterone qualified their position by stating that it might be different if they competed in the 800 m. According to one, "I don't really have a very strong opinion, I think it probably comes back to the fact that they're not running in my race," again assuming that women with high testosterone were only competing in specific events. Another ambivalent athlete, who stated she might "feel differently if this was my event," suggested further she "maybe didn't read enough, I would only see headlines or it would pop up on Twitter … it wasn't something that I cared to be one-hundred percent informed on." But even women 800 m runners I interviewed typically acknowledged not being fully informed, such as one who stated, "I have less knowledge than I should on the whole topic … I get kind of embarrassed about that."

National federations encouraged this kind of avoidance amongst athletes. For example, ahead of the Rio Olympic Games, one middle-distance runner described being advised by her federation's communications staff:

> … to avoid all questions related to the topic. They literally gave us a list of ways to deflect the topic … For those of us who ran 1500, it was "just say

it's not your event, not something you need to worry about or waste energy on…" Just kind of appearing neutral on the issue was the recommended approach.

For my interviewees, this was typically the extent of official directions provided by national federations. But it contrasted with their approach to other issues, where federations more readily assumed the role of educator. As observed by one Rio track-and-field Olympian:

> We have never in a team setting had the discussion with a medical person, or one of the coaches come and say, 'look, we recognize there's been talk about this… The [CAS] ruling is this because of this.' With other issues, like the plumbing issues, the building, the venues in Rio, mosquitos, Zika, what not, we were given so much education.

A track-and-field Olympian from a different country similarly reflected that "we get random briefings on different topics, but [hyperandrogenism] was never brought up on any of the teams that I've been on in the past three or four years, so it wasn't something that our governing body felt the need to tell us about." Thus, while some athletes had sought to become more informed, the majority appeared to actively avoid arriving at a definitive or informed stance on the topic, an approach that was encouraged by their national governing bodies.

The degree to which athletes have sought an informed opinion is an important concern, since the IAAF argued during the 2015 CAS appeal that "what is unfair is decided, to a large extent, by the community of athletes and other stakeholders who understand and love the sport" (CAS 2015, 82). But rather than correct misinformation, or draw attention to the breadth of opinions regarding the complexity of sex difference and testosterone's role in athletic performance, the IAAF and other leadership bodies appear to readily avoid such education efforts. Within this institutionally sanctioned culture of avoidance, the policy of excluding women with high testosterone goes unquestioned.

Discussion and Conclusion: Ignorance and Epistemological Resistance

This chapter is motivated by a broad question: how do people ignore epistemologies of the sexed body that contradict their beliefs, in this case, the alternative scientific accounts of sex difference—as non-binary, dynamic, indeterminate, and irreducible to a single biological factor—espoused by feminist scholars and some members of the scientific community? Sport has emerged in recent decades as a key institutional sphere where definitional battles over binary sex and gender categories are unfolding with increasing regularity and intensity. This is partially due to various international governing bodies' strict commitment to regulating gender eligibility *in spite of* the absence of supportive scientific evidence and the presence of alternative scientific and ethical perspectives (Cavanagh and Sykes 2006; Sullivan 2011; Pape 2017). In other words, this is a case of ignorance under conditions where it is possible to know sex and testosterone differently, as opposed to a situation where such knowledge has not yet been identified or produced (Frickel et al. 2010).

Under such circumstances, ignorance can usefully be conceptualized as an institutional process in which stakeholders collectively "turn away" from knowledge claims that are uncomfortable or disruptive, sometimes deliberately so, but often without reflection. As revealed in this study, ignorance relies on epistemic alignment among the diverse stakeholders that comprise an institutional sphere, in this case, the sport's governing bodies, affiliated scientists, athletes, coaches, team staff, managers, and media personnel connected to elite track-and-field. Together, these stakeholders co-construct and legitimize particular epistemologies of sex difference and testosterone, while actively excluding alternative accounts through strategies of misinformation, selective and ideologically driven interpretation of evidence, and avoidance. Interestingly, those interviewees with a background in sports science were more willing to recognize the presence of scientific debate. This suggests that efforts to protect binary representations of sex and testosterone are not driven by an investment in "science" per se, but in the gendered ideologies that underpin these regulatory practices.

It is important to consider the affective dimensions of such rule-making efforts. The "political geography" of this issue is arguably *not* shaped primarily by corporate or industry interests, as often comes to the fore in ignorance studies (Frickel et al. 2010; Kleinman and Suryanarayanan 2012; McGoey 2012), though such interests no doubt shape gender relations in international sport (Lenskyj 1986). Rather, the epistemic investments at stake concern lived experiences of sex as a binary form of embodied difference: an understanding of one's body that has been created within a specific institutional environment, but which is nevertheless "felt" as real and meaningful on a daily basis (Connell 1987). Testosterone, too, has become part of athletes' daily embodied experience and self-understanding, given the prominence of anti-doping regulation and narratives in elite sport (Henne 2015; Karkazis and Jordan-Young 2018). That these stakes are felt as deeply personal is evidenced by the often-emotional reaction of interviewees when asked about the issue of women with high testosterone. This affective dimension is also likely fundamental to the widespread will to ignore—rather than know differently—when it comes to this issue and warrants further examination.

While diverse stakeholders participate, the forms of ignorance identified in this study are legitimated and enabled by the actions of the IAAF and IOC and—to a lesser but still important extent—national federations, all of whom have the resources and structures to engage in education efforts. Through their actions, governing bodies not only select sympathetic scientific experts, and materially support their research agendas, but also prevent the recognition of alternative claims. This insight highlights the importance of an expanded feminist STS agenda: one that goes beyond revealing the gendered biases embedded in scientific claims about binary sex, or supporting feminist biologists to pursue more complex research agendas, to include critical examination of the institutional mechanisms by which feminist claims about biological difference are granted or denied legitimacy in other settings. Studies of ignorance, like that presented in this chapter, are one way by which feminist scholars can reveal the considerable institutional work that goes into preventing the production and recognition of alternative forms of scientific knowledge (Tuana 2004, 2006).

Notes

1. While the IOC and IAAF have rules in place to regulate the participation of transgender women, these are distinct from the type of regulation that is the focus of this chapter, which concerns those women with high testosterone presumably resulting from "intersex" traits. Since these women may not identify as intersex, I refer to them as women with high testosterone.

2. Consistent with the approach of the World Anti-Doping Agency (WADA) (WADA 2018, pp. 36–37), in this chapter, I use "exogenous testosterone" to refer to both: (a) forms of testosterone that do not occur naturally in the body; and (b) forms of testosterone that *do* occur naturally in the body but have been artificially elevated (i.e. exogenously administered). A key debate during the Chand appeal was whether these two forms of testosterone behaved differently in the body when compared to *naturally occurring levels* of *endogenous* testosterone.

3. The Hyperandrogenism Regulations of the IOC specified a limit of 8 nmol/L (IOC 2012).

4. The CAS adjudicating panel observed that "this remains an unresolved issue that would benefit from further exploration" (CAS 2015, p. 142).

5. IAAF researchers claim a correlation between testosterone levels and performance in the women's hammer throw, pole vault, 400 m, 400 m hurdles, and 800 m. By contrast, the subsequent proposed (and then suspended) "Eligibility Regulations for Female Classification" apply to the women's 400 m, 400 m hurdles, 800 m, 1500 m, and mile (Bermon and Garnier 2017; IAAF 2018).

6. The World Athletics Congress is the biannual meeting of the IAAF and its constituent member federations.

7. In a separate research project, I accessed the IOC archives at the Olympic Studies Centre in Lausanne where several files contain correspondence from the 1930s until the 1980s on the topic of eligibility regulation for women athletes.

8. Letter from Dr. Eduardo Hay (IOC Medical Commission) to Dr. Albert de le Chappelle, 25 April 1983, p. 3.

References

Acker, J. (1990). Hierarchies, jobs, bodies: A theory of gendered organizations. *Gender & Society, 4*, 139–158.

Bermon, S., & Garnier, P. Y. (2017). Serum androgen levels and their relation to performance in track and field: Mass spectrometry results from 2127 observations in male and female athletes. *British Journal of Sports Medicine, 51*, 1309–1314.

Birrell, S., & Cole, C. C. (1990). Double fault: Renee Richards and the construction and naturalization of difference. *Sociology of Sport Journal, 7*, 1–21.

Bohuon, A. (2015). Gender verifications in sport: From an East/West antagonism to a North/South antagonism. *The International Journal of the History of Sport, 32*, 965–979.

Cavanagh, S. L., & Sykes, H. (2006). Transsexual bodies at the Olympics: The International Olympic Committee's policy on transsexual athletes at the 2004 Athens summer games. *Body & Society, 12*, 75–102.

Connell, R. (1987). *Gender and power: Society, the person, and sexual politics.* Palo Alto, CA: Stanford University Press.

Cooky, C., Dycus, R., & Dworkin, S. L. (2013). "What makes a woman a woman?" versus "our first lady of sport": A comparative analysis of United States and the South African media coverage of Caster Semenya. *Journal of Sport and Social Issues, 37*, 31–56.

Court of Arbitration for Sport (CAS). (2015). CAS 2014/A/3759 Dutee Chand v. In *Athletics Federation of India (AFI) & The International Association of Athletics Federations (IAAF).* Lausanne: Court of Arbitration for Sport.

CAS. (2019). *Semenya, ASA and IAAF: Executive summary.* Lausanne: Court of Arbitration for Sport.

Fausto-Sterling, A. (2000). *Sexing the body: Gender politics and the construction of sexuality.* New York: Basic Books.

Fausto-Sterling, A. (2012). The dynamic development of gender variability. *Journal of Homosexuality, 59*, 398–421.

Frickel, S., Gibbon, S., Howard, J., Kempner, J., Ottinger, G., & Hess, D. J. (2010). Undone science: Charting social movement and civil society challenges to research agenda setting. *Science, Technology, and Human Values, 35*, 444–473.

Frickel, S., & Vincent, M. B. (2007). Hurricane Katrina, contamination, and the unintended organization of ignorance. *Technology in Society, 29*, 181–188.

Fujimura, J. (2006). Sex genes: A critical sociomaterial approach to the politics and molecular genetics of sex determination. *Signs, 32*, 49–82.

Gross, M. (2007). The unknown in process: Dynamic connections of ignorance, non-knowledge and related concepts. *Current Sociology, 55*, 742–759.

Henne, K. (2014). The 'science' of fair play in sport: Gender and the politics of testing. *Signs, 39*, 787–812.

Henne, K. (2015). *Testing for athlete citizenship: Regulating doping and sex in sport.* New Brunswick, NJ: Rutgers University Press.

Henne, K., & Pape, M. (2018). Dilemmas of gender and global sports governance: An invitation to southern theory. *Sociology of Sport Journal, 35*, 216–225.

Hess, D. J. (2007). *Alternative pathways in science and industry: Activism, innovation, and the environment in an era of globalization.* Cambridge, MA: MIT Press.

International Association of Athletics Federations (IAAF). (2011). *IAAF regulations governing eligibility of females with hyperandrogenism to compete in women's competition. Appendices.* Monaco: IAAF.

IAAF. (2018, April 27). IAAF introduces new eligibility regulations for female classification. Retrieved from https://www.iaaf.org/news/press-release/eligibility-regulations-for-female-classifica.

International Olympic Committee (IOC). (2012). *IOC regulations on female hyperandrogenism.* Retrieved from https://stillmed.olympic.org/Documents/Commissions_PDFfiles/Medical_commission/2012-06-22-IOC-Regulations-on-Female-Hyperandrogenism-eng.pdf.

Jasanoff, S. (1990). *The fifth branch: Science advisers as policymakers.* Cambridge, MA: Harvard University Press.

Kane, M. J. (1995). Resistance/transformation of the oppositional binary: Exposing sport as a continuum. *Journal of Sport and Social Issues, 19*, 191–218.

Karkazis, K., & Jordan-Young, R. (2018). The powers of testosterone: Obscuring race and regional bias in the regulation of women athletes. *Feminist Formations, 30*, 1–39.

Karkazis, K., Jordan-Young, R., Davis, G., & Camporesi, S. (2012). Out of bounds? A critique of the new policies on hyperandrogenism in elite female athletes. *American Journal of Bioethics, 12*, 3–16.

Kleinman, D. L., & Suryanarayanan, S. (2012). Dying bees and the social production of ignorance. *Science, Technology, & Human Values, 38*, 492–517.

Lenskyj, H. (1986). *Out of bounds: Women, sport, and sexuality.* Toronto, ON: Women's Press.

Longman, J. (2016). Understanding the controversy over Caster Semenya. *The New York Times*. August 18. Retrieved from https://www.nytimes.com/2016/08/20/sports/caster-semenya-800-meters.html.

Lopez, J., & Scott, J. (2000). *Social structure. Buckingham*. Philadelphia: Open University Press.

Lorber, J. (1993). Believing is seeing: Biology as ideology. *Gender & Society, 7*, 568–581.

Magubane, Z. (2014). Spectacles and scholarship: Caster Semenya, intersex studies, and the problem of race in feminist theory. *Signs, 39*, 761–785.

Martin, E. (1991). The egg and the sperm. *Signs, 16*, 485–501.

McGoey, L. (2007). On the will to ignorance in bureaucracy. *Economy and Society, 36*, 212–235.

McGoey, L. (2012). The logic of strategic ignorance. *The British Journal of Sociology, 63*, 553–576.

Pape, M. (2017). The fairest of them all: Gender-determining institutions and the science of sex testing. In V. Demos & M. T. Segal (Eds.), *Advances in Gender Research 24: Gender Panic, Gender Policy* (pp. 177–202). Bingley: Emerald Books.

Parker, C., & Braithwaite, J. (2003). Regulation. In M. Tushnet & P. Cane (Eds.), *The Oxford handbook of legal studies* (pp. 119–145). Oxford: Oxford University Press.

Pieper, L. (2016). *Sex testing: Gender policing in women's sports*. Urbana, IL: University of Illinois Press.

Proctor, R. N., & Schiebinger, L. (Eds.). (2008). *Agnotology: The making & unmaking of ignorance*. Stanford, CA: Stanford University Press.

Richardson, S. (2013). *Sex itself: The search or male and female in the human genome*. Chicago: University of Chicago Press.

Ritz, S. A. (2018). Complexities of addressing sex in cell culture research. *Signs, 42*, 307–327.

Sanz, V. (2017). No way out of the binary: A critical history of the scientific production of sex. *Signs, 43*, 1–27.

Sullivan, C. F. (2011). Gender verification and gender policies in elite sport: Eligibility and "fair play". *Journal of Sport & Social Issues, 35*, 400–419.

Tacke, V. (2001). BSE as an organizational construction: A case study on the globalization of risk. *The British Journal of Sociology, 52*, 293–312.

Tannenbaum, C., & Bekker, S. (2019). Sex, gender, and sports. *British Medical Journal, 364*(8192), 1120.

Timmermans, S., & Tavory, I. (2012). Theory construction in qualitative research: From grounded theory to abductive analysis. *Sociological Theory, 30*, 167–186.

Tuana, N. (1988). The weaker seed: The sexist bias of reproductive theory. *Hypatia, 3*, 35–60.

Tuana, N. (2004). Coming to understand: Orgasm and the epistemology of ignorance. *Hypatia, 19*, 194–232.

Tuana, N. (2006). The speculum of ignorance: The women's health movement and epistemologies of ignorance. *Hypatia, 21*, 1–19.

van Anders, S. M. (2012). Testosterone and sexual desire in healthy women and men. *Archives of Sexual Behavior, 41*, 1471–1484.

Wackwitz, L. (2003). Verifying the myth: Olympic sex testing and the category woman. *Women's Studies International Forum, 26*, 553–560.

Westbrook, L. (2016). Transforming the sex/gender/sexuality system: The construction of trans categories in the United States. In N. Fischer & S. Seidman (Eds.), *Introducing the new sexuality studies* (pp. 33–42). New York: Routledge.

World Anti-Doping Agency (WADA). (2018). *Athlete biological passport operating guidelines.* Version 6.1, July 2018. Retrieved from https://www.wada-ama.org/sites/default/files/resources/files/guidelines_abp_v61_2018_jul_en.pdf.

World Medical Association (WMA). (2019). WMA reiterates advice to physicians not to implement IAAF rules on classifying women athletes. Retrieved May 3, 2019, from https://www.wma.net/news-post/wma-reiterates-advice-to-physicians-not-to-implement-iaaf-rules-on-classifying-women-athletes/.

Screening Saviors?: The Politics of Care, College Sports, and Screening Athletes for Sickle Cell Trait

Mary G. McDonald

Since 2013, the National Collegiate Athletic Association (NCAA) has required that all athletes be screened for sickle cell trait. NCAA administrators and supportive member institutions justify screening as necessary to ensure the care, health, and safety of student-athletes given that the inherited condition can interfere with blood flow and oxygen uptake under extreme conditions such as during intense exercise. Once identified through the NCAA's screening program, affected athletes are then asked to monitor themselves—with assistance from trainers and coaches—during physically demanding sporting activity to ensure their well-being. However, the American Society of Hematology (ASH) has criticized the decision to screen college athletes as overly broad and unnecessary. ASH has argued that the screenings be stopped and replaced with a preventative model similar to that developed by the US military. This model offers a different focus suggesting the need to care for the safety and well-being of all athletes regardless of sickle cell trait status. This "universal precau-

M. G. McDonald (✉)
Georgia Institute of Technology, Atlanta, GA, USA
e-mail: mary.mcdonald@hsoc.gatech.edu

© The Author(s) 2020   **247**
J. J. Sterling, M. G. McDonald (eds.), *Sports, Society, and Technology*,
https://doi.org/10.1007/978-981-32-9127-0_11

tion" protocol emphasizes that sporting environments be structured to allow for heat acclimatization, hydration, and proper periods of rest for players during practices and games to best protect all athletes from illnesses related to athletic exertion (Thompson 2012).

ASH's initial concern over the NCAA's approach of identifying and monitoring individual athletes versus mandating changes in performance cultures suggests broader politics at play within NCAA structures of care and thus, the need for additional scrutiny. This is all the more complicated given that sickle cell trait and disease have been differently represented and understood both historically and within contemporary time. Such an examination is also difficult given that sickle cell trait is often falsely conflated with sickle cell disease (the latter is often referred to as sickle cell anemia). While connected, the two typically produce different health outcomes. Before turning greater attention to the politics at play related to the NCAA sickle cell screening program, it is thus important to first distinguish between sickle cell trait and disease, and consider how to best approach these complex constellations.

Duster (2003, p. 43) characterizes sick cell anemia as an autosomal recessive disorder which "appear in the offspring only when both parents contribute a gene that, when paired, causes the disorder." Identified over 100 years ago, sickle cell anemia is thus an inherited condition in which abnormal hemoglobin causes red blood cells to take on unique "C" or "sickle" shapes. These sickling cells can inhibit blood flow that cuts off the supply of oxygen, which in turn may produce extreme pain and infections. Those with sickle cell anemia have shorter life expectancies. According to the ASH website: "Complications of sickle cell disease occur because the sickled cells block blood flow to specific organs. The worst complications include stroke, acute chest syndrome (a condition that lowers the level of oxygen in the blood), organ damage, other disabilities, and in some cases premature death" (Sickle Cell Disease n.d.).

In contrast, those with sickle cell trait have inherited a single gene and typically experience minimal health consequences. However, according to ASH, "extreme conditions such as severe dehydration and high-intensity physical activity can lead to serious health issues, including sudden death for individuals with sickle cell trait" (Sickle Cell Trait n.d.).

According to the NCAA website: "Unlike heat-related or cardiac conditions, athletes with sickle cell trait may present as being fatigued and can often talk, but may be experiencing ischemic pain and weakness in their muscles. Pushing the athlete to continue beyond this point for 'toughness' or discipline can lead to a fatal collapse" (Sickle Cell Trait: A Factsheet for Coaches n.d.).

Bob Carson and Simon Dyson have aptly analyzed the NCAA's sickle cell trait screening program (2015) by using actor-network theory (ANT), a popular theory and method within Science and Technology Studies (STS). The authors reveal the unstable and changeable assemblages of human and non-human (both animate and inanimate) actors linked through this process in which sickle cell trait materializes as both possible negative health consequences for some athletes and as a potential litigation threat. Indeed, the NCAA apparently initiated the screening program in response to a lawsuit settlement. While helping to make visible the networked non-human agency of sickle cell trait, Caron and Dyson (2015, p. 75) also discuss the limitations of ANT which they suggest fails "with a double cost: a view of agency that does not distinguish sufficiently between its human and non-human forms and, a corollary of this view of agency, an insubstantial view of social structure." Their criticism points to ANT's inadequacy of fully engaging the powerful salience of the racialized labor structures and practices that enable college sports.

While the NCAA positions itself as an entity that cares about student-athletes with administrators, staff, coaches and athletic trainers providing quality care for athletes, Carson and Dyson's (2015) critique, much as with ASH's early criticisms, invites additional analyses into NCAA's affective performances and conceptualizations of care. Importantly, feminist STS scholars have been at the forefront in theorizing not just care—but the politics of care—in regards to biomedical technoscientific interventions, postulations that are important for this analysis of the NCAA's sickle cell trait screening (see, for instance, Puig de la Bellacasa 2011; Murphy 2015). Notable here is Murphy's (2015, p. 721) conceptualizations of the complicated practices of care as articulated through technoscientific interventions. Murphy points out at least four different but interrelated sets of meaning. Care first, refers to the state of being emotionally attached to or fond of something; second, it means to provide for, look after, sustain, and be responsible for something; third, it indicates attention and concern, to be careful, watchful, meticulous, and cautious; while its fourth meaning (and the first in the *Oxford English Dictionary* entry) is to be troubled, worried, sorrowed, uneasy, and unsettled.

While mapping out these different notions, Murphy (2015, p. 719) also cautions against an unreflective embrace of emotionality, particularly in equating the provision of care "with affection, happiness, attachment, and positive feeling as political goods." She uses the case of women's self-help health initiatives such as the "pap smear" to support her position. During the 1970s, feminist health practitioners in Western nations promoted both clinical and self-exams encouraging "good patients" to screen their bodies for cervical cancer.

Yet Murphy reveals how these attempts to positively nurture and empower women were still embedded in class and racial inequalities. Subsequent attempts to eradicate cervical cancer across the globe are also overdetermined by histories of heteronormativity, colonialization, and capitalism. Hegemonic protocols and paternalistic, neoliberal practices emanating from the West are not simply about eradication of cervical cancer, but also embedded in choreographed "affective economies" which often dictate "how to relate, how to feel and how to live at a transnational scale" (Murphy 2015, p. 731). Influenced by postcolonial, feminist, and anti-racist theorizing, Murphy thus argues the need to trouble and unsettle dominant notions of care. This includes the need to historicize and critique "the painful complicities of technoscience" with entangled, unequal social relations without "equating care with affection and nurturance" (Murphy 2015, p. 732).

While analyzing different practices than Murphy does, this analysis draws upon critical STS feminist sensibilities, particularly as articulated through the politics of care, to unsettle dominant ideologies and practices made through the NCAA's sickle cell trait screening program. Thus, this chapter makes visible the ways in which the NCAA's mandatory screening program is also embedded in historical and contemporary politics of difference. Frequently characterized as a "black disease" this chapter engages the ways in which the testing practices link to a longer history of technoscientific biomedicine as a site for the production of racial difference. This means building upon Carson and Dyson's (2015) insights to more fully expose the commodified, racialized, and gendered biopolitics surrounding practices of care regarding sickle cell anemia and sickle cell trait screening both historically and within recent NCAA testing discourses.

This analysis is also informed by what Safai (2013) has termed the sport safety-industrial complex, that is the surveillance regimes of contemporary biomedicine, sport medicine, and their axillaries each seeking to mitigate "risk." Similar to the arguments of Carson and Dyson (2015), this narrow notion of risk, provided under the guise of health care, deflects broader attention away from systems of stratification within college sport particularly in regard to racialized labor practices, unsafe working conditions, and other health-related concerns which negatively impact many NCAA athletes.

Organizationally the remaining portions of this chapter are divided into three interrelated sections. The first section offers a brief historical context to reveal the ways in which this genetic condition and related screening practices—including the NCAA's sickle cell trait screening program—at times rely upon, remake, and subvert commonsense classification systems related to race. These systems are in turn historically embedded "in a racialized popular culture" which "sees genetics as a new form of alchemy, revealing the 'essence' of a person, and uses that essence to define difference, for good or for ill" (Gilman 2008, p. viii). The second section makes visible the broader commodified contexts of NCAA sport through which the screenings take place and communicate meanings—while simultaneously veiling the powerful control of athletes enacted through the NCAA's rules and structures. The chapter concludes with a discussion of biopower as articulated via broader technoscientific screening practices. This includes analysis of the production of NCAA athletes as "biosubjects" (Gerlach et al. 2011) as well as the broader implications of this contingent subject position both within the NCAA and in the wider culture. In totality, this chapter also makes visible the often precarious use of health screenings within sport spaces while also helping to trouble commonsense notions of (dis)ability, health, and risk.

Inheriting (Dis)Orders and Meanings

At first glance the impetus for the advent of mandatory testing for sickle cell trait appears to be the result of a legal settlement between the NCAA and Dale and Bridgette Lloyd (Zards 2010). The Lloyds' son, Dale Lloyd II, a freshman football player at Rice University collapsed and subsequently died in 2006 after running 16 consecutive 100-yard sprints. The cause of the African American player's death was linked to sickle cell trait. While over 20% of NCAA Division I (the highest level of competition) gridiron football programs were screening for sickle cell trait at that time, the NCAA did not require testing and Rice University did not have such a program (Zards 2010).

Another lawsuit was filed in 2013 against the NCAA and university in regard to the sickle cell trait-linked death of Slippery Rock University basketball player Jack Hill Jr. in 2012 when the test was not yet mandatory for Division II athletes. According to the complaint, Hill collapsed and died after participating in an "insanity" workout, which served as punishment for the team and reportedly the late-night workout was the third workout of the day (Ward 2013). His parents allege that their son, an African American, would still be alive had the school administered a pre-season sickle cell screening test and provided competent medical care. The Superior Court of Pennsylvania ultimately ruled that litigation in this case could target the NCAA given the organization's ability to set regulations regarding player health and safety. This decision thus provided additional points to consider in a broader, ongoing debate over the NCAA's "legal duty to care" (Ehrlich 2018, p. 1).

USA Today (Zards 2010, par. 5) captured the emotional response of Dale Lloyd's mother in suggesting why her family sought legal remediation from the NCAA and Rice University:

> We lost Dale. And we shouldn't have. Other people are losing their kids, and they shouldn't be losing their kids… You have to know your status and the precautions, because your son could be my son. Your daughter could be my son and not be here. And you'll live with that. And that's nothing you want to live with, trust me.

This understandably demonstrative plea captures some of the potential reasons why the Lloyds sought legal redress as a means to prevent future pain, suffering, and even death for those with sickle cell trait in the family's quest to optimize athlete health and well-being. As part of a wrongful death settlement filed by the Lloyds, representatives of Rice University brought legislation to the NCAA membership to require that all athletes demonstrate their trait status and if unknown take a blood (sickle cell solubility) test; however, the subsequent policy, enacted over time within different divisions of competition, would still allow athletes to sign a waiver or to provide documentation of previous results (e.g. newborn screening) exempting them from the test.[1] While teams are increasingly using biometric wearable technology to capture athletes' performance data (e.g. heart rate recovery), this policy means that sickle cell trait screening is the NCAA's "only health test mandated for all athletes" (Zards 2010, para. 30).

Read from this perspective the mandate to screen for sick cell trait seems a caring, benevolent endeavor, if not a pragmatic response in the face of litigation. However, following Murphy (2015) it is important to look beneath the affective economies of care that circulate through this case in order to examine important social relations. While new meanings have formed in regard to NCAA screening practices, closer inspection reveals the persistent notion that sickle cell trait potentially indexes "a genetically flawed 'black body'" (Caron and Dyson 2015, p. 60) as well as the ways in which this notion has been challenged and remade by diverse groups of actors. That is, the NCAA policy is the product of a long history fraught with ideological significance and misunderstanding as well as with competing practices and interests.

A foundational misrepresentation can be traced to the turn of the twentieth-century constructions of sickle cell offered by hematology experts as a biological malady particular to the "Negro race" (Roberts 2011). As the sociologists Omi and Winant (1994) might explain, this early characterization of sickle cell trait and anemia is an example of the process of racialization or "the extension of racial meaning to a previously unclassified social group or set of social practices" (Omi and Winant 1994, p. 18).

This early characterization of an inherited biological malady is further embedded within racist sciences' mobilization of white supremacist ideologies positioning blacks as "carrier and vector" whose presumed disregard for health infected their communities with disease and illness (Wailoo 2001). For example, according to dominant racist understandings, black and white differences in infant and child mortality, to which sickle cell disease contributed, were not thought by whites to reside in unequal social structures, but thought to communicate the inherent weaknesses of blacks. The advent of laboratory medicine and the rise of hematology within the 1920s and 1930s helped to recreate new meanings suggesting that the capacity to create sickled cells was a unique and inherent feature of "Negro blood" (Wailoo 2001).

During the middle portions of the twentieth century, scientists increasingly characterized sickle cell anemia as a "molecular disease" (Wailoo 2001, p. 5). As Abu El-Haj (2007) suggests sickle cell took on complex cultural connotations as both a black disease and a molecular disease. For example, when presented with white patients with sick cell disease, medical practitioners would apply the "one-drop rule" suggesting the patient actually possessed "unknown" black ancestors. This "molecularization of race" continues into the twenty-first century in other forms and formats including the marketing and production of race-based pharmaceuticals such as BiDil, designed to treat congestive heart failure in African Americans (Fullwiley 2007; Pollock 2012). In this way we see a shift from the categorization of particular phenotypes characteristic of racist science to the particular confusing articulation of racial categorization onto racialized genotypes (Abu El-Haj 2007).

In contrast to this process of racialized biomedicalization, the black power movement of the 1960s and 1970s helped mobilize sickle cell disorders as emblematic of the US government's neglect of black health (Nelson 2011; Wailoo 2001).[2] The Black Panther Party hosted community screening events and offered genetic counseling while also characterizing the disease as both biological as well as social given the government's long-standing neglect of the disorder. Members of the Party helped to elevate the "illness narratives" of poor and working-class blacks with the disease as a part of their organizing (Nelson 2011). This period of politicization, education, and increased visibility featured additional actions to raise awareness, including those promoted by celebrities such as Bill Cosby and Sidney Poitier. Black athletes also took part in this celebrity advocacy, most prominently the Pittsburgh Pirates star pitcher Doc Ellis who himself was a "carrier" of sickle cell trait. Ellis testified before Congress and joined over 30 other athletes to found the advocacy group, the Black Athletes Foundation for Sickle Cell Anemia. Other advocates discussed how individuals with sickle cell trait and anemia were discriminated against in the workplace (Wailoo 2001).

While athletes like Ellis and teammate Willie Stargell spread awareness, other African Americans critiqued the increasingly disproportionate attention given to sickle cell trait and disease as distracting attention away from unequal social conditions, which contributed to racial health disparities. Indeed, Wailoo (2001) documents the ways in which President Richard Nixon co-opted the increasing visibility of the disease as part of his broader initiatives to reorganize and shift state expenditures thus appearing to be interested in black health all the while ensuring that very little new federal money was used to address other more pressing—and significantly more costly—matters of public health. The Black Congressional Caucus supported legislation around sickle cell anemia but recognized Nixon's regressive agenda insisting that "the twisted priorities of government and grant seeking institutions for concentrating on sickle cell anemia should be condemned, when essentially hypertension kills more Blacks in one year then sickle cell in twenty" (Wailoo 2001, p. 192).

Throughout the later portions of the twentieth century, the rise of patient advocacy would again impact public understanding of the disease and provide a platform for sufferers to have their symptoms and pain taken seriously (Wailoo 2001). Given these and similar examples, Wailoo suggests that one way to understand the historical salience of the disease is as a commodity. This conceptualization emphasizes "its place in a network of exchange relationships, where, much like any object—the disease concept and the illness experience acquire value and could leverage resources, money or social concessions" (Wailoo 2001, p. 9).

For the purposes of this focus on the NCAA, the history of sickle cell as a black molecular disease and as a commodity are particularly relevant within subsequent NCAA discourses in relationship to sickle cell trait screening. While I will expand more fully on the commodity relationship in the next section, relatedly it is important to note that representations of sickle cell trait associated with the NCAA's screening program continue to draw from, sometimes refute, and then again add to a subtle type of genotype essentialism in representations of sickle cell as a black malady.

On the one hand, that all athletes are screened suggests a type of "color evasive logic" and individual focus in which race does not seem to matter in relationship to trait status. On the other hand, when interviewed "white athletes had mixed reactions to the policy, but most were unsure about why they had to be screened" (Bediako and Moffitt 2011, p. 423). Indeed in a study of NCAA athletes' responses to the screening, athletes at one university characterized sickle cell trait as "predominately in African Americans" and "in the blood" (Lawrence et al. 2015, p. 180). Other responses included "Isn't it in type O blood? A lot of African Americans have type O" and "Caucasians can't get it" (Lawrence 2010, p. 131). Additional representations further reaffirm the illusion of racial genotypes. For example, while elaborating upon their testing procedures NCAA materials cite common statistics regarding sickle cell trait noting that: "Sickle cell trait occurs in about 8 percent of the U.S. African-American population, and between one in 2,000 to one in 10,000 in the Caucasian population" (Sickle Cell Trait: A Factsheet for Athletes n.d.).

The authority of seemingly straight forward statistical language in regard to prevalence coupled with the notion of the rarity among whites subtly reaffirms the notion that sickle cell trait is largely an index of blackness. However, the absolute failure of race as a commonsense biological category is apparent given other evidence that suggests those with the trait receive protection against malaria and thus have inherited the trait via ancestors who live or who once lived in malarial regions. In this way sickle cell is not a race-specific disorder as is still commonly imagined but rather represents a geographical genetic adaptation (Roberts 2011). Consider this alternative understanding offered by cultural critic Dorothy Roberts (2011, p. 113) who suggests simply linking together two world maps,

> one highlights the regions around the globe where malaria is prevalent, the other highlighting areas where sickle cell disease is present. The maps

mirror each other perfectly. By comparing them, it is plain to see that malaria and sickle cell aren't restricted to Africa and that much of Africa is unaffected. High frequencies of the trait also occur in parts of Europe, Oceania, India and the Middle East, all places where there is malaria.... If frequency of sickle cell gene determined racial boundaries, it certainly would not prove there is a black race. Rather, Roberts (2011, p. 113) cites Jarad Diamond in suggesting that if categorizations were made based upon the presense or absence of the sickle cell gene, then "we'd place Yemenites, Greeks, New Guineans, Thai and Dinkas in one 'race,' Norwegians and several black African peoples into another."

Clearly the context of sport in the US contributes racialized knowledge given the overdetermined process of racialization as the most visible professional and college sports including men's basketball, football, and women's basketball are numerically over-represented by players who identify as African American. The power of these imaginings is all the more pernicious when you consider the lingering sporting illusion, posited by racist science in the early portions of the twentieth century, suggesting that black athletes have a natural advantage over whites.

A story in the NCAA magazine, *Champion*, featuring the experiences of Eckerd University basketball player Lance Kearse is emblematic of the representational politics that feature sickle cell trait as a commonsense short-hand for blackness. The narrative suggests a point at which Kearse's body fails him as he experiences the painful symptoms associated with the disorder (Hendrickson 2011). The text serves as an advertisement for the usefulness of screening protocols that allow Kearse to gain a greater understanding of his condition, thanks to the NCAA:

But Kearse has emerged as an example of the benefits of awareness, proper treatment and education. His playing time has returned to normal. He no longer fears the burns and cramps, or questions if he's risking his life. (Hendrickson 2011, p. 30)

A visual image of Kearse's shirtless muscular body accompanies the text. In contrast to the images of infirmary imagined through the black body by early twentieth-century racist science and in alignment with lingering understandings of "natural" black athleticism, Kearse's body is an enticing depiction of black masculinity—presumably due to the NCAA's care—

seemingly healthy, athletic, and even "buff." In comparison to the Black Panther's promotion of illness narratives decades earlier, the NCAA represents Kearse's story as a sign of (black) health and as a contemporary success story. On the surface this depiction further creates exchange value for the NCAA in positioning the organization as concerned about athlete well-being.

Commodity Relations and the NCAA

ASH's public opposition to NCAA mandated screening programs points toward deeper problems with NCAA structures of care. In January 2013, then ASH President Janis Abkowitz issued a statement proclaiming that "ASH believes the NCAA policy is medically groundless—perhaps even dangerous—and is focused more on protecting the NCAA from legal liability than protecting the health of student-athletes" (cited in ASH Opposes 2013). Abkowitz further states that the policy is overly "broad and insufficient" and "attributes risk imprecisely, obscures consideration of other relevant risk factors and can lead to stigmatization or racial discrimination" (cited in ASH Opposes 2013). Abkowitz additionally notes that "while neither screening nor universal precautions will provide complete protection, universal precautions will mitigate risk and have no potential harm." (cited in ASH Opposes 2013). Members of the NCAA, ASH, and the American College of Sports Medicine did subsequently discuss these issues with the NCAA making modifications to "rules limiting intensity and duration of preseason football practices" and hopefully moving college sports closer toward universal precautions (Abkowitz 2013, p. 1).

Potential additional harms alluded to by Abkowitz include ethical concerns such as the confidentiality of screening results, the unreliability of cheaper screening tests as well as inadequate educational programming for those who test positive for the trait. The possibility of stigmatization and discrimination based upon trait status are long-standing ethical concerns. While athletes can opt out of the screening, many may feel pressure to conform to the expectations of their institutions and coaches. Others may have inadequate knowledge of sickle cell trait and thus see the screening as an essential part of their pre-season physical exam necessary to clear them to play college sport (Lawrence et al. 2015; Ferrari et al. 2015).

The extent to which significant changes have been made to sport conditioning cultures as ASH advocates is, at best, open to debate. For example, in 2016 the University of California admitted liability for the 2014 death of football player Ted Agu due to "acute sickle cell crisis" after an intense workout where players grabbed a heavy rope and repeatedly moved up and down a campus hill (Veklerov 2016). The $4.75 million settlement reached by Agu's parents also now forbids the University of California coaches to demand "high–risk physical activity" (Giknis 2016). This case occurred after the advent of screening practices were in place and Agu's trait status was apparently known to coaches and trainers, further raising concerns about the efficacy of screening programs as solutions to concerns about the excessive physical demands too often required of players.

In 2018, University of Maryland football player Jordan McNair collapsed and died from exertional heat stroke due to the lack of care he received from the coaching and athletic training staffs (Almsay 2018). His death was not connected to sickle cell trait, but still suggests that universal precautions advocated for by ASH are needed for all sports. One social commentator has additionally questioned the value of the wide-spread practice of coaches using physically grueling training sessions as a method of punishment for mistakes and as a means to instill discipline (Giknis 2016).

These examples cast doubt on the screening program's overall efficacy and speak of the long-standing need to change training cultures for the benefit of all athletes' health. These examples also suggest the salience of further applying Wailoo's (2001) aforementioned theorizing about the value of commodities, in this case, of sickle cell trait screening. While there is no doubt that some athletes have benefited from screening programs and related shifts in some training regimes, without large-scale changes in sporting environments, the screening programs might best be characterized as a type of public relations campaign. Sickle cell trait screening has additional exchange value given the NCAA's current troubles.

Important issues facing the NCAA include (but are not limited to) ongoing calls to dismantle the current amateur model and to pay athletes

beyond their scholarships given the estimated $13 billion annually gener-
ated through college sport. Aligned with these calls are issues related to
the athletic arms race including the rising costs of athletic facility debt
(Nocera and Strauss 2018). One might also mention long-standing gender inequalities as well as the inattention too frequently paid to academic
integrity seen most clearly in the University of North Carolina academic
fraud case, which did not result in NCAA sanctions. Another concern is
the recent federal investigation around men's assistant basketball coaches
and representatives of shoe companies inappropriately paying athletes
while also steering them to professional agents—all of which are against
NCAA amateurism regulations. These examples indicate the exploitation
of elite athletes that currently exists within Big Time college sports
(Nocera and Strauss 2018).

Especially important to this discussion are criticisms directed toward
the NCAA regarding important matters of health. This includes the lack
of care for some student-athletes when they suffer injuries. For example,
colleges are not required to pay for sport-related injuries and several former college athletes have large medical bills as a result ("National College
Players" n.d.). Despite criticisms over the NCAA's delayed response to
the "concussion crisis" and traumatic brain injuries that disproportionately occur within collision sports, the NCAA and its Sport Science
Institute continue to proclaim that "NCAA student athletes deserve a
safe and healthy college experience" (Sport Science Institute n.d.).
Screening for sickle cell trait is similarly represented.

As sport scholars have long argued, the alleged benevolent sphere of
US college amateur sport is a façade that hides a cartel-like structure that
in turn exploits athletes' unpaid sporting labor. This is especially apparent
in the most visible levels of college sport including the Division I Football
Bowl Subdivision and men's and women's basketball (Sage 1990). This
stratified structure is all the more complicated, when you consider that
Big Time athletic programs frequently value black (especially male)
athletes for "their athletic competency, but not their academic potential"
(Harris 2000 p. 45; see also Hawkins 2013).

While scholars continue to demonstrate the racialized, gendered, and
commodified processes at work within collegiate sport, NCAA information and promotional sessions about sickle cell trait position the organi-

zation as an advocate for athletes' health and well-being. And given the racial politics previously discussed, this is a complicated and contradictory process involving both re-racialization and a paternalistic sense of care. Much as with President Richard Nixon's mobilization of sickle cell decades ago, the NCAA appears to be concerned about black health, without sufficient attention to more costly matters and structural issues including racialized labor practices that in turn negatively impact player well-being. Consistent with Murphy's discussion of the pap smear, sickle cell trait screening serves as a technoscientific intervention ensconced in a politics of care in need of continuous critique and unsettling.

It is important to note that alongside the projection of care associated with the screening process, there are also other movements at play. For example, college football players at Northwestern University started a process to unionize and listed health concerns as one reason for organizing a union. Although their initial efforts to unionize were not successful, the National College Players Association (NCPA), derived from the Northwestern effort, lists their own mission as working "to protect future, current and former college athletes" ("National College Players" n.d.). Specific goals of the NCPA include helping to "raise scholarship amounts to cover all costs, eliminate restrictions on employment, and increase graduation rates for NCAA athletes" ("National College Players" n.d.). Matters of care in regards to health include the need to "establish mandatory health and safety standards to minimize college athletes' risk of abuse, serious injury, and death from brain trauma, heat illness, and other conditions; prevent players from being stuck with sports-related medical expenses; prohibit universities from using a permanent injury suffered during athletics as a reason to reduce/eliminate a scholarship" ("National College Players" n.d.).

NCAA supporters suggest that recent changes to the governance structure that gives more power and autonomy to the five richest sport conferences is a necessary step toward addressing some concerns raised by critics such as those by the NCPA. Time will tell what, if any, material effect these changes will make in regards to athletes' health and well-being; however, it is again important to note that sickle cell trait screening persists.

Concluding Thoughts: Screening Practices Matter

As demonstrated throughout this chapter, there are important histories and significant problems which help to animate the NCAA's sickle cell screening protocols. Testing programs, mandatory across all divisions of NCAA athletic competition as practices of care, are actually narrowly defined practices of care. These important matters are additionally entangled with inequitable social relations both within and beyond college sport.

An additional context worth mentioning here is the larger cultural appeal of medical screening practices. As Nelkin and Tancredi (1994, p. 9) argue the appeal of testing practices are embedded in two broader tendencies within American society "the actuarial mind-set, reflective in the prevailing approach to problems of potential risk, and the related tendency to reduce these problems to biological or medical terms." The actuarial mind-set reduces individuals to "statistical aggregates," a state of affairs which in turn transforms bodily materials and tissues into valuable economic and political resources (Nelkin and Tancredi 1994, p. 8).

In their analysis of contemporary problems with biotechnologies such as testing for genetic disorders, Gerlach et al. (2011) discuss the ways in which the power-knowledge regimes of contemporary molecular biology help produce biosubjects who are additionally fixed under the powerful gaze of the State. While at first glance it seems that the State is beside the point in this discussion of the NCAA, broader regimes of power-knowledge still play a significant role in contemporary governance. The NCAA has devoted a good deal of time, money, and effort in implementing a screening process to mobilize an image of concern, while failing to fully address other academic, health, and financial structures that greatly impact athletes—physically, mentally, socially, and politically. In this way, one effect is similar to other cases demonstrating a broader shift to "risk-responsibility" discourse. That is, increasingly individuals are asked to control and manage any personal health troubles and risks. Dramatic cases of this include neonatal screening where parents are expected to engage if they are in a "risk category" for birth defects due to age, family history, genetic predisposition, etc.

This technique of responsibilization is also evident in NCAA discourses where testing procedures privilege the efficacy of the biotechnology of screening in contrast to large-scale efforts to enact changes in the sport structure and/or a real commitment to give greater agency to players to voice their health and academic concerns. *The New England Journal of Medicine* makes the case that screening athletes for sickle cell trait is a social experiment for:

> there is now great interest in genetic-based risk profiling and personalized medicine. Although the NCAA program shares some elements with these new approaches to care, it differs from them in many ways: the screening takes place outside the physician–patient relationship, the "patient" is undergoing testing because his or her genetic makeup may produce an adverse reaction in circumstances related to a chosen avocation, and the possible corrective "intervention"—modification of practice and training regimens—could require a shift in the culture of sports. (Bonham et al. 2010, p. 998)

In the absence of a broader connection between the processes of racialization and the political economic contexts of college sports, the epistemological focus of the NCAA at times reinscribes the "medicalization of symptomless-at-risk states" (Davison 1996 p. 327; see also Abu El-Haj 2007). Much like elements of genomic medicine itself, the NCAA testing policy too frequently hail subjects to submit to monitoring processes and when necessary, to act in seemingly rational ways to work on themselves in the pursuit of health. And much like similar technoscientific interventions and elements of genomic medicine, this practice transforms the binary between health and pathology making all persons potential "'patients in waiting' (even if some persons are more risky than others) as carriers of those few disease-causing mutations that have been identified to date" (Abu El-Haj 2007, p. 291). And with a host of testing agencies and pharmaceutical companies this means that the patients are also consumers-in waiting. This framing is all the more powerful in the broader culture considering the role of neoliberal logic, which champions the decline of State welfare and colludes with risk-responsibility culture to demand that individuals act rationally and efficiently as accountable for their own personal health (Safai 2013).

In the ever-expanding world of biotechnologies, and in the business as usual world of NCAA sports, one can only hope that this chapter has offered a moment of interruption in thinking through the politics of care. That is, what I hope to have promoted here are different, unsettling ways of thinking toward the goal of ultimately challenging these economic forms of governance and racialization, while also disrupting the NCAA's imagined role as benevolent caretaker.

Notes

1. Screening for sickle cell disease for all US newborns is based upon the argument that early detection and intervention (e.g. penicillin to prevent infection) helps reduce morbidity and mortality. This context is much different than NCAA sickle cell trait screening practices (Abkowitz et al. 2014).

2. Due to multiple factors, there has been a shift in life expectancy for those with sickle cell anemia. In 1977, the life expectancy was in the mid-teens for those with the most severe forms of the disease. By the 1990s this number had risen to age 42 for men and 48 for women according to estimates from the Cooperative Study of Sickle Cell Disease. While there is no doubt that social conditions influence levels of access and the quality of care, medical personnel attribute this shift to a variety of interventions including newborn screening programs that identify patients for prophylactic penicillin treatment from birth to age six (Platt 2018). According to Platt (2018), other shifts contributing to this expansion of life expectancy: "the advent of pneumococcal vaccine, transcranial doppler ultrasound screening with transfusions to prevent stroke, chest syndrome recognition and prevention, comprehensive pediatric care and hydroxyurea."

References

Abkowitz, J. L. (2013). Presidents column—Sickle cell trait and sports: Is the NCAA a hematologist? *The Hematologist: ASH News and Reports, 10*(3), 1.

Abkowitz, J. L., Connor, F. G., Deuster, P. A., & Thompson, A. A. (2014). Sickle cell trait and safe athletic participation: The way forward. *Current Sports Medicine Reports, 13*(3), 192–193.

Abu El-Haj, N. (2007). The genetic reinscription of race. *Annual Review of Anthropology, 36*, 283–300.

Almsay, S. (2018, September 22). Maryland football player who died from heat stroke needed cold immersion therapy. *CNN*. Retrieved from https://www.cnn.com/2018/09/22/us/maryland-jordan-mcnair-death-report/index.html.

ASH opposes extension of NCAA sickle cell trait screening policy. (2013, February 25). *Helio*. Retrieved from https://www.healio.com/hematology-oncology/hematology/news/print/hemonc-today/%7Bd1224f40-5e91-4163-8f1b-70c661b42722%7D/ash-opposes-extension-of-ncaa-sickle-cell-trait-screening-policy.

Bediako, S., & Moffitt, K. (2011). Race and social attitudes about sickle cell disease. *Ethnicity & Health, 16*(4–5), 423–429.

Bonham, V. L., Dover, G. J., & Brody, L. C. (2010). Screening student athletes for sickle cell trait—A social and clinical experiment. *The New England Journal of Medicine, 363*, 997–999.

Caron, B., & Dyson, S. M. (2015). Actor network theory, agency and racism: The case of sickle cell trait and US athletics. *Social Theory and Health, 13*(1), 62–77.

Davison, C. (1996). Predictive genetics: The cultural implications of supplying probable futures. In T. Marteau & M. Richards (Eds.), *The troubled helix: Social and psychological implications of the new human genetics* (pp. 317–330). Cambridge: Cambridge University.

Duster, T. (2003). *Backdoor to eugenics* (2nd ed.). New York: Taylor and Francis.

Ehrlich, S. C. (2018). Gratuitous promises: Overseeing athletic organizations and the duty to care. *Jeffrey S. Moorad Sports Law Journal, XXV*(1), 1–49.

Ferrari, R., Parker, L. S., Grubs, R. E., & Krishnamurti, L. (2015). Sickle cell screening of collegiate athletes: Ethical reasons for program reform. *Journal of Genetic Counseling, 24*(6), 873–877.

Fullwiley, D. (2007). The molecularization of race: Institutionalizing human difference in pharmacogenetics practice. *Science as Culture, 16*(1), 1–30.

Gerlach, N., Hamilton, S., Sullivan, R., & Walton, P. (2011). *Becoming biosubjects: Bodies. Systems. Technologies*. Toronto: University of Toronto Press.

Gilman, S. (Ed.). (2008). *Race in contemporary medicine*. London: Routledge.

Giknis, F. (2016, April 18). Is physical activity as punishment acceptable in college athletics? *College AD*.

Harris, O. (2000). African American predominance in sport. In D. Brooks & R. Althouse (Eds.), *Racism in college sport: The African American athlete's experience*. Morgantown: Fitness Information Technologies.

Hawkins, B. (2013). *The new plantation: Black athletes, college sport and predominately white NCAA institutions*. New York: Palgrave Macmillan.

Hendrickson, B. (2011, October 1). The monster within. *NCAA Champion Magazine*.

Lawrence, R. H. (2010). *Athlete and coach knowledge, attitudes, and perceptions of sickle cell trait and National Collegiate Athletic Association Testing: Recommendations for intervention*. Dissertation.

Lawrence, R. H., Scott, A., Haywood, C., Robinson, K., & Mason, M. (2015). Social and behavioral implications of National Collegiate Athletic Association sickle cell trait screening: The athletes' perspective. *Journal of Georgia Public Health Association, 15*(2), 177–183.

National College Players Association. (n.d.). Mission and Goals. *National College Players Association*. Retrieved from https://www.ncpanow.org/mission-and-goals.

Murphy, M. (2015). Unsettling care: Troubling transnational itineraries of care in feminist health practices. *Social Studies of Science, 45*(5), 665–690.

Nelkin, D., & Tancredi, L. (1994). *Dangerous diagnostics*. Chicago: University of Chicago.

Nelson, A. (2011). *Body and soul: The Black Panther Party and the fight against medical discrimination*. Minneapolis: The University of Minnesota.

Nocera, J., & Strauss, B. (2018). *Indentured: The battle to end the exploitation of college athletes*. New York: Portfolio/Penguin.

Omi, M., & Winant, H. (1994). *Racial formation in the United States*. New York: Routledge.

Platt, A. (2018, January). Stopping the sickle cycle-Where are we? *American Sickle Cell Anemia Association*. Retrieved from http://www.ascaa.org/research.php.

Puig de la Bellacasa, M. (2011). Matters of care in technoscience: Assembling neglected things. *Social Studies of Science, 41*(1), 85–106.

Pollock, A. (2012). *Medicalizing race: Heart disease and durable preoccupations with difference*. Durham: Duke.

Roberts, D. (2011). *Fatal invention: How science, politics and big business re-create race in the twenty-first century*. New York: The New Press.

Safai, P. (2013). Sports medicine, health and the politics of risk. In D. L. Andrews & B. Carrington (Eds.), *A companion to sport* (pp. 112–128). Oxford: Blackwell.

Sage, G. (1990). *Power and ideology in American sport*. Champaign, IL: Human Kinetics.

Sickle Cell Disease. (n.d.). *American Society of Hematology*. Retrieved from https://www.hematology.org/Patients/Anemia/Sickle-Cell.aspx.

Sickle Cell Trait. (n.d.). *American Society of Hematology*. Retrieved from https://www.hematology.org/Patients/Anemia/Sickle-Cell-Trait.aspx.

Sickle Cell Trait: A Factsheet for Athletes. (n.d.). *NCAA*. Retrieved from http://www.ncaa.org/sites/default/files/NCAASickleCellTraitforSA.pdf.

Sickle Cell Trait: A Factsheet for Coaches. *NCAA*. Retrieved from https://www.ncaa.org/sites/default/files/NCAASickleCellTraitforCoaches.pdf.

Sport Science Institute. (n.d.). Health and safety. *NCAA*. Retrieved from http://www.ncaa.org/health-and-safety.

Thompson, A. (2012). Division (I): ASH opposes NCAA requirement for screening. *The Hematologist: ASH News and Reports, 9*(2). Retrieved from https://www.hematology.org/Thehematologist/Features/1185.aspx.

Veklerov, K. (2016, January 29). UC admits liability in 2014 death of Cal football player. *San Francisco Chronicle*.

Wailoo, K. (2001). *Dying in the city of the blues*. Chapel Hill, NC: The University of North Carolina.

Ward, P. (2013). Lawsuit targets Slippery Rock. Pittsburgh Post Gazette. Retrieved from http://www.postgazette.com/education/2013/09/07/Lawsuit-targets-Slippery-Rock/stories/201309070229.

Zards, B. (2010, July 20). Lawsuit prompts NCAA to screen athletes for sickle cell. *USA Today*. Retrieved from https://usatoday30.usatoday.com/sports/college/2010-06-30-sickle-cell-ncaa-cover_N.htm.

Index[1]

---

[1] Note: Page numbers followed by 'n' refer to notes.

© The Author(s) 2020
J. J. Sterling, M. G. McDonald (eds.), *Sports, Society, and Technology*,
https://doi.org/10.1007/978-981-32-9127-0